T0281251

Pro SQL Server
Disaster Recovery

James Luetkehoelter

Apress®

Pro SQL Server Disaster Recovery

Copyright © 2008 by James Luetkehoelter

Softcover re-print of the Hardcover 1st edition 2008

All rights reserved. No part of this work may be reproduced or transmitted in any form or by any means, electronic or mechanical, including photocopying, recording, or by any information storage or retrieval system, without the prior written permission of the copyright owner and the publisher.

ISBN-13: 978-1-4842-2040-5

ISBN-10: 1-59059-967-5

ISBN-13: 978-1-4302-0601-9 (eBook)

ISBN-10 : 1-4302-0601-2 (eBook)
DOI 10.1007/978-1-4302-0601-9
9 8 7 6 5 4 3 2 1

Trademarked names may appear in this book. Rather than use a trademark symbol with every occurrence of a trademarked name, we use the names only in an editorial fashion and to the benefit of the trademark owner, with no intention of infringement of the trademark.

Lead Editor: Jonathan Gennick
Technical Reviewer: Steve Jones
Editorial Board: Clay Andres, Steve Anglin, Ewan Buckingham, Tony Campbell, Gary Cornell,
    Jonathan Gennick, Matthew Moodie, Joseph Ottinger, Jeffrey Pepper, Frank Pohlmann,
    Ben Renow-Clarke, Dominic Shakeshaft, Matt Wade, Tom Welsh
Project Manager: Kylie Johnston
Copy Editor: Nicole Abramowitz
Associate Production Director: Kari Brooks-Copony
Production Editor: Kelly Gunther
Compositor: Linda Weidemann, Wolf Creek Press
Proofreader: Elizabeth Berry
Indexer: Broccoli Information Management
Artist: April Milne
Cover Designer: Kurt Krames
Manufacturing Director: Tom Debolski

Distributed to the book trade worldwide by Springer-Verlag New York, Inc., 233 Spring Street, 6th Floor, New York, NY 10013. Phone 1-800-SPRINGER, fax 201-348-4505, e-mail orders-ny@springer-sbm.com, or visit http://www.springeronline.com.

For information on translations, please contact Apress directly at 2855 Telegraph Avenue, Suite 600, Berkeley, CA 94705. Phone 510-549-5930, fax 510-549-5939, e-mail info@apress.com, or visit http://www.apress.com.

Apress and friends of ED books may be purchased in bulk for academic, corporate, or promotional use. eBook versions and licenses are also available for most titles. For more information, reference our Special Bulk Sales–eBook Licensing web page at http://www.apress.com/info/bulksales.

The information in this book is distributed on an "as is" basis, without warranty. Although every precaution has been taken in the preparation of this work, neither the author(s) nor Apress shall have any liability to any person or entity with respect to any loss or damage caused or alleged to be caused directly or indirectly by the information contained in this work.

This book is dedicated to Ken Henderson (1967–2008).

Contents at a Glance

Contents

About the Author

JAMES LUETKEHOELTER has been fascinated with data and information quality his entire life. After exploring a myriad of scholastic disciplines (starting in music, of all things), he finally got his degree in philosophy, focusing most on logic and epistemology (the study of knowledge). Out of college, he quickly was drawn into the database arena, where he has lived ever since. He has been a frequent speaker at SQL Server conferences in the United States and Europe.

James is the president of Spyglass LLC, a small data-centric consulting firm. In his spare time, he enjoys cataloging the various pronunciations of "Luetkehoelter." He has well over 2,000 discrete variations documented.

About the Technical Reviewer

■STEVE JONES is a founder and editor of SQLServerCentral.com, one of the largest SQL Server communities on the Internet. He writes regular articles and a daily editorial in addition to answering questions from people on all aspects of SQL Server. Steve is a Microsoft MVP, lives near Denver, and regularly attends the Professional Association for SQL Server (PASS) Community Summit as well as local user group meetings in his area.

Introduction

This is a very different technology book compared with others on the shelf next to it. Most technology writing is, well, technical—and at times, only technical. Technical reference information or books that introduce a new technology are important, but technical books usually focus only on the *how* of any technology.

This book focuses more on the *what* than the *how*.

Knowing *how* to do something provides little insight into knowing *what* to do. Knowing how to set the time on your DVD player does not tell you what time to actually set; the time you should set depends on what time zone you're in, whether your time zone observes daylight savings time, and so on. Technology is no different.

Knowing how to perform a backup/restore of a SQL Server database does not impart instructions on what to do with that knowledge. How often should a database be backed up? How about the transaction log? These questions differ depending on your specific business environment. Perhaps a single nightly backup is sufficient. Or perhaps a nightly backup is impossible due to the size of the database. Restore requirements might focus on minimizing downtime, or they might stress as close to zero data loss as possible. Knowing the *what* involved with any technology is the key to being successful as a technology professional.

Thus, I will endeavor to present you with less how and more what in this book. In the coming pages, I'll present you with my concept of what disaster recovery is, the tools available to SQL Server to deal with disaster recovery, and my process for disaster recovery planning and dealing with disaster scenarios. This book is heavy on my point of view and lighter on the technical specifics. If you're looking for technical specifics, Books Online (http://msdn2.microsoft.com/en-us/library/ms130214.aspx) will do nicely.

As you read, you may find yourself disagreeing with a recommendation I make or my technical description of some process. Excellent! If you disagree with me, that shows you're thinking about disaster recovery. I'm happy with you disagreeing with my book as long as you have your own approach to disaster recovery.

One other item about this book: the term *best practices* is deliberately absent. I speak at a number of SQL Server conferences, and I attend Microsoft Tech•Ed every year—in other words, I see lots of presentations. However, I seldom hear specific ideas about what to do with a particular technology, other than a slide or two talking about best practices. The truth of the matter is, there is no such thing as a best practice; every situation is different, and what can be a good idea in one environment can lead to bedlam in another.

Who This Book Is For

If you're a database administrator, either by choice or by necessity, understanding disaster recovery should be at the top of your to-do list. The problem is that disaster recovery is often either seen as a complicated, expensive process or it is minimized to the role of a basic backup/recovery plan. If disaster recovery isn't a part of your ongoing job as a process requiring continual improvement, read this book. If you lose sleep worrying about whether your database will fail, read this book.

How This Book Is Structured

This book is divided into three logical sections: the backup/recovery process, various disaster mitigation techniques, and practical tips for approaching disaster recovery within your own environment. The backup/recovery process is a necessary component to any disaster recovery plan. Disaster mitigation techniques, such as database mirroring, are powerful yet optional. Determining how backup/recovery and mitigation play in to your own disaster recovery plan (and how to create that plan) means the difference between a successful plan and losing your job.

Chapter 1 introduces my interpretation of disaster recovery. Although short, this chapter is extremely important, because it spells out the premises I work with throughout the rest of the book. Disaster recovery is not simply a backup/restore process, it is not simply high-availability techniques, and it is not a project to be completed. Disaster recovery is a daily job duty of a database administrator.

Chapter 2 focuses on truly understanding the database backup process. There are many misleading aspects to the backup process, so without a thorough understanding of just how a backup works, you run the risk of building the foundation of your disaster recovery plan on crumbling bricks.

Chapter 3 builds on Chapter 2 by exploring how to use database backups to restore a database. As with the backup process, you can often be misled while performing a restore. If you aren't familiar with the pitfalls ahead of you, a restore process could take much longer than you anticipated (and much longer than your manager wants).

Chapter 4 explores more complicated backup and recovery techniques using file-groups. As a database grows in size and functionality, it may be necessary to break up the backup process into smaller steps; a full nightly backup just may not be physically feasible. From a restore perspective, you may have data you'd like available before the entire database is restored. Filegroups are the key to both highly customized backups and piecemeal restores.

Chapter 5 shifts from a more technical discussion to the practical activity of creating a backup/recovery plan. Approaching backup without considering what the restore requirements might be (such as how much downtime and potential data loss is acceptable) is irresponsible. Backup and restore always go hand in hand, particularly when planning.

Chapter 6 begins the discussion of mitigation techniques, starting with log shipping. Up to this point in the book, I've talked about how to react to disasters with backup/recovery. You can use log shipping to create a standby database to minimize the impact of a number of disasters, including catastrophic environmental issues.

Chapter 7 continues with a technical discussion of database clustering, another mitigation technique. Also used to minimize the impact of a disaster, database clustering focuses specifically on server failure. Although limited in its usefulness, database clustering should be considered in any disaster recovery plan.

Chapter 8 focuses on database mirroring, which is basically a combination of log shipping and database clustering. By keeping an up-to-date standby database at a remote location, database mirroring can protect against a wide variety of possible disasters, from hardware issues to an actual tornado. Better yet, it can provide a consistent user experience by immediately redirecting clients to the standby database.

Chapter 9 briefly discusses database snapshots. An often-overlooked aspect of disaster recovery is user error, which is unpredictable and potentially devastating. You can use database snapshots as a mechanism to recover from a user error or potentially retrieve altered or deleted data.

Chapter 10 combines a technical discussion of some of the hardware implications you may face with practical approaches you can use to work through those hardware issues. Although this chapter is in no way intended to make you an expert at hardware, it should at least make you conversant enough to discuss potential problems with those who are experts.

Chapter 11 discusses how to approach disaster recovery planning. This completely nontechnical chapter discusses how to combine backup/recovery planning with disaster mitigation techniques to prepare a thorough disaster recovery plan. This chapter includes sample disaster scenarios and potential approaches that could prevent or minimize the impact of the disaster.

Chapter 12 discusses the nontechnical roadblocks you may face when undertaking disaster recovery planning—namely, working with others. The human variable is usually the biggest issue when it comes to disaster recovery planning. I discuss selling the concept to management and colleagues, as well as attaining success while working with problematic areas of the business, whatever they may be.

Contacting the Author

You can reach James Luetkehoelter via e-mail at JL.questions@gmail.com or through his posts on the blog at http://sqlblog.com.

CHAPTER 1

■■■

What Is Disaster Recovery?

One of the greatest frustrations I've faced is discussing (or arguing) a topic for hours, only to realize near the end that my audience and I have completely different views as to what the topic actually is. With that in mind, I hope to make clear what I consider to be *disaster recovery*. My goal is to establish a common understanding of the topic being discussed.

In this chapter, I'll establish what disaster recovery means for the purposes of this book. To accomplish this successfully, I'll discuss

- Disaster recovery from a procedural perspective

- How disaster recovery relates to similar terminology—specifically, *business continuity* and *high availability*

- Exactly what is considered a disaster

- Disaster recovery from a technical perspective

Defining Disaster Recovery

Working as a consultant, one of the most difficult situations to handle is restoring life to a downed SQL Server. It's a stressful situation for everyone involved. When clients call me, it means they have a significant issue. Usually they're unclear as to what the exact problem is or how to proceed.

There are five words that I never want to ask but sometimes have to: "When was your last backup?" From the answer, I can immediately determine if this client has a clear understanding of disaster recovery. Some immediately spring into action, pulling backup tapes out to begin their own documented restore process. But all too often, the question is met with silence and blank stares.

Over the years, I've been in this situation dozens, if not hundreds, of times. Looking back, what jumps out at me is how differently everyone views SQL Server disaster recovery. Here are some of the various interpretations that I've encountered:

- Making sure your data is backed up

- Having a backup/recovery scheme

- Having a *documented* backup/recovery scheme

- Having a documented backup/recovery scheme with directions so thorough that a ten-year-old could follow them

- Off-site data storage

- Planning and documenting all procedures to respond to any type of outage

As this list implies, some view disaster recovery somewhat simplistically, while others see it as a massive project. All interpretations can be valid, but bear in mind that one interpretation might encompass too much, while another interpretation might leave important aspects out.

For the purposes of this book, I'll define disaster recovery as encompassing the following:

- The process involved in returning a downed instance or server to a functioning state

- The process of restoring a damaged database to a functioning state

- The process of restoring lost data

- Mitigation of risks for downtime or loss of data

- Identification of cost, either due to mitigation steps taken or downtime/data loss

- Some level of planning and documenting these processes and mitigation steps

- Consultation with the business owner of the data

Consulting with the business owner of the data is a critical step. The owner is the only one qualified to determine how much downtime or data loss is acceptable. That ties in closely with cost; usually the business side of the equation wants to see zero data loss and zero downtime. This is often an extremely costly goal to achieve. If you don't put cost into the equation from the beginning, it's unlikely you'll get approval for the cost when it comes time for implementation.

This list is still a little vague, but I'll make things clearer in Chapter 12 when I discuss overall disaster recovery planning.

Disaster Recovery, High Availability, and Business Continuity

These three terms sometimes are used interchangeably and often have "floating" definitions. Of the disaster recovery planning projects I've seen that have failed (or at best, limped), the primary reason for the failure was a lack of consensus as to what the project was trying to accomplish. What usually happens is that the basic disaster recovery portion of the project gets a severe case of scope creep, followed by mass confusion and unrealistic expectations.

The following are my definitions for these three terms:

- *Business continuity*: The process of ensuring that day-to-day activities can continue regardless of the problem. It encompasses both technical and nontechnical disasters, such as a worker strike or a supply-chain issue.

- *High availability*: The process of ensuring that systems remain available as long as possible no matter what the cause might be for downtime. This includes disasters, but it also includes events such as regular maintenance, patches, and hardware migration.

- *Disaster recovery*: The process of mitigating the likelihood of a disaster *and* the process of returning the system to a normal state in the event of a disaster.

Figure 1-1 shows the relationship between the three terms.

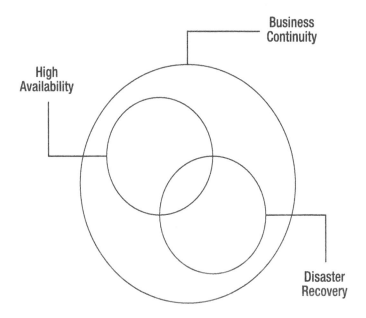

Figure 1-1. *The relationship between business continuity, high availability, and disaster recovery*

Remember, the result of failed disaster recovery projects is often massive scope creep and communication chaos. In the following sections are some specific examples of such failures, taken from real situations that I've either faced or helplessly witnessed.

The Commandeered Project

At a large company, the database administration (DBA) team decided it needed to formalize its backup and recovery operations. The goal was to clearly document its procedures and establish a periodic disaster recovery drill. All of this was confined to the context of the database environment. This was a large undertaking for the team, but it had a clear goal and realistic deliverables.

Every item of work had to be associated with a project, so the team leader entitled the project "Database Disaster Recovery." Eventually, through the miracle of status reports, this project title reached an executive who was so impressed with the initiative and dedication of the DBA team that he rewarded them with the usual: more work. The company announced that the DBA team leader would become the project manager for a new company-wide disaster recovery project.

As you might imagine, the result was the Never-Ending Project. The DBA team leader was not a project manager by profession. Nearly every technical department in the company had a representative present at meetings, which were consumed by continual discussion of every possible scenario that the project needed to address. There was little structure to the project, no clearly defined goals or deliverables, and certainly no sense of order.

After two years and only a list of horrific disaster scenarios to show for it, the project finally faded into memory as fewer and fewer departments sent representatives to meetings. The DBA team was finally able to return to its initial project, which was newly entitled "Database Documentation."

The "We Were Supposed to Do That?" Project

A much smaller manufacturing company took a top-down approach to disaster recovery. At a company meeting, the owner of the company asked the staff to put together a plan of action to return the business to a functioning status in the event of a disaster. The technical staff did a fine job assessing risks and documenting workarounds and recovery steps for a variety of disaster scenarios. The documentation was assembled, and the task was considered complete.

Months later, workers at the trucking company that delivered raw materials to the plant walked off the job. The owner of the manufacturing company had orders to fill without the ability to manufacture the products. He quickly picked up the disaster recovery documentation and looked for a section regarding an interruption in the supply chain. You guessed it: there was no such section. The technical staff addressed only the technical issues. When the owner asked for a disaster recovery plan, he was really looking for a business continuity plan. As a result, the company lost customers who couldn't wait three weeks while the manufacturer found a secondary supplier.

The High Availability/Disaster Recovery Project

The owner of a promising Internet startup hired a consulting company (for the record, not me) to help ensure that the startup could get as close as possible to 99.999% uptime for its web site. The contract specified that the consulting company was to design the system such that there would be no more than 30 minutes of downtime in the event of any single failure. The consultants came in and did a fantastic job of setting up redundant servers, network connections, and even a colocation. The 30-minute threshold would easily be met.

Business took off for the startup until one day when the main data center suffered a massive power outage caused by flooding in the building. Even the backup generators failed. Luckily, the company had an identical system on standby at another facility. A few name changes and domain name system (DNS) entries later, the system was back online.

Weeks later, the owner started receiving hundreds of complaints from customers who had ordered products but never received them. Upon investigation, he discovered that neither the customers nor their orders were in the system. Frustrated, he called the consulting company, demanding an explanation. It turned out that the system that was colocated was only updated every 30 minutes. When the flood occurred and the standby system was activated, the company ended up losing 20 minutes' worth of data. The ultimate financial impact: $79,000, plus more than 200 customers who would never return.

The issue of data loss and its financial impact was never discussed. The consulting company did its job, but no one even thought to question the risk of data loss.

The Price of Misunderstanding

The previous scenarios are just a few examples of what can happen when terms aren't clearly defined. Wasted time, frustration, financial loss, and the perception of failure can all be avoided by simply being clear when using terminology.

Now that I've established what I mean by the term *disaster recovery*, I'll clarify what constitutes a disaster.

Disaster Categories

I find it useful to categorize various types of disaster. This isn't simply due to my compulsive need to categorize (hey, I'm a database guy). It's useful to understand exactly what is meant by a *media failure* or a *hardware failure* and to appreciate what sort of events can cause them. I'll walk through each of the categories and offer some real examples that I've encountered over the years. Then I'll compare the categories in terms of the following criteria:

- Probability of occurrence

- Predictability of the event

- Overall impact (usually measured from a financial perspective)

Tip I find it useful to clearly identify the problem before even thinking about a solution. When looking at a disaster scenario, be sure you know the root cause. If you don't, your solution might just be a Band-Aid on a larger issue.

Environmental

As the name implies, environmental disasters are ones in which the environment of the server has been affected in some way. These can come in a wide range of variations. Here are a few real-life scenarios I've encountered:

- *Poor server-room design*: I once encountered a client who had poor ventilation within the server room. It wasn't out of negligence; the server environment simply grew more quickly than the client's capacity to house it. Due to the heat, servers would fail randomly throughout the day.

- *Natural disaster*: A tornado swept through southern Wisconsin, randomly destroying buildings (as they like to do). One of the buildings it hit had servers in it, which ended up in pieces in trees more than a mile away.

- *Accident*: A water pipe running close to a rather large (and well-constructed) server room burst, flooding the floor. Luckily, the flooding was contained and only a few items were affected; however, some of those items were terminals to manage the servers themselves. This was before Microsoft came out with its Terminal Services product, so there was no means of managing them other than hooking heavy CRT monitors to each server.

Hardware

Hardware includes not only the server itself, but also any associated hardware, including network devices and other dependent hardware such as domain controllers. The following are some examples of hardware disasters:

- *Failed motherboard*: A server with a single power supply simply shut down. After multiple attempts to boot, the client called a vendor technician to bring in a replacement power supply. Still, the server wouldn't clear a *power-on self-test* (*POST*). After further investigation, it appeared the problem was a damaged motherboard.

- *Damaged cables*: A newly purchased cluster was implemented for redundancy. The client tested it for months before moving it to production. Once in production, nodes would fail randomly. It turned out that the SCSI cables were bound so tightly that they were shorting out, briefly disrupting communication with the disk array and causing random failure events.

- *Complete network failure*: Construction crews accidentally severed a primary fiber-optic line that carried all network traffic between a larger organization and its more than 4,000 satellite offices. The primary business tools were located at the main office, so all work essentially stopped until the line was repaired.

Media

Hard drives and tape drives have one major weakness—they're magnetic media, which means they can be corrupted easily if put in the proximity of a magnetic field. These devices also contain moving parts, which are prone to break. Here's a list of some types of media failures that you might encounter in the field:

- *Failing disk drive*: In this simple and common failure, a single drive in a disk array begins to acquire bad sectors. Within a week, it fails outright.

- *Corrupted active backup tape*: An active tape used in a backup rotation becomes corrupted, retaining only a portion of the information it should be storing.

- *Damaged archival tape*: An archived tape, being stored offsite, becomes damaged and entirely unreadable, probably due to being dropped or placed on top of a TV or monitor.

Process

I define process errors a little differently than most. A process can be one of these two things:

- An automated program or script that runs unattended

- A manual process performed on a scheduled basis, either reoccurring or once

You might argue that a mistakenly executed manual process is a form of user error, but these types of errors fit more closely with automation in terms of likelihood, impact, and predictability. For example, when performing a database upgrade for an application, you usually have the opportunity to assess the likelihood and impact of a failure. You can plan accordingly to mitigate risks. Since you know exactly when this process is going to occur, you can, in a sense, "predict" a failure.

Here are some examples of process failure:

- *Service pack installation issues*: While installing a service pack, a cryptic error message occurs. From that point on, SQL Server doesn't start in normal mode.

- *Manual task not performed*: At a satellite office, one of the formal jobs of the office manager is to change the backup tape daily. The office manager goes on vacation and forgets to instruct someone else to change the tapes. A failure occurs, prompting a restore to two days ago. Unfortunately, there is only one tape, and it has been continually overwritten each morning. Thus, the only backup you have is from that same morning; you have nothing from two days previous.

- *Automated backup failure*: A SQL Server backup job has been automated to run every night at 4 a.m. Failure notifications go to a single DBA. The DBA has been out sick for four days when a failure occurs and a restore is required. Nobody was aware of the problem, because the one person who received the failure notification e-mails had been out sick and not checking his e-mail. A system administrator goes to the server to restore the SQL databases only to discover that the automated job has failed the past three days.

User

User error is the most difficult category to deal with. User errors are unpredictable and potentially devastating in their impact. Users can come up with a seemingly unending number of creative ways to cause havoc. Here are a few examples:

- *"Where is the WHERE?"*: Most of us are guilty of this at one time or another. We forget to put a WHERE clause on a DELETE or UPDATE statement. In one particular case, an ad hoc change was required to the database—three child records needed to be associated with a different parent record. Needless to say, the change occurred for every record in the database.

- *"I didn't delete that"*: A data entry clerk accidentally deletes the largest customer from the database. Cascading deletes had been turned on, so every order that customer made was deleted.

- *Too much power in the wrong hands*: My favorite disaster of all time happened to me personally. I was working as a DBA at a small consulting company with only one SQL Server. A colleague came into my office with the following speech: "Hey, I was going to upload those new files we got from that client, and there wasn't enough room, so I tried to delete *something something dot something*, but it said it was in use, so I disabled a service and then I was able to delete it. Now I can't connect to the SQL Server. Did you make some changes?" Enough said.

Predictability, Probability, and Impact

I'm sure many of you are reading through these examples and thinking "This one is easy to remedy" or "Well, if you designed the application properly. . . ." If you're thinking that, fantastic! Problem solvers unite! I, however, approach things a bit more cynically. I look at each example and think about what other things might go wrong or roadblocks to implementing some sort of mitigation solution. Whatever your outlook is, let's take things one step at a time and simply identify potential disasters.

I previously said these categories revolve around the likelihood of occurrence, the predictability of an event, and the impact of the failure. Table 1-1 summarizes the category breakdown.

Table 1-1. *Probability, Predictability, and Impact of Various Failure Types*

Failure Type	Probability	Predictability	Impact
Environment	Very low	Natural disasters are impossible to predict, but a poorly constructed server room may be an entirely different matter.	Usually catastrophic.
Hardware	Low	Some server monitoring tools warn of impending failure.	Downtime and data loss; how much depends on what failed.
Media	Low	Most RAID controller software provides some means of predicting an impending drive failure. Type storage is rarely accessed, making it extremely difficult to predict impending failure.	Ranges from relatively no impact when losing a single RAID 5 drive to significant downtime and potential data loss.

Continued

Table 1-1. *Continued*

Failure Type	Probability	Predictability	Impact
Process	High	There's always some level of predictability, because the events happen at a fixed time.	Could range from embarrassment to major downtime and data loss.
User	Usually low, depending on training and application design	Almost impossible to predict, although poorly trained staff and a poorly designed application may be a hint.	Could range from a minor annoyance to catastrophic.

Probability, predictability, and impact together help to prioritize disaster recovery planning. If a disaster has a low probability, is difficult to predict, and has a relatively low impact, there's no sense in placing it at the top of the list of action items (or placing it on the list at all).

I'll refer back to these categories and scenarios throughout the book, applying specific technical features to each particular category and the example scenarios.

Disaster Recovery from a Technical Perspective

Up to this point, I've been approaching the question of disaster recovery from an abstract, procedural level. While it's important to think about the subject in an abstract way, this is a technical book. I established that, for the purposes of this book, disaster recovery encompasses reducing the likelihood of the disaster and returning the system to a functioning state. Simply put, disaster recovery is mitigation and response.

SQL Server has long had technologies in place to handle mitigation and response. SQL Server 2005 includes new technologies and improvements that have completely changed the way we should think about disaster recovery. Having a backup and recovery plan can and should be augmented by other techniques. Given the increasing size of the average database, a straightforward full backup is becoming an untenable technique on which to rely.

Mitigation Technologies

Certain technologies center only on reducing the likelihood or impact of any particular disaster. These I classify as *mitigation technologies*. Here are some examples:

- *Clustering*: A longtime feature in SQL Server, clustering allows you to set up additional failover servers to take control of the database should the primary server fail.

- *Log shipping*: A technique that has been used manually in the past, log shipping is the process of copying log backups and moving them to a standby server that continually restores them. If the primary server fails, users can be redirected to the standby server manually.

- *Database mirroring*: A completely new technology in SQL Server 2005, database mirroring provides automatic failover. Unlike clustering, there is no shared data, and the standby database can be on any server in any location.

Response Technologies

If this were a perfect world, mitigation techniques would always protect our systems and data from disaster. This is not a perfect world. While mitigation techniques in disaster recovery planning are useful, having a response plan is a requirement. Here are some examples of response technologies:

- *Backup and restore*: No database platform would be complete without functionality to back up and restore a database. SQL Server 2005 provides additional functionality such as mirrored backups and checksum validation.

- *File/filegroup backup and restore*: SQL Server allows you to back up individual data files or filegroups, though this method isn't used frequently. It can aid tremendously in designing a backup scheme for a very large database (VLDB).

- *Database snapshots*: Also new to SQL Server 2005, a database snapshot lets you revert back to a specific point in time without having to go through an entire restore process.

A wide range of technologies apply to disaster recovery. As responsible DBAs, we should be using every option at our disposal to approach any potential disaster situation. Given the number of disaster categories and the technologies available to address them, it's time to be creative and think outside of the "backup/restore" box.

Caveats and Recommendations

Common understanding is the key to any meaningful discussion. Before undertaking any major initiative, it's critical that all parties be clear on terminology and objectives. In this chapter, I've attempted to clarify disaster recovery as it pertains to this book.

The following are some additional thoughts to keep in mind as you work to implement a sound disaster recovery process in your own environment:

- *Stay simple*: Don't make things too elaborate or define terms in a complex way. The key is to break everything down into base concepts, leaving as little room as possible for implicit interpretation. Complex terminology or objectives are usually the primary cause of misunderstanding.

- *Agreement is not a requirement for action*: I'm sure that some of you who are reading this don't quite agree with how I've categorized things or how I've defined disaster recovery. That doesn't mean the rest of the book doesn't have value. The key is that you understand my position before moving forward. The same applies to any undertaking.

- *Categorization isn't just show*: Being a database professional, categorization is almost a compulsive need for me, but there is a real purpose behind it. If individual topics or problems have commonality, it is likely that approaches to discussing them have the same commonality.

Summary

I've established that disasters can be categorized in five basic ways: environmental, hardware, media, process, and user. Each individual disaster scenario has a certain probability, predictability, and impact, which together determine the priority of actions taken. Disaster recovery is the process of reducing the probability or impact of a disaster and the actions taken to respond to that event.

Now that I've spelled out the basic procedural structure for disaster recovery, I'll explain the technical options available to you and how they relate to this basic structure.

CHAPTER 2

■■■

Making Database Backups

In terms of disaster recovery planning, creating a backup is the one step that is non-negotiable—unless, of course, complete data loss is an option for you (and if so, you probably bought the wrong book). Whether your database is 20MB or 20TB, this is the first step in dealing with disaster recovery. Any discussion of disaster recovery planning or restoring databases is incomplete unless you first have a solid understanding of the backup process.

This chapter will focus primarily on Transact SQL (T-SQL) backup techniques and features. (There are, of course, techniques other than T-SQL commands that you can use to back up a database.) First, I'll briefly review the SQL Server storage model and database recovery modes. Then, I'll look at options for the destination of the backup, including backup devices. Finally, I'll explore the various backup commands, including both their technical and practical usage.

For any backup technique to be valid, it must abide by the following guidelines:

- *The backups must be portable*: If you can't move your backup from point A to B, it won't do you much good if your original server is literally on fire (yes, I've seen it happen).

- *The backups must be securable*: This can be as simple as placing a backup tape in a safe. If your backup involves simply replicating the entire database to 4,000 laptops used by sales staff, security becomes an issue.

- *The backups must be the result of a repeatable process*: I've witnessed some fairly amazing recoveries using "accidental" backups. One example involved moving a disk array that was attached to a development server to the failed production server. It just so happened that production had been copied over to the development environment the previous night, so there was very little data loss. In this example, no repeatable process occurred—just fortuitous timing.

These guidelines are achieved primarily by using SQL Server T-SQL backup commands, which will be the focus of this chapter. I'll also discuss a number of other feasible backup techniques. Before getting into specific backup commands, I'll clarify a few other items first:

- How SQL Server stores information

- SQL Server recovery modes

- Backup devices and backup location implications

A Brief Review of SQL Server Storage

To understand the requirements of any SQL Server backup technique, it is critical to understand how SQL Server stores data and writes it to disk. This is an extremely high-level review; we should all know this like the back of our hands, right?

At this point, I won't be looking at filegroups; I'll cover them in depth in Chapter 4. For the purposes of this chapter, filegroups don't exist. Instead, I'll focus on the following types of database files:

- *Primary data files*: Every database has a single, primary data file with the default extension of .mdf. The primary data file is unique in that it holds not only information contained in the database, but also information *about* the database. When a database is created, the location of each file is recorded in the master database, but it is also included in the primary data file.

- *Secondary data files*: A database can also have one or more secondary data files that have a default extension of .ndf. They are not required, nor do they hold any file location data. Generally, you use secondary data files either to create storage space on drive letters separate from the primary data file or to keep the size of each individual data file at a practical maximum size, usually for portability.

- *Transaction logs*: A database must have at least one transaction log file with a default file extension of .ldf. The log is the lifeblood of the database—without an accessible transaction log, you can't make any changes to the database. For most production databases, a proper backup scheme for a transaction log is critical.

When you make a change to the database, you do so in the context of a *transaction*: one or more units of work that must succeed or fail as a whole. Transactions surround us in our daily life. Simply going to the store to buy a pack of gum involves a transaction;

you give your money to the cashier, who in turn gives you the gum and your change. Everything must happen as a single unit of work to be acceptable to both parties. Obviously, it's unacceptable to the cashier if you just take the gum, and you wouldn't accept not receiving change for your purchase.

When you make a change to the database, data isn't written directly to the data files. Instead, the database server first writes your change to the transaction log on your behalf. When the transaction is complete, it is marked as *committed* in the transaction log (a step you often initiate by explicitly executing COMMIT TRAN). *This does not mean that the data is moved from the transaction log to the data file.* A committed transaction only means that all elements of the transaction have completed successfully. The buffer cache may be updated, but not necessarily the data file.

Periodically, a *checkpoint* occurs. This tells SQL Server to ensure that all committed transactions, whether held in the buffer cache or in the transaction log file itself, are written to the appropriate data file(s). Checkpoints can occur in several ways:

- Someone literally issues a CHECKPOINT command.

- The Recover Interval instance setting has been reached (this indicates how often checkpoints occur).

- You make a database backup (when in Simple Recovery mode).

- The database file structure is altered (when in Simple Recovery mode).

- The database engine is stopped.

The normal process for writing data to disk occurs automatically, as shown in Figure 2-1. However, it isn't written directly to an .mdf or .ndf file. All data first goes to the transaction log.

Normal write operations act accordingly. Although this is simplified greatly, write operations follow these basic steps:

1. The user issues some sort of INSERT, UPDATE, or DELETE statement.

2. The data is immediately written to the internal log cache.

3. The log cache updates the physical transaction log file (.ldf) and makes changes in the data buffer cache.

4. The data buffer is eventually cleared of all "dirty" buffers, and the data files (.mdf or .ndf) are updated.

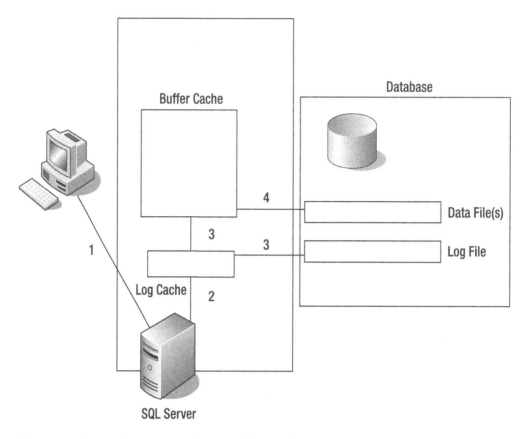

Figure 2-1. *The ongoing process of writing data to the disk in SQL Server*

When a database backup occurs, only the actual data and transaction log files are written to disk. Committed transactions not yet written to disk remain in the transaction log and are rolled forward during the recovery process as the database is brought back online. Incomplete transactions are rolled back during recovery. In Chapter 3, I'll further discuss this process of recovery that occurs when the database is brought online.

SQL Server Recovery Modes

Each individual database can be set in one of three distinct recovery modes: Full Recovery, Simple Recovery, and Bulk-Logged Recovery. Each mode determines how the transaction log should behave, both in active use and during a transaction log backup, which I'll discuss in detail shortly.

Full Recovery

Full Recovery mode is the default recovery mode for a newly created database. All transaction history is maintained within the transaction log, which you must manage. The advantage to Full Recovery mode is that you can restore up to the moment a database fails or up to a specific point in time. The drawback is that if you leave it unmanaged, the transaction log can grow rapidly. If the transaction consumes the disk, it could cause the database to fail. Is there anyone who hasn't had this happen at one time or another?

Full Recovery mode offers no automated maintenance of the transaction log. It continues to grow, as shown in Figure 2-2. The only way to clear it is to either switch to Simple Recovery or back up the transaction log.

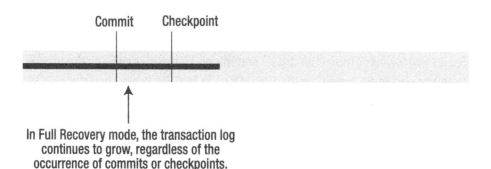

Figure 2-2. *Transaction log behavior in Full Recovery mode: a recipe for disaster if the transaction log is not maintained*

Simple Recovery

The oft-maligned Simple Recovery mode clears the active transaction log of committed transactions during a checkpoint, as shown in Figure 2-3. The advantage is that the transaction log maintains itself and needs no direct management. The drawback is that in the event of a disaster, you're guaranteed some level of data loss; it is impossible to restore to the exact moment of failure.

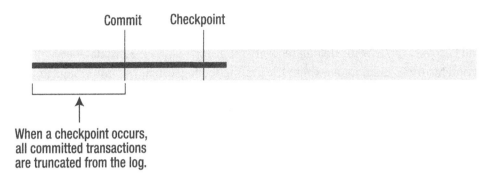

Figure 2-3. *In Simple Recovery, the transaction log is more or less self-maintaining.*

Even though Simple Recovery mode truncates the transaction log periodically, this doesn't mean that the transaction log won't grow. You may size the transaction log file at 100MB, but if a bulk-insert comes along, SQL Server will treat it as a single transaction. SQL Server will log every individual INSERT statement, sometimes causing the transaction log to grow to enormous sizes (I've seen 100MB go to 160GB). When this happens, you must manually shrink the transaction log down to a reasonable size. This can be a frustrating process, because you often must run the shrink command multiple times or in conjunction with other functions. Lots of material is available both on Microsoft's Knowledge Base and in the SQL community itself, so I won't go into details here. Suffice it to say that Simple Recovery is not necessarily the answer for log maintenance. That's where Bulk-Logged Recovery comes in.

■**Note** Many claim that you should never use Simple Recovery mode for a production database. I'll challenge this notion in later chapters.

Bulk-Logged Recovery

Bulk-Logged Recovery mode has always been misunderstood. Most DBAs have a general idea of what it does and how it works, but when it comes to articulating the specific details and implications of its use, clear speech usually devolves into a semiaudible mumbling.

When using Bulk-Logged Recovery, the transaction log behaves exactly as if it were in Full Recovery mode, with one exception: bulk operations are minimally logged. Bulk operations include:

- Bulk imports of data, such as those you might perform using Bulk Copy Program (BCP), the `BULK INSERT` command, or the `OPENROWSET` command with its `BULK` clause

- Large object (LOB) operations, such as `WRITETEXT` or `UPDATETEXT` for `TEXT`, `NTEXT`, and `IMAGE` columns

- `SELECT INTO` statements

- `CREATE INDEX`, `ALTER INDEX`, `ALTER INDEX REBUILD`, or `DBCC REINDEX`

As all of these operations are logged in Full Recovery mode, the transaction log can grow tremendously. The advantage to the Bulk-Logged Recovery mode is that it prevents unwanted or unanticipated log growth.

Whenever a bulk-logged operation occurs, SQL Server only records the IDs of the data pages that have been affected (see Figure 2-4). SQL Server pages have internal IDs, such as 5:547, so you can squeeze a larger amount of page IDs into a small portion of the log.

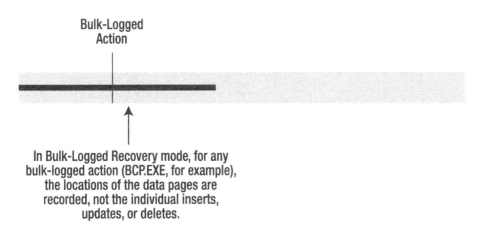

Figure 2-4. *Bulk-Logged Recovery is designed to minimize the use of the active transaction log.*

While Bulk-Logged Recovery is a savior when it comes to managing the transaction log for data warehouses and systems that include a large amount of bulk operations, it isn't without its downside.

The disadvantage is that point-in-time recovery is not technically possible; you can only restore to the point of the last transaction log backup. It is still possible to recover bulk transactions, as long as the transaction log that contains them has been backed up. While the active transaction log in Bulk-Logged Recovery mode is smaller, the log backups themselves hold copies of the pages altered during the bulk load process. The result is potentially large transaction log backups.

The key to using this mode effectively is to invoke it only when needed, then move back to Full Recovery mode for point-in-time backup. This is a risky procedure. If you do choose to move between Bulk-Logged Recovery and Full Recovery, always follow these steps:

1. Switch from Full Recovery to Bulk-Logged Recovery.

2. Perform your bulk-logged operation.

3. After the bulk-logged operation completes, immediately move back to Full Recovery mode.

4. Perform a full database backup.

Changing Recovery Modes

You can easily change between recovery modes by typing in this code:

```
ALTER DATABASE AdventureWorks SET RECOVERY BULK_LOGGED
```

You can also change recovery modes from the administrative GUI. Figure 2-5 shows the drop-down menu that you would use.

Figure 2-5. *You can set each database to use either Full Recovery, Simple Recovery, or Bulk-Logged Recovery.*

You don't need to restart SQL Server for the change to take effect. Let me say that again: *you don't need to restart SQL Server for the change to take effect.* Think about that statement—is this a good thing?

Well, it certainly is convenient; no downtime occurs when you change the recovery mode. However, there are implications when you move from one mode to another. For example, if you move from Simple Recovery to Full Recovery and simply set up transaction log backups, those backups will be completely useless until a full or differential backup occurs. Without a complete transaction history from a full or differential backup, point-in-time recovery cannot occur.

SQL Server 2005 Books Online (BOL) has excellent recommendations for pre and post actions when switching between recovery modes. I'll revisit changing recovery modes in Chapter 5 when I show you how to begin building a cohesive backup/restore strategy.

T-SQL Backup

Most people consider using T-SQL commands to be the ideal way to initiate and manage database backups. Making backups involves a number of considerations. You'll want to give thought to your naming conventions so that you can better keep track of which backup is which. Then there is the rather obvious issue of where to place your backups. You'll also want to consider the use of logical backup device definitions.

Naming Conventions

Whether you use a logical or explicit physical name for your location, you need to use a naming convention that provides some level of information about the contents of the file or device. Here are some of the conventions I've run into over the years:

- `DatabaseName_BackupType` (e.g., `AdventureWorks_Full.bak`): This is one of the most common formats used. The file itself has a datetime stamp, so this is probably your best choice if you don't need to remove the backup files programmatically.

- `DateTime_DatabaseName_BackupType` (e.g., `0713051113_AdventureWorks_Full.bak`): This technique is usually used when custom scripts maintain the backup history.

- `DatabaseName_BackupType_ExpiryDateTime` (e.g., `AdventureWorks_Full_091305.bak`): If someone needs to create a backup out of the regular backup schedule, this format allows you to programmatically remove the files that are no longer needed.

- `DatabaseName_BackupType_BackupReason` (e.g., `AdventureWorks_Full_PreUpgrade.bak`): This naming convention is similar to the previous one in that it represents a backup created out of the regular backup schedule. I find this technique more useful than the previous one because it describes the reason for the backup, not just when you can delete it.

- `DatabaseName_BackupType_3rd-PartyFormat` (e.g., `AdventureWorks_Full_<<Backup application name>>.bak`): If you use a third-party application to create backups for compression or encryption reasons, it's nice to see the name of the application (or an abbreviation) in the name of the backup file.

You can use similar conventions as in the preceding list, but with logical naming, simply remove the `.bak` extension. Most importantly, pick a naming convention and stick to it as best you can. When disaster strikes, it can make a world of difference.

Backup Locations

Before you create a backup, you need to determine where the backup will go. Ultimately, you only have two choices: TO DISK or TO TAPE. However, when it comes to disk, you have a few different options to think about.

Local Disk

You can always specify a file when writing to disk. The syntax is quite simple:

```
BACKUP DATABASE AdventureWorks
TO FILE='D:\Data\AdventureWorks_Full.bak'
```

When backing up locally, you want to avoid placing the backup file on the same disk array as the database itself. In the event of media failure, you'd lose both the database and the backup of the database. Note that I said disk array, not drive letter. It's possible (and sometimes common) to have most of the local drive letters on the same physical disk array.

Tip A common practice (and one I tend to favor) is backing up locally to disk, then copying the backup file off to a network location or backing it up to tape. In the event of a process or user error, you have a copy of the backup already on the server. You don't need to search for a backup tape, which is an overall slower restore process in most cases.

Mapped Network Drive Letter

In previous versions of SQL Server, mapped drive letters didn't appear in the file-selection dialog when choosing a backup file location; under SQL Server 2005, they do. The problem is that when you're configuring a backup, you see the network drives that are mapped for that particular session. The backup will work if you test it, but once SQL Server returns to running as a service, the backup will fail if the same drives aren't mapped in the context of the SQL Server service account. You can work around that potential problem by simply mapping your backup drives using an XP_CMDSHELL job once SQL Server starts.

When writing backups directly to network shares, the advantage of using a drive letter is similar to using a backup device—you now have a logical reference to the share. If you need to move the share to another server, you only have to change the drive mapping, not the backup job itself.

The syntax for the basic command is exactly the same as for a local disk file. Simply change to the mapped drive letter:

```
BACKUP DATABASE ADVENTUREWORKS
TO FILE='G:\Data\AdventureWorks_Full.bak'
```

UNC Share

Although it doesn't have the advantage of a logical reference that a mapped drive does, backing up directly to a Uniform Naming Convention (UNC) path is the preferred method of backing up to a network resource. The syntax remains the same as with a local or mapped network drive:

```
BACKUP DATABASE ADVENTUREWORKS
TO FILE='\\Fileserver\Data\AdventureWorks_Full.bak'
```

Be sure that the SQL Server service account has permission to write files on the network share.

■ **Tip** For a long time, backing up directly to network shares was ill advised. Despite the advantage of immediately moving the backup file off of the server, a single hiccup could corrupt the entire backup file. Network technology continues to advance, and while I have issues with backing up to a file share via a wireless network connection, a gigabit/second network connection directly to the file server may be a reasonable approach.

Tape

Although backing up directly to tape is common, I seldom encounter situations where a T-SQL job is written explicitly for this purpose. Usually third-party backup software agents handle this type of backup. If you do intend to back up directly to a tape device, you have a number of options to choose from that only apply to tape-based backups, including REWIND|NOREWIND and NOUNLOAD|UNLOAD.

One potential problem when backing up directly to tape is the speed. The longer a process takes to complete, the more opportunities it has to fail. Actually, creating the backup file on the tape takes longer than simply copying a file to tape. If drive space is available, it may be better to back up to disk first, then back up the disk file to tape. For larger databases, this may not be an option.

> **Tip** Most third-party backup agents do nothing more than send T-SQL commands directly to the database. If your environment requires you to back up directly to tape or has a large number of databases to back up, then third-party agents are worth the additional cost. You don't need to worry about T-SQL syntax errors, and the cataloging features of third-party software simplify locating and initiating a restore. If your environment doesn't have these requirements, the agent software is probably an unneeded expense.

Comparison of Backup Locations

As you've seen, there are a variety of options when it comes to backup locations. So how do they stack up? Table 2-1 breaks it down, comparing backup speed, backup reliability, and storage reliability.

Table 2-1. *Comparison of Backup Locations*

Location Type	Speed	Backup Reliability	Storage Reliability
Local disk	Typically the fastest	Since it runs quickly, it's less likely to have errors occur during the backup process.	Storing backups locally is a risk to disaster recovery. Environmental, hardware, and media disasters compromise not only your active system, but also your means of restoring it.
Tape	Typically the slowest	Tape is generally a more delicate medium than a hard disk, plus the process is slow. Both factors increase the possibility for problems during the backup.	Although delicate, you may store tapes off-site in a secure location. This is usually the only way to mitigate environmental disasters.
Network (UNC)	Slow, depending on network bandwidth and latency	Networks have so many variables associated with them that it's difficult to generalize about availability. A UNC path is a better method of referencing a location since it is nearly always resolvable.	By keeping the backup files on the network, any disaster event that affects SQL Server itself doesn't compromise disaster recovery.
Network (mapped drive)	Slow, depending on network bandwidth and latency	Mapped drives require that the mapping be done under the context of the SQL Server service account. It is possible that mapping could be lost, causing the backup to fail.	Although mapped drives have the benefit of storing the backup off of SQL Server, you can't rely on the drive letter alone in a disaster situation. The actual UNC location must be recorded somewhere.

A mapped network drive is generally the only undesirable location out of those listed in Table 2-1. Clients sometimes request the use of network drives, but usually because either they don't know where a UNC location is or because the UNC location changes periodically.

Combining multiple locations is usually the best method. I usually recommend creating a backup file locally, then either backing it up to tape or copying it to a network location. Combining techniques will be a recurrent theme throughout this book; focusing on a single option is often what creates problems in overall planning.

Logical Backup Devices

You can create logical backup device names, usually referred to as just *backup devices*. They provide an alternative to specifying a file or tape location explicitly in a BACKUP command. People who use the default backup directory structure created by SQL Server (Drive Letter:\Program Files\Microsoft SQL Server\...) obviously don't take advantage of backup devices. One of the primary advantages to using backup devices is that you can change the definition of a backup device, and thus of your backup location, without having to find and change all the commands in your backup and restore scripts. Instead, you change just the logical device definition.

Creating a Backup Device

Create a backup device by invoking the built-in sp_adddumpdevice procedure—for example:

```
EXEC sp_adddumpdevice @devtype='disk',
@logicalname='AWBackup',
@physicalname='D:\backup\AWBackup1.bak'

EXEC sp_adddumpdevice @devtype='tape',
@logicalname='AWTapeBackup',
@physicalname='\\.\tape0'
```

WHY DUMP?

When developers talk about backup devices, they never use the word *dump*. So why are stored procedures named sp_adddumpdevice? The answer goes back to SQL Server 6.5 and earlier, when the concept of devices (preallocated disk space) was the norm, and the actual command to perform a backup was DUMP DATABASE or DUMP LOG. The convention is now used for backward compatibility. Three versions later, isn't it time for a more appropriate name for that stored procedure?

Dropping a Backup Device

Dropping a backup device is even simpler than creating one:

```
Sp_dropdevice @logicalname='AWBackup'
```

This command only removes the backup device definition—it doesn't automatically delete the files contained therein. Use this command to remove all the files in addition to the device definition:

```
Sp_dropdevice @logicalname='AWBackup', @devfile='DELFILE'
```

The literal `'DELFILE'` is required for completely dropping the device and all the files associated with it—not the most intuitive command. A simple Y|N or 0|1 flag would make more sense. Keep in mind that just dropping the device doesn't remove the files and won't reclaim space. If you delete a backup device, you'll be asked whether you want to delete the files.

Advantage of Backup Devices

Again, the main advantage to using a backup device is to provide a logical name for the backup location. That way, if you change or add hardware and need to change the location of the file or tape, you won't need to modify your backup command. Consider the following command:

```
BACKUP DATABASE AdventureWorks
TO AWBackup
```

This command backs up a database to the device represented by AWBackup. The actual, physical device could be a tape drive or a disk file, and it can hold multiple backups and all backup types (including full, differential, and log). Everything depends on the definition that you, the DBA, give to AWBackup, and you can change that definition over time independently of your BACKUP DATABASE commands.

Managing Backup Devices

One thing no DBA or server administrator ever likes to see is a full disk drive. Whether backups are stored in a named backup device or kept separately as distinct files on disk, you need a way to maintain them and remove old and invalid files. Previous to SQL Server 2005, you needed to use either a maintenance plan or a custom script to perform this maintenance. In SQL Server 2005, you can now specify how long until a backup should be removed, or you can specify a date after which a backup expires (meaning it is no longer needed and should be removed)—for example:

```
BACKUP DATABASE AdventureWorks
TO AWBackup
WITH EXPIREDATE = '12/05/2007'
```

or

```
BACKUP DATABASE AdventureWorks
TO AWBackup
WITH RETAINDAYS=7
```

The first option causes that specific backup to be removed after December 5, 2007 (at midnight, to be precise). The second option forces that particular backup to be removed after seven days have passed.

Media Sets and Backup Sets

Every backup belongs to a backup set, and every backup set belongs to specific media set. I have rarely encountered anyone who uses these features explicitly. Backup "agent" software that integrates with a larger backup management tool often creates names just for the purpose of internal organization:

```
BACKUP DATABASE AdventureWorks
TO BACKUPDEVICE1
WITH RETAINDAYS=7,
NAME='Full',
MEDIANAME='ALLAWBackups'
```

NAME refers to that specific backup set, and MEDIANAME is a label for BACKUPDEVICE1. Unless you're in the practice of storing multiple backup files within a single backup device or file, it's best not to use these. If you're using a third-party backup agent, let the agent control the MEDIANAME and NAME properties.

■ **Tip** Although there is an advantage to using a file-based backup device from an organizational perspective, I generally avoid doing so. I prefer a single file for each distinct backup, whether it's a full backup, a differential, or a log. The larger a file grows, the longer it will take to be moved, and the opportunity for corruption to the entire backup set grows.

Full Backup

Regardless of the recovery mode used, you need to start with a full backup. Both log backups and differential backups require a full backup to use as a starting reference point. *No backup scheme is complete without at least one full backup.*

I ran into one situation where the only resolution was to restore to a specific point in time. The client said, "No problem. We keep six months' worth of backups on tape." It turned out to be six months' worth of transaction log backups; there were no full backups anywhere on tape. Explaining to the client that there was no way I could restore the transaction logs was one of the most painful discussions I've ever had as a consultant.

Creating a simple, full backup statement in T-SQL is intuitive:

```
BACKUP DATABASE AdventureWorks TO DISK = 'D:\data\AW.bak'
```

There is a very serious issue with this statement, however. The default behavior for a backup command is to append to the existing file. If you use the previous statement in a recurring job, the `AW.bak` file will continue to grow until it consumes all of the disk space. Once that happens, future backups will fail. To ensure that the backup file contains only a single backup, you need to include the `WITH INIT` clause:

```
BACKUP DATABASE AdventureWorks TO DISK='D:\data\AW.bak' WITH INIT
```

This ensures that every time the backup is performed, the file is overwritten. Accidentally appending backups to a single file is a common mistake for new DBAs.

Log Backup

In Full Recovery or Bulk-Logged Recovery mode, log backups are essential not only for recovery purposes but also for managing the size of the active transaction log. Simple Recovery mode is the only one that actually deletes committed transactions periodically. If never backed up, transaction logs for a database in Full Recovery and Bulk-Logged Recovery mode will continue to grow until they consume all available disk space. If the disk is filled completely, the database will stop.

The command for backup log files is nearly identical to a full backup:

```
BACKUP LOG AdventureWorks_Log TO DISK = 'D:\data\AW.trn'
```

The name referenced is the logical name for the transaction log file, not just the name of the database. `.trn` is also the most common extension used to identify a log backup. Every action against a database is assigned a Log Sequence Number (LSN). To restore to a specific point in time, there must be a continuous record of LSNs. *An uninterrupted chain of log backups is absolutely critical for recovery purposes for databases in Full or Bulk-Logged recovery mode.*

Differential Backup

Restoring log backups tends to be a slow operation, especially if your full backup is a week or more old. Differential backups are intended to decrease recovery time. DIFFERENTIAL is actually an option for the BACKUP DATABASE statement:

```
BACKUP DATABASE Adventureworks TO DISK = 'D:\data\AW.dif' WITH DIFFERENTIAL,INIT
```

In this example, AW.dif contains all the changes made since the last full backup. You can use it during the restore process in addition to transaction log backups. First, restore the full backup, then restore the latest differential, then restore any transaction logs that follow it.

Consider the following items when using differential backups:

- *If you perform full backups infrequently, differential backups will grow significantly in size for an operational database*: Remember, differential backups contain all changes since the most recent full backup. The longer the time between full backups, the more changes in your differentials.

- *A differential backup is directly tied to a specific full backup*: Performing an ad-hoc full backup outside of the normal backup schedule can render a differential backup useless.

- *Thoroughly examine the frequency of differential backups when establishing a backup plan*: When the database changes frequently, differential backups can consume a significant amount of space. Be sure to balance the necessary recovery speed of the database with the available space. If the recovery speed isn't a concern, you don't need to use differential backups.

■**Note** When discussing backup methods with server/network staff, clarify the distinction between a differential backup and an incremental backup. Many file server backup applications include both a differential and an incremental mode; the differential includes all of the data that has changed since the last full backup, while the incremental includes all of the data that has changed since the last differential or full backup. SQL Server has no direct equivalent to an incremental backup.

Backup File Sizes

You must consider the size, or potential size, of individual backup files. Keep in mind that your server/network administrators create backups as well, so it's crucial to understand the amount of space used by each backup technique. In one situation, the size of the backups exceeded the capacity of a tape drive, and it took almost two months before the server administrator noticed that some full database backups made to disk were not being backed up to tape. Luckily, no disaster of any kind occurred during that time frame. It did make management nervous, though.

Full backups tend to be nearly the same size as the database itself. They are slightly smaller, but for practical purposes, just plan on the backup file being the same size as the database. You can reduce the size of an individual backup by using file or filegroup backups, which I'll discuss at length in Chapter 4.

Differential backup sizes can vary greatly, depending primarily on the amount of time that passes between the differential and the last full backup. A differential contains a copy of every page that has changed since the last full backup, so without frequent full backups, the differential backup could theoretically grow to nearly the size of a full backup.

Log backups are usually the smallest of the three types, although sometimes a single log backup can exceed a differential or even a full backup in size. In Full Recovery mode, log backup sizes are fairly consistent with differential backups as long as the use of the system is consistent. However, the log backup can grow significantly when large amounts of data are added to or removed from the database.

THIRD-PARTY BACKUP TOOLS

A number of third-party tools can replace the native SQL Server backup, providing improvements such as reduction of backup size, speed enhancements, and encryption. I have personally tested every such product on the market, as long as it has a demo version to download. Of course, some are better than others, but in general, most work as advertised. I even use one such product and recommend it to some of my clients. Such products can be a wise investment given the needs of your specific environment.

This sidebar, however, is the extent of my discussion about these tools. Using these types of tools is perfectly valid to help address SQL Server disaster recovery. However, they don't address the base issues of disaster recovery; instead, they enhance solutions that are already in place. When approaching disaster recovery, always assume the worst-case scenario. That includes assuming that the native SQL Server tools are the only option available to you. You can always use third-party tools to enhance your disaster recovery process, but you should never consider them as a starting point.

Error Checking

The backup process can perform verification of the data as it is being backed up, either checking for torn pages or validating checksums. You must enable whichever option you desire at the database level, as shown in Figure 2-6 for checksum validation.

Figure 2-6. *Page Verify options allow you to choose between no verification, checksum validation, and torn-page detection.*

Torn-page detection simply checks each data page to see if a write process completed in its entirety. If it finds a page that has only partially been written to (due to some sort of hardware failure), it simply flags it as "torn."

Checksum validation is a new page-verification technique. It adds a value for each data page, essentially identifying the exact size in bytes of the page. While this seems like it would be an expensive operation as far as performance goes, it's actually quite efficient in SQL Server 2005 (if it weren't, they wouldn't make it the default behavior). It effectively acts as torn-page detection as well.

The backup process can validate checksums by comparing the value stored in the database with the value associated with the data page written to disk. However, it doesn't do this by default. If checksum validation is enabled, you can force the backup process to perform this validation:

```
BACKUP DATABASE AdventureWorks
TO DISK = 'D:\data\AW.bak'
WITH CHECKSUM
```

When an error is encountered during checksum validation, SQL Server writes a record to MSDB..SUSPECT_PAGE. The default behavior is to STOP_ON_ERROR, allowing you to attempt to correct the problem and continue issuing the same command with the addition of RESTART.

The other checksum-validation option is to CONTINUE_ON_ERROR. When this is enabled, the backup simply writes the error to the MSDB..SUSPECT_PAGE table and continues on. However, the SUSPECT_PAGE table has a limit of 1,000 rows, and if that is reached, the backup will fail.

Enabling checksum validation obviously has a performance impact on your backup process. If you have the luxury of a large maintenance window, checksum validation can save you a lot of time and misery by avoiding the need to deal with a partially corrupted backup file.

I'll examine the `MSDB..SUSPECT_PAGE` table and approaches to dealing with errors generated by either torn-page validation or checksum validation in detail in Chapter 3.

Securing Backups

The `BACKUP DATABASE` and `BACKUP LOG` statements support a `PASSWORD` property:

```
BACKUP DATABASE AdventureWorks
TO DISK = 'D:\data\AW.bak'
WITH PASSWORD='monona'
```

This password is not strongly stored with the backup, and any hacker worth his salt can break it. It is intended more to prevent the accidental restore of an incorrect backup set.

You can truly secure a backup by placing it on an encrypted file system or physically securing a tape in a safe. Of course, third-party backup tools can encrypt backup data as the backup is occurring.

You can secure data by encrypting the actual columns in the database before a backup even begins. SQL Server 2005 supports native encryption, using industry-standard encryption algorithms. If your database contains extremely confidential information, such as credit-card information, it is probably better to encrypt it within the database rather than simply relying on some sort of backup encryption or password.

Striped Backup

Sometimes databases are so large that creating a full backup on a single tape or disk array is next to impossible. In these instances, you can use *striped backups*, sometimes known as *multiplexing*. Figure 2-7, for example, shows a backup being striped (or written simultaneously) across four tape drives. The advantage is that each device is being used to its fullest capacity to create the backup. The disadvantage is that in the event of a failure, all tapes or files will need to complete a restore.

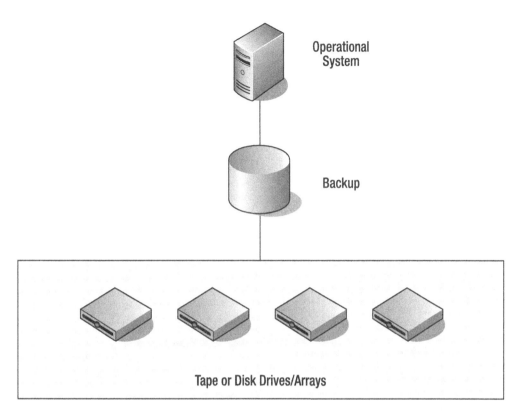

Figure 2-7. *A striped backup configuration: the backup is split into pieces among the various backup devices.*

Striped backups are *too* easy to create, in my opinion:

```
BACKUP DATABASE AdventureWorks
TO DISK ='D:\data\AW.bak',
E:\data\AW.bak',
'F:\data\AW.bak' WITH INIT,
CHECKSUM,
CONTINUE_ON_ERROR
```

In this particular example, the backup is being spread across all three files. Since striping is above all a performance optimization, this example would have little impact on performance if D:, E:, and F: were all on the same data array.

One of the most common mistakes I've encountered is when a GUI-centric DBA creates a striped backup by mistake. It's easy to do, and I've accidentally done it myself (yet another reason to move from using SQL Server's GUI interface to T-SQL whenever possible). Here's what happens: a junior DBA begins his or her journey down the wrong path by looking at the dialog shown in Figure 2-8.

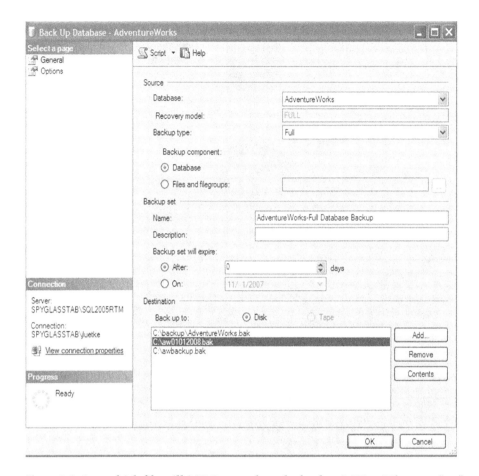

Figure 2-8. *Into which file will SQL Server place the backup? (Hint: What you "see" may not be what you get.)*

The junior DBA looks at the destination area on the dialog box in Figure 2-8 (the destination areas in 7.0 and 2000 are similar) and thinks, "I want to back up to this file on `C:\aw01012008.bak`. I've got it highlighted, so that should work." He sets the process up as a recurring job and finds that `C:\AW.bak` and `C:\backup\adventureworks.bak` are slowly growing in size. Since these locations aren't where he's backing up his data, he deletes them. Subsequent backups fail.

The backup is striped in between all three files in a round-robin fashion. No single file has the entire backup; each has a third of the full backup. Since each file would be required for a restore, the DBA is dead in the water if he encounters a failure.

Mirrored Backup

Mirrored backups are a new feature in SQL Server 2005 that allow you to write the same backup file to multiple locations, as Figure 2-9 illustrates. Mirroring is a fantastic technique to mitigate media failures.

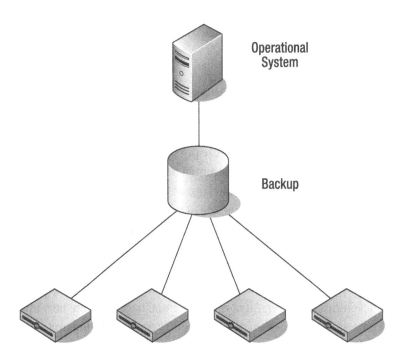

Figure 2-9. *Mirrored backup configuration*

The command to create a mirrored backup is similar (almost *too* similar) to creating a striped backup:

```
BACKUP DATABASE AdventureWorks TO DISK='D:\data\AW.bak
MIRROR TO DISK = 'E:\data\AW.bak'
MIRROR TO DISK = 'F:\data\AW.bak'
WITH INIT,CHECKSUM,CONTINUE_ON_ERROR
```

I'm using a full backup in the example, but mirrored backups are best suited for transaction log backups. When in Full Recovery or Bulk-Logged Recovery modes, transaction logs are critical; being able to immediately back them up to more than one location plays a huge role in mitigating both media and hardware errors.

The one restriction to backing up to multiple locations is that the underlying devices must be identical. In particular, multiple tape drives must all be of the same model from the same manufacturer.

I don't advocate using mirrored backups for full backups, but they're a must, not a maybe, for log backups. You must protect transaction log backups at all costs if you want to have point-in-time recovery. In my opinion, you can never have enough copies.

Copy-Only Backup

In the introduction to this chapter, I mentioned that you can use backups for purposes other than disaster recovery. A typical use is to use a backup to move a copy of the database to a development environment. I suffered dearly from this practice.

I had one client who required the fastest restore possible; naturally, I made frequent differential backups. As you've already seen, differential backups are tied directly to a single full backup. This client frequently took full backups of the production database and restored them to a development box. Due to the size of the backup file, the client immediately deleted it once the database was restored. Initially, this didn't worry me, because I was taking differential backups each hour. As you may have already guessed, the server went down, destroying the database in the process. When I went to begin my "quick" restore process, I discovered that the server had gone down just after a full backup was taken for use on the development server. All of my differential backups were now invalid. I had to use the previous night's full backup and apply every transaction log up to the point of failure.

If only copy-only backups existed back then. A new feature in 2005, the copy-only backup does *not* reset the backup chain. As far as differential backups go, the copy-only backup never happened. Any backup made outside of the standard backup scheme should be done as a copy-only backup:

```
BACKUP DATABASE AdventureWorks
TO DISK='D:\data\AW.bak'
WITH INIT,
CHECKSUM,
COPY_ONLY
```

While this is a useful feature, you still must specify it explicitly. If you don't have tight control over who has the right to back up a database, it can be difficult to control when the COPY_ONLY feature should be used.

Additional Backup Considerations

Before leaving this chapter, you need to at least be aware of some additional backup types. The following subsections explain them.

Structure Backup

I find it useful to create a backup of the T-SQL script that could re-create the structure of the database itself. There are times when a database becomes corrupted in such a way that there is no way to bring it online, but only to start it in what is termed *emergency mode*. While in that mode, you can copy data out of the database, but that's about it. If you don't have an empty, clean destination for that data, the emergency mode won't do you any good.

I ran into this exact problem with a SQL Server 2000 database, where the emergency mode is an undocumented technique that should only be used while working with Product Support Services (PSS) technicians. I was able to get all of the client's data exported, but the client had no build script of the structure of the database. Tables were filled with data, but indexes, triggers, and stored procedures were still missing. If the client had created a structure backup at some point in the past, we could have returned the database to a functional state within a reasonable amount of time. Instead, what should have taken eight hours took four days.

Cold Backup

I've run into situations where the DBA performs a cold backup only—that is, he stops SQL Server, backs up all of the data files, and then restarts the SQL service. The obvious problem is that the technique makes the database unavailable while the backup is occurring. Unless you have a large window for backup operations, this may not be an option.

Full-Text Backup

In SQL Server 2000, full-text catalogues were not included in any backup unless the appropriate directories were backed up with the Microsoft Search service turned off. In SQL Server 2005, full-text catalogues are backed up automatically whenever a full or filegroup backup occurs (given that the catalogues are associated with the filegroup being backed up). It can be convenient to have those catalogues included automatically, but they can increase the size of the full or filegroup backup significantly. If your database makes use of full-text search, be sure to keep this fact in mind.

I'll cover filegroup backups and how they relate to full-text search in detail in Chapter 4.

Backup and Disaster Categories

So how do recovery modes, recovery locations, and individual backup options apply to the disaster criteria I've already established? How do they help or hinder in mitigating the impact of the disaster?

Recovery Modes

Failure can occur in a number of different categories. Your choice of recovery mode affects the ease with which you can recover from a problem within each category:

- *Environmental*: The recovery mode doesn't matter for this category. A tornado doesn't care if your database is in Simple Recovery or Full Recovery mode.

- *Hardware*: There really isn't a direct correlation between recovery modes and a hardware failure; you're facing the same challenges regardless.

- *Media*: Failure here has the same results regardless of the recovery mode.

- *Process*: Here's where the recovery mode has an impact. If Simple Recovery mode is used, it is impossible to restore to a point in time; it is impossible to go back to just before the failure occurred. Bulk-Logged Recovery might help, but you can only restore to the point of the last transaction log backup, not to a more granular point in time. To mitigate process failure, Full Recovery mode is the optimal option.

- *User*: Similar to process failures, Simple Recovery mode is of no help. Because user failures are unpredictable, Bulk-Logged Recovery might not even be an option. Full Recovery is the only mode that lets you restore to a specific point in time.

Backup Locations

The following list discusses the impact of backup location on the ease of recovery. Again, I've broken this list down into category of failure.

- *Environmental*: The backup location is one of the only means of mitigating environmental failures. The only way to recover from a tornado strike is if you put your backups on a tape and either take them offsite or place them in a fire-resistant safe cemented into the foundation of the building.

- *Hardware*: Again, location is the key to mitigating hardware failure. Whether it's keeping a backup on another server or another tape, location addresses most hardware failure scenarios.

- *Media*: Location itself doesn't mitigate media failure; the key is using *multiple* locations.

- *Process*: The location for process failures is only relevant in the protection of transaction log backups.

- *User*: Again, location only affects user failure in that it can help protect transaction log backups.

Backup Methods

This time, this list is centered around how your backup method impacts your recovery options:

- *Environmental*: None of the backup methods mentioned help if a tornado destroys your facility.

- *Hardware*: Mirrored backups are a great way to minimize the risk of hardware failure. If you mirror your backups to four tape drives, any one can fail without impacting your recovery capabilities.

- *Media*: Using checksum validation at least notifies you of the possibility of media failure. Mirrored backups also minimize risk so that no single media device disrupts your recovery capabilities.

- *Process*: Copy-only backups play a role in dealing with process error; however, their role in such a scenario is only to speed the restoration effort. An effective log backup scheme is still the key to protection against process failure.

- *User*: As with process failures, copy-only backups can have an impact from a performance perspective (assuming differential backups are used). Again, the key to mitigating user failure is proper log backups.

Caveats and Recommendations

I've learned a lot about backup and recovery in my career. The following list summarizes some lessons learned and gives recommendations to help guide you in constructing a disaster recovery plan for your databases:

- *Time is the ultimate enemy*: No matter what type of backup and what process you used, you're dealing with magnetic media and mechanical devices such as hard disks and tape drives. The longer a mechanical device is in operation or magnetic media written to, the higher the chance of a failure. All backups should have a basic goal of completing as quickly as possible.

- *Mirror transaction log backups*: In Full and Bulk-Logged Recovery modes, the transaction log is the lifeblood of the database. A continuous history of transactions is required for point-in-time recovery. If you lose a single transaction log backup, that ability is lost. Always mirror transaction log backups.

- *Mirror to multiple physical devices*: Whenever possible, be sure to use different physical devices when using mirrored backups. This means separate RAID arrays, network locations, or tape drives. Backing up to different drive letters may just be backing up to the same RAID array; if that array fails, both backups will fail.

- *Beware striped backups*: Using multiple physical backup locations and striping a backup amongst many files can significantly improve performance. However, you now need every backup file to do any type of restore. Only use this approach if you need very fast performance and/or if you have a large database (multiterabyte). You should first explore other techniques for improving performance, one being file/filegroup backups, which I'll discuss in Chapter 4.

- *Don't fear Simple Recovery mode*: Some say that any production database should be in Full or Bulk-Logged Recovery mode. I don't necessarily agree with that. As you'll see in later chapters, if the business unit truly understands the implications of Simple Recovery mode (meaning the amount of data lost) and is comfortable with those implications, why put yourself through the trouble of managing transaction log backups?

- *Manage backup devices and sets*: While it may be tempting to store more than one backup in a single device or file, make sure that you manage how many copies you keep. It can be easy to append too many backups to one file and fill the hard disk or tape on which it is stored.

- *Follow a naming convention*: It doesn't really matter what technique you use, but stick to a naming convention. One that incorporates the database name, the type of backup, and the time of creation is usually best.

Summary

As you've seen, there are a number of different methods to back up a database, each with its own benefits and drawbacks. The location, recovery mode, and backup technique all play different roles in addressing individual disaster categories.

Each backup option has its own benefits and drawbacks, but you need to at least have one single full backup. Log backups are critical for point-in-time recovery, and differential backups can speed the restore process significantly. Having explored the process of backup, I'll now show you how you can restore these backups should disaster strike.

CHAPTER 3
■ ■ ■

Restoring a Database

Performing a backup is not only a relatively simple task, but it's also a relatively safe task. Rarely as a DBA do you fret over whether performing a backup will have negative consequences on your database. Restoration, on the other hand, is a completely different matter. It isn't a routine task, so unless you have a very unstable environment and get practice on a regular basis, restoration can tend to feel unfamiliar. Combine that general uneasiness with a complicated process, the likelihood of an executive looking over your shoulder, impatient users wanting the system back, and the knowledge that an incorrect choice in restore options could be detrimental, and the result is stress. Unfortunately, stress breeds more stress.

I've been in this situation countless times with my internal servers, when working for a private-sector company, and as a consultant being called in for assistance. I'd like to say that the process becomes easier with time, but it doesn't. Even when you have a documented plan in place and have practiced it, something new usually crops up. It could be damaged hardware, it could be invalid backup files, or it could just be not being able to access the disaster recovery documentation. Whatever happens, it is rarely straightforward, even in the simplest of restore scenarios. If you have yet to be in a restore situation, be patient—you will.

Are you uneasy now? Good. That unease helps keep you on your toes. However, it's also the key to why a restore process can unravel. The restoration process is inherently filled with emotion and pressure from management, creating a need for teamwork and constant communication with business users. In this book, I'll talk about all of these aspects, but first you need to understand the technical process, devoid of any external factors or pressures. In Chapter 5, I'll discuss overall planning, and Chapter 13 will focus on the types of business and interpersonal pressures that can make this job so difficult. To successfully understand the entire process, you need to first break it down to its key elements.

In this chapter, I'll focus on the technical aspects of a restore—primarily, the T-SQL RESTORE command. I'll examine ways to perform restores from within the GUI, but I'll emphasize how to perform a restore using T-SQL. I'll cover the basic scenarios of full, differential, and point-in-time restores, as well as a new SQL 2005 feature: page-level restore (spoiler: this feature is not for the faint of heart). I'll describe issues surrounding the restoration of system databases, and I'll offer a detailed look at the dreaded "suspect" database state. As always, I'll conclude by showing you how this all fits in with general disaster recovery categories, and I'll discuss major caveats and recommendations.

Restore vs. Recovery

It's important to understand the difference between a restore and the process of recovery. Misunderstanding this distinction can account for significant loss of time during a restore process.

RESTORE is a T-SQL command that recreates a database or a portion of a database from a backup file created with the T-SQL BACKUP command. It has nothing to do with changing the state of a database, such as offline or online.

Recovery is the process of bringing a database from an offline or restoring state to an online state in which the database is available for use again. Recovery occurs every time SQL Server starts. Before bringing any database online during a startup, SQL Server checks each database's transaction log for committed and uncommitted transactions. If it finds any committed transactions after the last checkpoint is performed, it "rolls" them forward. It automatically rolls any uncommitted transactions back. The same thing occurs during a restore operation. Once the database is brought back to an online status, no further database files may be restored.

THE DATABASE MYTH OF THE MASSIVE DELETE

I've heard this story a number of times, and it has the taste of an urban myth ("I know a guy whose brother . . ."). According to the story, two consultants are updating a database, and they need to delete a few invalid records. Consultant #1 types in DELETE FROM Order and executes, gasping in shock as he does; he realizes that he just issued a DELETE command for the entire table, which contains more than 14 million order records. Consultant number #2 immediately runs to the server room, finds the SQL Server, and unplugs the power.

When SQL Server restarts, it sees that DELETE statement as an uncommitted transaction (it wouldn't commit until the final row was deleted). It reverses the DELETE that was issued by rolling back all of the rows it had deleted successfully. Consultant #1's job is saved, and all is well throughout the land.

Looking at these simple descriptions, you may be thinking, "I already knew that" or "That's not so confusing." The problem is that RESTORE is an explicit statement, whereas recovery will occur implicitly if it's not controlled manually. If only a single, full backup file is being restored, recovery isn't something you need to concern yourself with. However, once you start including multiple files to restore (differential and log backups), the potential for an unwanted or unexpected restore surfaces.

Recovery is an option for a RESTORE statement. If I'm recovering the AdventureWorks database from a full backup and don't include the RECOVERY option, the operation will default to WITH RECOVERY. The GUI presents the same default, as shown in Figure 3-1. Be careful only to use the first option (RESTORE WITH RECOVERY) if you're sure that no further restore operations are required.

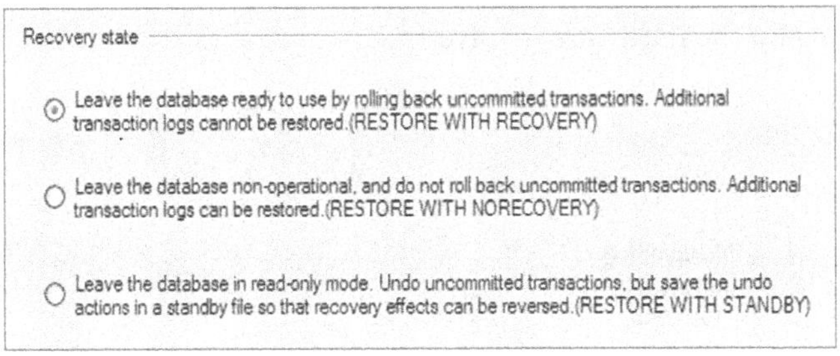

Figure 3-1. *The default* RECOVERY *option as displayed on the Options tab of the* RESTORE *dialog box in SQL Server Management Studio (SSMS)*

If you accidentally leave the RECOVERY clause out of a BACKUP statement or quickly go through the GUI to do a restore, you'll have to start over if you were supposed to include differential or log backups. While that might not seem like an earth-shattering development, go back and reread the second paragraph of this chapter. No matter how large or how small the database is, if the business feels it is important, there will be pressure and stress. Telling an executive or business lead that you need to start the restore process over because the database did a recovery before you could apply additional backup files will not earn you gold stars or a prime parking spot. That's, of course, if the database is around 10GB or less in size. If the database is 500GB or more than 1TB, you might be looking for a new job.

▪**Tip** In the same way that I would recommend always including a WHERE clause in a DELETE statement to avoid accidental mass deletion, I also recommend always including the RECOVERY clause, even if it's just restoring a full backup. Even if the default is WITH RECOVERY, I type in this code:

```
RESTORE DATABASE AdventureWorks
FROM AdWorksDevice
WITH RECOVERY
```

By explicitly specifying WITH RECOVERY or WITH NORECOVERY every time you execute a RESTORE statement, hopefully including a RECOVERY clause will become second nature. I can't count how many times early in my career I forgot to specify WITH NORECOVERY. The process of recovery brings the database back online, so you don't need to apply any further differential or log backups.

Availability During Recovery

Normally, as a database is recovering, it remains unavailable to users. With SQL Server 2005 Enterprise Edition, a database is made available immediately after committed transactions are rolled forward. This process is illustrated in Figure 3-2. The database is available online to users, while the rollback process proceeds. This might seem like trivial functionality, but imagine the case of the massive delete; rolling back millions of rows could mean hours, depending on the hardware involved.

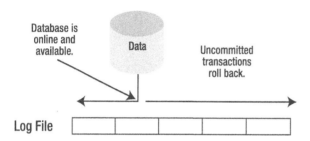

Figure 3-2. *After committed transactions in the log file are rolled forward, the database is online, but only when using fast recovery in SQL Server 2005 Enterprise Edition. If fast recovery isn't available, you may be waiting awhile while the database finishes the complete process of recovery.*

By making the database available immediately after the roll-forward process, you can increase the uptime significantly in the event of some sort of disaster. The roll-forward process is usually quite fast.

Periodically, the database forces committed transactions to be written to the database. This process is usually referred to as a *checkpoint*. You can force a checkpoint to occur by simply issuing the command CHECKPOINT; otherwise, the checkpoint frequency will be determined by the database setting RECOVERY INTERVAL. You can adjust this with the sp_configure command:

```
Sp_configure 'Show Advanced Options' ,1
Sp_configure 'Recovery Interval' , 5
RECONFIGURE WITH OVERRIDE
Sp_configure 'Show Advanced Options',0
```

This example changes the checkpoint process to occur every five minutes. By default, the recovery interval is set to 0, meaning SQL Server dynamically manages how often a checkpoint occurs. The higher the value, the longer the roll-forward portion of recovery will take.

Once the roll-forward is complete, the rollback operation occurs, removing uncommitted transactions from the transaction log. When fast recovery is available (Enterprise Edition only), the database is considered recovered and available for incoming requests while the rollback process occurs.

T-SQL's RESTORE Command

T-SQL's RESTORE command can provide all sorts of functions—not just replacing database files. You can retrieve information about the files contained in the actual backup file or tape, get general information about the database within the backup file, or check the backup file/tape for potential errors.

Information Contained in the Backup File

One of the most important items to remember is that the primary backup file (.mdf) retains information about the structure and state of the original database. Why is this important? If you're simply restoring over an existing database with a regularly created backup, it's unlikely that you'll run into any problems. However, if you're restoring to a new location or a new server where the original location doesn't exist (perhaps the new data drive letter is E instead of D), the RESTORE commands will become much more complicated. Luckily, the RESTORE HEADERONLY, RESTORE FILELISTONLY, RESTORE LABELONLY, and RESTORE VERIFYONLY commands give you a great deal of information about the backup file itself.

RESTORE HEADERONLY

The amount of information contained in the backup header is staggering. More important, the file header information has "hooks" to tables within the MSDB database. When you're performing a restore with the GUI, some of the information displayed is a combination of both the information contained in the backup header and the information within MSDB (which I'll cover shortly).

You can normally issue the RESTORE HEADERONLY command simply by referencing the backup file:

```
RESTORE HEADERONLY
FROM DISK='D:\SQLBackups\AWFull.bak'
```

If you're referencing a tape device, you may also specify the options of UNLOAD|NOUNLOAD and REWIND|NOREWIND. These options go in the RESTORE command's optional WITH clause and don't apply to disk-based backup files.

Also, keep in mind that RESTORE HEADERONLY returns *all* backups contained on the device referenced, whether it's simply a file that contains more than one individual backup, a logical backup device, or a tape volume. To view an individual backup set or file, use WITH FILE or WITH MEDIANAME (for tapes) to filter the result set.

Rather than discuss every property returned by this command (there are more than 30), I'll focus on the ones that are either very useful or potentially misleading. Some of these attributes are confusing because they could be referring to either a native SQL Server backup or a third-party backup.

THE ALL-IMPORTANT LSN

The LSN, or Log Sequence Number, is the key to a successful restore operation. To have any sort of point-in-time restore, you must have an unbroken chain of LSNs, either via full, differential, or log backups, or in some scenarios, the active transaction log. If you lose a single LSN, you may be stuck restoring up to that point. When running the RESTORE HEADERONLY command, you'll see a number of different LSN entries, including one associated with having multiple restore "branches." The bottom line is that LSNs, which ultimately get written to the transaction log, are the lifeblood of restore and recovery. Make sure that your transaction logs are complete, secure, and structurally intact.

Some undocumented commands let you look at log entries and such, but I'm not going to share them, because it's easy to make things worse than better by using them (I know this from experience—trust me). If you ever believe that you have an invalid "broken chain" of LSN entries, call PSS before attempting anything.

LSNs also make point-in-time restore possible. As long as there is an uninterrupted string of sequential LSN numbers and the database is in Full Recovery mode, you can recover the database up to the last committed transaction. Even though SQL Server 2005 records all transaction details (including before and after images) in the transaction log, that log is in the form of a binary file and cannot be browsed without a third-party tool.

MSDB contains a great deal of information about backup operations—not just scheduled backup operations, but also any backup operations that occur any time a BACKUP or RESTORE statement is issued. You could query MSDB system tables to read information on the contents of backup files, but it's much better to interrogate the individual backup file(s) themselves. You can do that using the RESTORE HEADERONLY command, and Table 3-1 describes some of the information that you can get back. Commands such as RESTORE HEADERONLY read information directly from the backup file(s). That information is similar to what's in MSDB, but do remember that the information from the backup file header should be considered the authoritative source of data.

Table 3-1. *Information Revealed by* RESTORE HEADERONLY

Field Label	Information Returned
BackupType	Multiple, numeric codes are listed here, some of which correspond to a SQL Server native backup, some to a third-party backup type. The SQL Server types are: 1) Database, 2) Transaction Log, 4) File, 5) Full Differential, 6) File Differential, 7) Partial, and 8) Partial Differential. For non-SQL Server backup types, there is 1) Normal, 5) Differential, 16) Incremental, and 17) Daily. If you have a non-SQL Server type, be sure that Differential and Incremental mean what you think they mean, as discussed in Chapter 2.
ExpirationDate	If a datetime is present, it shows when the backup file (not the backup set, which includes all backup files) will expire. If the backup file is on a tape device, expiration means that you can overwrite the backup. If the backup file is on a file-based device, SQL Server will delete that file after the expiration date.
Compression	Currently, SQL Server doesn't support compression; there should be a 0 here. If there's anything other than a 0, it's a third-party backup tool.
Position	A simple integer identifies which backup this is in a backup device (tape- or file-based).
DeviceType	This is a list of both physical and logical type codes, including file-based backups (2 for logical, 102 for physical), tape (5 for logical, 105 for physical), and virtual devices (7 for logical, 107 for physical). A virtual device usually indicates a third-party backup utility.
FirstLSN, LastLSN, CheckpointLSN, DatabaseBackupLSN	These fields are entries for the corresponding LSN numbers; consider these fields for internal use only.
SortOrder, Codepage, UnicodeLocaleID, UnicodeComparisonStyle	These fields represent the configuration at the *server* level. Keep in mind that you can create different collations at the database and column level.
BackupStartDate, BackupFinishDate	These fields indicate the times that it starts and finishes writing to media, not necessarily the entire time needed by SQL Server for the backup. They aren't without value, but there is more time involved. MSDB is a better place to look for execution times.
SoftwareVendorID	4608 references a SQL Server backup. Anything else indicates a third-party backup.
Flags	This bitmap specifies information such as whether a backup has bulk-logged data or whether a backup is damaged. This information is also given in other, more specifically labeled columns of the report. Don't rely on the bitmap, as the meanings could change in the future. Instead, focus on the actual columns.
Collation	This is the *database*-level collation, not the server-level collation. Keep in mind that different collations can exist all the way down to the column level.

The attributes listed in Table 3-1 aren't the only attributes returned by the RESTORE HEADERONLY command, but the others are either self-explanatory or of marginal use. Much of the information is repeated within MSDB, which is a good place to look if you're collecting data for trend analysis.

RESTORE FILELISTONLY

When more than one backup is written to the same device, you'll need to use the following command to identify the position of any given backup:

```
RESTORE FILELISTONLY
FROM DISK = 'D:\SQLBackups\AWFull.bak'
```

Far fewer fields of information are returned by this command because it gives only general information as to the contents of a backup device (whether it's a file or a tape device). For the most part, the information is straightforward, with a couple of exceptions. Table 3-2 describes the most important of the fields returned.

Table 3-2. *Information Returned by* RESTORE FILELISTONLY

Field Label	Information Returned
LogicalName	The logical name of the backup file.
PhysicalName	The physical location of the backup file, not the physical location of the database file(s) being backed up.
Type	This can be a data file (D), a log file (L), or a full-text catalog (F). I'll cover the inclusion of full-text catalogs in backups in Chapter 4.
FileGroupName	This is the SQL Server filegroup name that contains this file. A full-text catalog is associated with a specific filegroup.
FileID	This corresponds to the Position field shown by the RESTORE HEADERONLY command.

Again, there are a number of other columns, but they're either used mostly internally (more LSN information) or stored in other locations as well (such as SizeInBytes). Given that the RESTORE HEADERONLY command displays all the backup sets if multiple backups are contained within the same file or tape, this command can save you a lot of time in quickly identifying the particular backup from which you need to retrieve information.

RESTORE LABELONLY

Use the RESTORE LABELONLY command to view the high-level label information for a tape backup—for example:

```
RESTORE LABELONLY
FROM TAPE ='\\TAPE0\\AWFull.bak'
```

Table 3-3 lists the more significant bits of data returned by the command. The results are typically most meaningful when dealing with tape backups. It's less common to need to look at high-level labels on backups made to disk.

Table 3-3. *Results of* RESTORE LABELONLY

Field Label	Information Returned
FamilyCount	The number of families present on the device. Tape backups are often divided into families.
FamilySequenceNumber	The number identifying the specific family being displayed. You'll see a row of output for each family.
MediaLabelPresent	This returns 1 for Microsoft Tape Format (MTF) or 0 for other— essentially a third-party format.
MirrorCount	For the specific backup set family, the number of mirrored backups that were created.

You won't find yourself using this command often, unless you use SQL Server to back up directly to tape. In most environments where that is the case, you'd use a third-party tool that provides its own method for examining the contents of the tape.

RESTORE VERIFYONLY

This verify-only option lets you interrogate and validate any particular backup file (and *verify* does mean what it implies—the restore operation doesn't actually restore any data). The RESTORE VERIFYONLY command is functionally equivalent to BACKUP VERIFYONLY. You simply specify the file to check:

```
RESTORE VERIFYONLY
FROM DISK = 'D:\SQLBackups\AWFull.bak'
```

There are significant improvements to the verification process. Initially, this command only verified the logical structure of the backup file; now it goes so far as to validate the structure of individual objects contained in the backup file. If various page-validation options, such as torn-page detection or checksum validation, are specified in the backup file, the RESTORE VERIFYONLY operation will go through and validate the actual data as well.

RESTORE VERIFYONLY differs from all the other RESTORE commands in that it won't return a discrete result set of different attributes. It simply declares a backup valid, fails and declares it damaged, or fails while populating the MSDB..SUSPECT_PAGE table.

Information Contained in MSDB

MSDB records a significant amount of information regarding the backup history kept in three main tables: restorefilegroup, restorefile, and restorehistory. You can also get timing information from tables related to SQL Agent jobs, but SQL Agent doesn't necessarily invoke the backups. These tables store information directly related to a RESTORE command issued against the server.

The restorehistory table MSDB table is one that I find most useful. It contains a record of any restore operation, even if it's just a verification operation. Table 3-4 describes some of the columns in the table. In an environment where there are multiple hands in the backup/restore process, the restorehistory table can play a critical role in diagnosing exactly what was done during a restore process.

Table 3-4. *Relevant Information in the MSDB* restorehistory *Table*

Column	Contents
Restore_Date	The datetime of the *start* of the restore operation.
Restore_Database_Name	The name of the *destination* database. If the WITH MOVE clause is included, this may not be the same as the original database name.
User_Name	The user, as it is known in SQL Server, who executed the RESTORE command. If the user was authenticated via a Windows group, the Windows group will be displayed.
Restore_Type	This can be a database (D), a file (F), a filegroup (G), a differential (I), VERIFYONLY, or a revert (R), which applies to a database snapshot (more on database snapshots in Chapter 9).
Replace	A 1 indicates that existing files were replaced with the WITH REPLACE option—the equivalent of the "Overwrite existing files" option in the GUI.
Recovery	A 1 indicates that the WITH RECOVERY clause was included. Remember, this is the default behavior as well.
Restart	A 1 indicates that this particular RESTORE command is associated with a previous backup that failed and was repeated with the RESTART command.
Stop_At	The point in time where the database was stopped.
Stop_At_Mark_Name	The log mark name, if that technique was used, where the restore stopped.
Stop_Before	1 indicates that it includes the transaction associated with the Stop_At_Mark_Name value, while 0 indicates that this transaction was not included in the restore.

This table is useful for diagnosing failed restore attempts (which I often end up deal-ing with). As long as the RESTORE command was used, a row exists.

The restorefilegroup and restorefile tables contain basic information regarding file and filegroup restores. I'll revisit them in Chapter 4.

Restoring Full Backups

With the exception of database snapshots, which I'll be discussing at length in Chapter 9, all restore operations start with the restore of a full backup. It isn't possible to restore only a differential or a log backup. Both need a point of reference—the LSN—to proceed.

Restoring in Simple Recovery Mode

This is the most basic restore scenario. While I do believe there can be a place for Simple Recovery mode for a production database (an argument I'll expand upon in Chapter 5), you're unlikely to face it for a production database. In most environments, Simple Recov-ery is reserved for development and quality-assurance systems, as well as for unplanned backup requirements, such as copying a database to a new development environment or performing a full backup before making a major change. The following command initi-ates a restore in Simple Recovery mode:

```
RESTORE DATABASE AdventureWorks
FROM DISK='D:\SQLBackups\AW.BAK'
WITH RECOVERY
```

Technically, you don't need to specify WITH RECOVERY, because it's the default. I included it here to remind myself that it *is* the default. If you have the feeling of déjà vu, it's because I already said that in this chapter. In my opinion, I can't reinforce strongly enough the need to explicitly specify either WITH RECOVERY or NORECOVERY. Don't rely on default behavior here. Be explicit.

Here I'm also assuming that the AW.BAK file contains only a single backup file. If you recall from the previous chapter, you need to append to the existing file (or logical backup device) when creating a backup. In Figure 3-3, you can see a single data file; the assumption might be that this file contains a single backup.

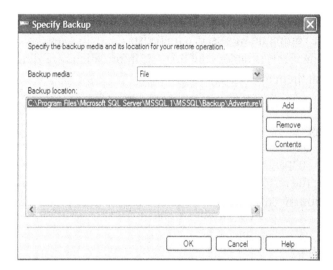

Figure 3-3. *This dialog appears when selecting a source from which to restore.*

As you can see in Figure 3-4, however, a single file may actually contain multiple backups.

If you store multiple backups within a single file, you must specify the number identifying the backup that you want to restore; otherwise, the restore attempt will fail.

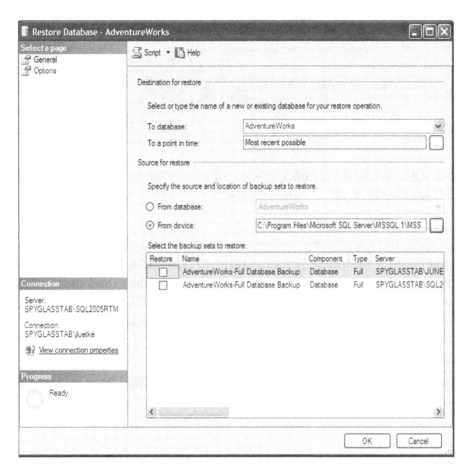

Figure 3-4. *The backup file contains more than one distinct backup, so you have to choose which one to restore. Make sure you know which file you want before continuing.*

Restoring in Full Recovery Mode

In most cases, you'll be dealing with databases in Full Recovery mode. This can complicate the restore process immensely if you want to restore as much data as possible. You need to include the full backup, any differential backups, any log backups, and the tail of the transaction log.

One of the most common mistakes users made with SQL Server 7 or 2000 was forgetting to back up the transaction log before beginning a restore. The tail of the log contains any transactions that occur after the most recent backup (full, log, or differential). If you restore the database with the REPLACE option, the transaction log will reset and those tail transactions will be lost.

SQL Server 2005 now prevents you from restoring a database without first backing up the log's tail. If you attempt such a restore, you'll receive the error shown in Figure 3-5.

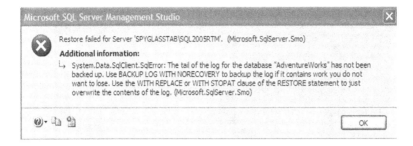

Figure 3-5. *SQL Server 2000 and earlier offered no warning that the tail of the transaction log would be overwritten. This is a nice addition.*

This addition of a simple error message should eliminate a common and costly mistake. While the error message suggests using WITH REPLACE or WITH STOPAT to bypass this error and proceed with the recovery, do *not* do so. Make it a habit to back up the tail of the transaction log every time you perform a restore. Using a different procedure to bypass the log's tail should clearly be an exception to the process.

■**Note** Replacing a database snapshot (discussed at length in Chapter 9) doesn't result in a prompt to back up the log's tail.

Restoring in Bulk-Logged Recovery Mode

When in Bulk-Logged Recovery mode, you can only restore to a point in time up to the most recent bulk-logged action. For a full restore, there is no difference in behavior from that of a database in Full Recovery or Simple Recovery mode.

Restoring/Moving to a New Location

Another common mistake made by new DBAs (and sometimes experienced ones) is the method for restoring a database to a new location. To do this within the GUI, you have to go to the Options page during the restore process, as shown in Figure 3-6. Notice the browse button next to the items in the Restore As column. If the database files need to reside in a different directory structure, you'll need to specify it. With SQL 2000 and earlier, you needed to actually type it out. The browse button is another nice addition.

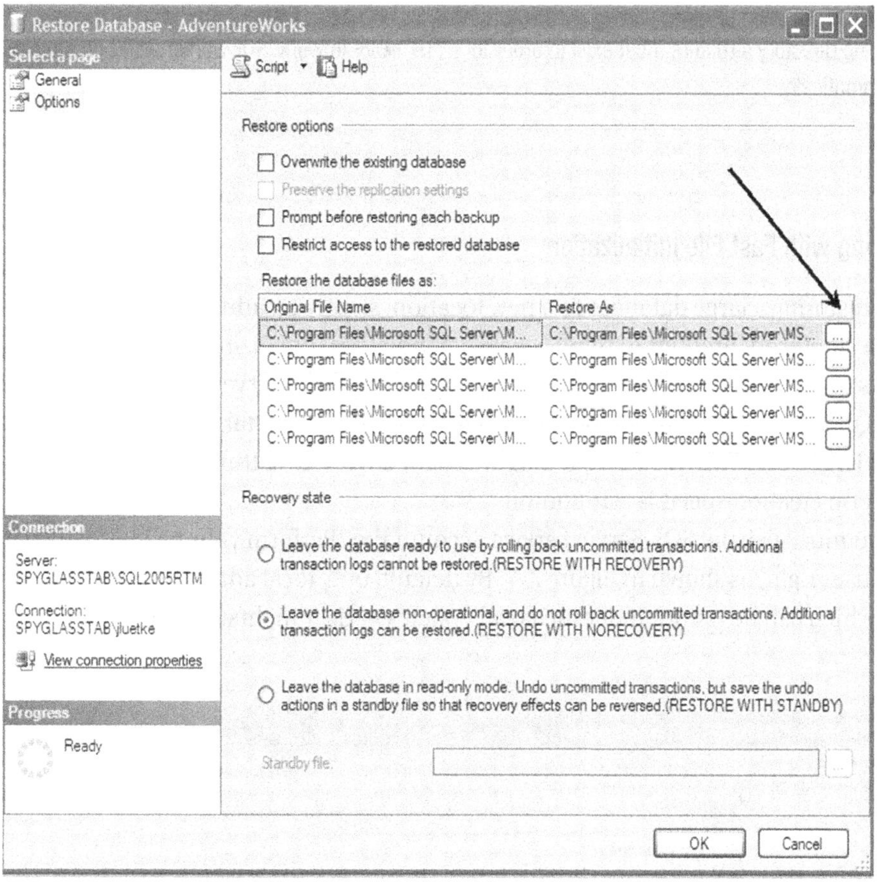

Figure 3-6. *Moving files under the Restore As column*

Of course, I prefer to use a restore script rather than the GUI. In the rush to begin, it's tempting to click OK without checking all of the settings. Keep in mind that you're giving the logical name of the file to be moved and the physical name of the new location. The key clause when moving data files is WITH MOVE—for example:

```
RESTORE DATABASE AdventureWorks
FROM DISK='D:\SQLBackups\AW.BAK'
WITH MOVE 'AWData1'
TO='E:\SQLData\AWData1'
MOVE 'AWLog1'
TO='F:\SQLLog\AWLog1'
WITH RECOVERY
```

Note again that I explicitly included the WITH RECOVERY clause, even though it's the default. Try to get yourself in that habit—it can be a lifesaver.

> **Tip** The directory structure must exist in order for WITH MOVE to work. SQL Server won't create directories automatically.

Restoring with Fast File Initialization

When restoring a large database to a new location, simply creating the data files can consume a significant amount of time, because Windows is initializing the file and setting all the bits to 0. If you're running SQL Server 2005 on Windows Server 2003 (or Windows XP, if it's SQL 2005 Express Edition or Developer Edition), you can take advantage of instant file initialization. With this feature, files are created without setting every bit to 0. The impact on creation speed is astounding.

You must give the SQL Server service account the "Perform volume maintenance tasks" user right, as shown in Figure 3-7. By default, only local administrators have this right, which can be found under the Local Policies ➤ User Rights Assignment.

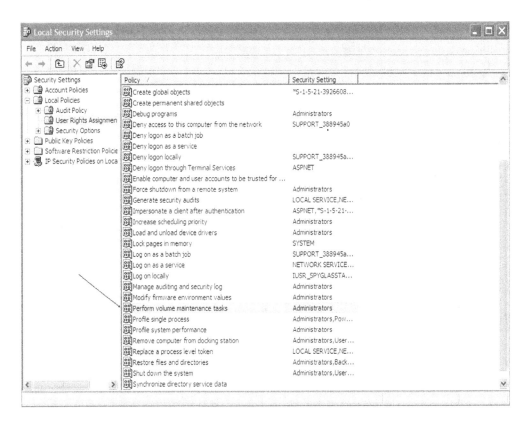

Figure 3-7. *As long as the SQL Server service account has permission for "Performance volume maintenance tasks," the database engine can create empty files quickly.*

Once you've added SQL Server to this list, you no longer need to initialize every bit in the file to 0. When SQL Server finally writes data to the file, it *won't* go back and change bits to 0 for empty spaces—only the current data is recorded.

Note You need local administrator rights to grant the right to perform volume maintenance tasks.

Restoring Differential Backups in Simple Recovery Mode

Many DBAs don't realize that you can restore differential backups in Simple Recovery mode. Remember a differential backup is simply the data pages that have changed since the last full backup. No transaction log is needed:

```
RESTORE DATABASE AdventureWorks
FROM DISK='D:\SQLBackups\AWFull.bak'
WITH NORECOVERY -- We aren't done with our Restore process

RESTORE DATABASE AdventureWorks
FROM DISK='D:\SQLBackups\AWDiff.bak'
WITH NORECOVERY
```

You don't need to restore more than one differential backup; you only need to restore the most current one. This isn't quite a point-in-time recovery, but it does allow you to get to a much more current state than the last full backup. Again, I still haven't recovered the database. If you were to look at the database in Management Studio, you would see that it's in a loading state. To bring it online, you just need to perform a recovery:

```
RESTORE DATABASE AdventureWorks
WITH RECOVERY
```

The database is now online and available for users. I generally like to keep the recovery process as a separate action.

Restoring Differential Backups in Full/Bulk-Logged Mode

Differential backups in Full Recovery or Bulk-Logged Recovery mode behave exactly the same as if they were in Simple Recovery mode, except that you will receive the tail-log error if you try to overwrite the database and restore just to the last differential. You can force an overwrite if you really want to restore just the full and the differential backup, but I've never seen that technique in action. Instead, you can start restoring transaction logs.

> **Note** Did you remember to use `WITH COPY_ONLY`? Differential backups are tied to the last full backup that occurred. If, for some reason, you create a full backup out of your normal backup scheme (to move to a development platform, for example), you can accidentally nullify the usefulness of including differential backups. I have personally experienced this frustration under SQL Server 2000 and 7.0 on multiple occasions. From this point forward, any "extra" full backup I make will include the `WITH COPY_ONLY` clause.

Restoring to a Point in Time

You can use three methods to restore the database to a specific point in time. First, you can obviously specify a specific time. Second, you can jump to the exact LSN number you want to restore to if you remember it (remember all those LSN entries when you ran a `RESTORE HEADERONLY`?). Third, you can create and specify named *log marks*, and then you can restore to one of those marks. Regardless of which option you chose, you can choose whether the restore should include the stopping point, or whether the restore should go up to, but not including, the stopping point. (For example, you can choose to restore up to *and including* a given LSN, or up to but *not including* the LSN.)

Restoring to a specific point does have implications. You can't apply any additional backups after a point-in-time recovery. Also, restoring log backups takes much longer than restoring a differential or even a full database backup if the log restore started from day one. A full restore replaces data pages, whereas a differential restore replaces pages that have changed since the last full backup. A transaction log restore literally replays the transactions that have occurred. Given the amount of transactions to restore, the process can take an unacceptable length of time. I'll talk more about optimal backup/restore plans in Chapter 5.

Time

Usually a request comes in to restore the database to a specific time. For example, "So-and-so accidentally deleted two million records, and we need to restore the way the database looked at 3:10 p.m." As you'll see in Chapter 9, there is another way to handle this.

Restoring log files is actually a separate command, but it's similar to the `RESTORE DATABASE` command. It does require that a full database restore and a differential (if needed) occur first. After that, you can restore as many files as you want as long as you have a sequential order:

```
RESTORE DATABASE AdventureWorks
FROM DISK='D:\SQLBackups\AWFull.bak'
WITH NORECOVERY -- We aren't done with our Restore process
RESTORE LOG AdventureWorks
FROM DISK='D:\SQLBackups\AWLog1.bak"
WITH NORECOVERY
RESTORE LOG AdventureWorks
FROM DISK='D:\SQLBackups\AWLog2.bak'
WITH RECOVERY, STOPAT 'Jan 10, 2006 3:10pm'
```

The previous example restores a full backup and two transaction logs and stops at 3:10 p.m. on January 10, 2006. Note that the STOPAT clause appears *after* the RECOVERY clause.

LSN

If you know the exact LSN at which you want to stop the restore, you can stop at that particular point. But how would you know what LSN to stop at? Well, you could have gotten it from RESTORE HEADERONLY, by calling PSS, or by receiving a specific error. I've seen this technique used only once, and it can only be performed via T-SQL:

```
RESTORE DATABASE AdventureWorks
FROM DISK='D:\SQLBackups\AWFull.bak'
WITH NORECOVERY -- We aren't done with our Restore process
RESTORE LOG AdventureWorks
FROM DISK='D:\SQLBackups\AWLog1.bak"
WITH NORECOVERY
RESTORE LOG AdventureWorks
FROM DISK='D:\SQLBackups\AWLog2.bak'
WITH RECOVERY, STOPATMARK LSN:2433:5422
```

Log Marks

You can create log marks before performing a transaction that allows you to restore directly up to the point where the log mark was created. The following example shows a transaction called LogMarkAfterUpdate that contains a log mark:

```
RESTORE DATABASE AdventureWorks
FROM DISK='D:\SQLBackups\AWFull.bak'
WITH NORECOVERY -- We aren't done with our Restore process
RESTORE LOG AdventureWorks
FROM DISK='D:\SQLBackups\AWLog1.bak"
WITH NORECOVERY
RESTORE LOG AdventureWorks
FROM DISK='D:\SQLBackups\AWLog2.bak'
WITH RECOVERY, STOPATMARK 'LogMarkAfterUpdate'
```

With both LSN and log-mark restores, you can specify STOPBEFOREMARK and STOPAFTERMARK. As you'll see in Chapter 5, the difference between those two options can be significant.

Mirroring Backups

In Chapter 2, you learned that SQL Server 2005 and higher supports mirrored backups. While mirroring full backups doesn't seem like an efficient use of I/O or disk space, mirroring transaction log backups should be a given (assuming that they're being written to different locations). With mirrored backups, you only need one location from which to restore. With the previous STOPAT example, you could mix and match copies of the log file backups. Let's say you're mirroring your backups between D: (a RAID 5 partition) and E: (a RAID 1 partition). If one of the backups becomes corrupted, you could simply reference the other mirror:

```
RESTORE DATABASE AdventureWorks
FROM DISK='D:\SQLBackups\AWFull.bak'
WITH NORECOVERY -- We aren't done with our Restore process
RESTORE LOG AdventureWorks
FROM DISK='E:\SQLBackups\AWLog1.bak"
WITH NORECOVERY
RESTORE LOG AdventureWorks
FROM DISK='D:\SQLBackups\AWLog2.bak'
WITH RECOVERY, STOPAT 'Jan 10, 2006 3:10pm'
```

In the previous example, AWLog1.bak ends up being deleted on the D: partition, whereas the AWLog2.bak file becomes corrupted on the E: partition. There's no interdependency required for restore purposes—any copy of the appropriate file will do.

Striping Backups

Striped backups require that all pieces of the backup be available at the same time. This is very different from mirrored backups. If you configure the striped backup properly, the speed of the restore should be significantly faster than a single-file restore. The catch is that all of the files in the backup stripe must exist:

```
RESTORE DATABASE AdventureWorks
FROM DISK='D:\SQLBackups\AWFull.bak',E:\SQLBackups\AWFull.bak
WITH NORECOVERY
```

If either of those files is missing, the entire backup will be lost. Use striped backups with caution. If you recall from the previous chapter, it can be easy to accidentally create a striped backup.

If you need to stripe a backup across multiple tape drives, it may be better to let the hardware itself handle that via a tape array or an autoloader. With large databases, you usually don't have a choice, and leaving the striping work to just the hardware may be a better choice. I'll discuss hardware-related subjects in Chapter 10.

Verifying Backups

SQL Server has always provided a means to verify backups, either with BACKUP VERIFYONLY or RESTORE VERIFYONLY. With versions 2000 and earlier, running these commands only did a basic scan of the structural integrity of the file. SQL Server 2005 runs a much more thorough check of the database structure itself. This occurs even if the page-verification option for the database is set to None.

When verifying a backup, you may want to include the clause CONTINUE_ON_ERROR instead of the default STOP_ON_ERROR. This gives the operation a chance to complete with the hope that only a handful of pages may be corrupted. Intuitively, this may seem to be waste of time, but restoring a database that you know will ultimately be incomplete can actually save time drastically. If, on the other hand, you go with the default of STOP_ON_ERROR, you may be pausing to correct a problem only to have another problem occur further in the restore process. You'll end up running longer and longer portions of the restore process, finding each error one at a time. It's often faster to choose CONTINUE_ON_ERROR and get a listing of all errors in one pass.

■**Note** You can even specify CONTINUE_ON_ERROR with regular BACKUP and RESTORE commands. You can specify the clause regardless of whether you also specify VERIFYONLY.

If you let a verification process continue after an error, it will record the corrupted pages to a new table in the MSDB database: the SUSPECT_PAGE table. Every time the VERIFYONLY command finds a suspect page, it will add a row to the SUSPECT_PAGE table, up to a maximum of 1,000 times. If a single backup file produces in excess of 1,000 suspect pages, then you have a serious problem to solve, and there's little point—or so SQL Server's designers believe—in continuing to record errors.

Restoring Data Pages

New with SQL Server 2005, you can replace individual data pages with the RESTORE command. You can do this either in offline or online mode. You would use online mode if you discover a suspect page during normal operations. In order to have any level of success with the page-level restore, the database must be in Full Recovery mode. Bulk-Logged Recovery mode may work, but for practical purposes, don't count on page restores working in that mode.

You can restore only actual data pages. This technique won't work for pages in log files, nor for Global Allocation Map (GAM) pages, Secondary Global Allocation Map (SGAM) pages, or Page Free Space (PFS) pages. Only data pages associated with a specific table or index will work.

The restore process is just like a full recovery. Once you know the page ID to be restored, you can begin a full restore and specify only the page IDs you need replaced. Be sure to apply all transaction log backups (including the tail-log backup), as changes to the pages being restored may have occurred after the full backup:

```
RESTORE DATABASE AdventureWorks PAGE '20:1570,20:1571,20:1572'
FROM DISK='D:\SQLBackups\AWFull.bak'
WITH NORECOVERY RESTORE LOG AdventureWorks

FROM DISK='D:\SQLBackups\AWLog1.bak"
WITH NORECOVERY

RESTORE LOG AdventureWorks
FROM DISK='D:\SQLBackups\AWLog2.bak'
WITH RECOVERY
```

Note that you can specify multiple pages to be restored. The maximum number of pages is 1,000, but something tells me that if more than 1,000 pages are damaged, you have bigger problems to deal with.

Of course, you need to get the internal page IDs before beginning the process. You might get an error during the restore, in which case it gets written to the MSDB..SUSPECT_PAGE table. You could also run the T-SQL database console command (DBCC) DBCC CHECKDB command, and use the results of that command. If you're going to attempt a page restore, make sure you have a complete list of damaged pages. If you run into an error during a RESTORE but don't have the CONTINUE_ON_ERROR option set, you may be restoring a single page only to discover more damage than you initially encountered. Only perform page restores with IDs collected from either a complete DBCC CHECKDB run or from MSDB..SUSPECT_PAGE.

Restoring System Databases

Many DBAs are familiar with restoring a user database, but what happens if you lose the entire instance? You had better be familiar with restoring system databases, and master databases in particular. The other system databases—MSDB, model, distribution, and resource (you do know about the resource database, yes?)—can be equally important, but the master is your starting point. Always.

Master

Every DBA should practice restoring a master database. The process is unlike any other database restore.

First, stop the SQL Server service via SQL Server Management Studio, SQL Server Configuration Manager, or the Services applet in the Control Panel. You need to stop it so you can restart the server in single-user mode.

Start SQL Server in single-user mode. From a command line, type sqlservr -m. You should see startup text in the command window, as shown in Figure 3-8.

Figure 3-8. *After you use* sqlservr -m *to open the database, the window remains open until the instance shuts down.*

Restore the master database. Open a database engine query session and issue the command shown in Figure 3-9. You may receive an error stating that a single session is already running. Click OK to get past the error.

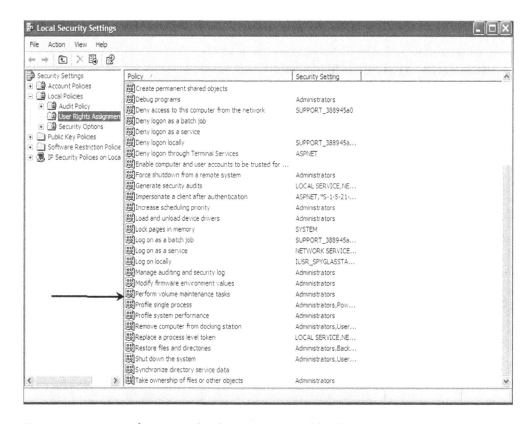

Figure 3-9. *Restoring the master database is only possible when in single-user mode (*`sqlservr -m`*). Any attempt to restore the master while the database is started normally fails.*

SQL Server will shut down automatically if the master restores successfully. Restart SQL Server normally using SQL Server Management Studio, SQL Server Configuration Manager, or the Services applet in the Control Panel.

MSDB

SQL Agent activity is the primary source of data contained in MSDB. Job definitions, schedules, operators, and alerts all make their home in MSDB.

SQL Server Integration Services (SSIS) can also save packages to the MSDB database. Be sure you're clear on whether packages are saved to MSDB or on the file system. Integration Services development is now presented as a Visual Studio 2005 project, so there may be a disconnect between you (the DBA) and someone creating that project.

Another impact of overwriting the MSDB database is that all job history information is lost. Many may not be concerned with this, but I find that the more historical information (and job history, in particular) I have on the operation of my system, the better prepared I am to address issues or plan for future needs.

First, you must stop SQL Agent. Once you stop it, you can restore it like any other database:

```
RESTORE DATABASE MSDB
FROM FILE=C:\msdb.bak
WITH RECOVERY
```

MSDB runs in Simple Recovery mode, so this will always be an easy restore from a full backup. Note how I continue to explicitly type in the WITH RECOVERY option, even though it's the default. If it's starting to annoy you, good—you've learned that specifying it explicitly is important.

Model

I see very few implementations that use the model database (that is, it's been changed from its default settings). Remember that with the model database, you can not only change the default settings for a new database—such as the initial file sizes and growth percentage—but you can also include actual tables. I often use custom statistic gathering for performance and capacity planning. Rather than create all of the custom tables I use for holding data (plus a few seed tables that hold code values), I just add them to the model database of a server.

If you work with the model database in any fashion, make sure you have the most current version backed up—it can save you a lot of time and headaches. In the scenario I just described where I had a significant number of customizations made to the model database, there was one instance when I forgot to back it up. The entire server crashed, and I had no written record of how I had it set up. It took a lot of manual work comparing reports and documentation I had delivered to a client to recreate the original model settings.

Note It may sound inane, but having something go wrong or making a blatant mistake is really the best way to learn. Most of the content of this book comes from my years of either watching the impact of other's mistakes or learning from my own. Mistakes, errors, and even disasters are the best drivers toward learning. The expression "hindsight is 20/20" is true—it's much easier to see what should have been done after you've seen the impact of failing to do it.

---

tempdb

Technically, you don't back up or restore tempdb. You can move it, however, and this topic often comes up during a restore operation. If you have a massive disaster incident that requires new hardware, you could be in a situation where you need to change the physical location of tempdb. Remember that the master maintains the location of tempdb. If you place your tempdb in a location other than its original, you'll need to update that information. You don't do this by backing up and restoring or by detaching and reattaching. You need to use an ALTER DATABASE statement. As with most database operations involving the actual files, you need to refer to the logical name of those files. Normally, it's TEMPDEV for the data file and TEMPLOG for the log file. To confirm, you can query the SYS.MASTER_FILES table. To place tempdb in a new location, you must first accept whatever location it is placed in when SQL Server is reinstalled, then use ALTER DATABASE to move it. You must execute this code from within the master database:

```
ALTER DATABASE tempdb
MODIFY FILE (NAME = tempdev, FILENAME = 'E:\SQLData\tempdb.mdf');

ALTER DATABASE tempdb
MODIFY FILE (NAME = templog, FILENAME = 'E:\SQLData\templog.ldf');
```

Once you run this code, you need to stop and restart SQL Server. After that, tempdb will be recreated in the specified location, with the settings, such as the initial data and log file size, stored in the master.

Distribution

If a server is used as a distributor for replication, and depending on the replication method used, you'll need to back up the distribution database on a regular basis. Transactional replication makes heavy use of the distribution database, while merge replication does not.

However, depending on the replication scenario, you may not need to restore the distribution database. Often replication is best "restored" by dropping subscriptions and publications and re-creating them. This was usually the case in SQL 2000, and could remain a preferable way of rebuilding replication rather than restoring the distribution database.

The one large exception to that would be in an elaborate replication topology. If you're replicating between a handful of servers, simply rebuilding the replication publications should suffice. If the topologies have thousands of subscribers, publishing subscribers, and large databases, restoring the distribution database will save hundreds of man hours.

Resource

You may have noticed that the size of the master database is considerably smaller in SQL Server 2005/2008 compared to SQL Server 2000 and earlier. That's because the code used to generate pseudotables and system views is now located in a hidden system database called resource. This database does *not* appear in SQL Server Management Studio, as you can see in Figure 3-10.

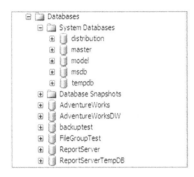

Figure 3-10. *The resource database is a system database, but you won't see it in SQL Server Management Studio. That doesn't mean you shouldn't back it up, though.*

However, if you look on the file system, you'll see two files: mssqlsystemresource.mdf and mssqlsystemresource.ldf, as shown in Figure 3-11. These two files represent your resource database. Unlike with other databases that are exclusively locked when the instance is running, you can copy and paste both of these files to a new location.

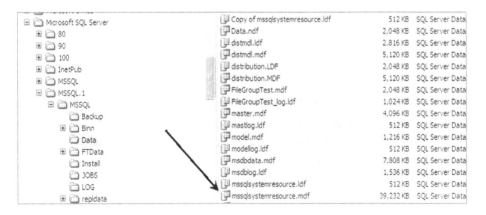

Figure 3-11. *The resource database files appear as normal database files, with both a data file (.mdf) and a log file (.ldf).*

Backing up the resource database is critical because SQL Server won't start without it present and in the same location as the master database. Unlike other databases, you can't back up the resource database with T-SQL commands; you must simply copy and paste the resource database to another file location, then back up those files to tape. Even though resource is locked while SQL Server is running, you can still copy and paste the open files without fear of data corruption.

As tedious as this sounds, you only need to back up the resource database any time you install a service pack, hotfix, or hotfix rollup on the server. If worse comes to worse, you could always find a server running at the same service pack/hotfix level and use that resource database as a backup from which to restore.

ReportServer

The ReportServer database doesn't simply hold configuration information. It holds report definitions, schedules, report snapshots, and more. Nearly every aspect of Reporting Services is stored within this database. If you use Reporting Services at all, you should treat this database as a production database within your organization. If you use report caching, subscriptions, or snapshots, you should prepare for point-in-time recovery.

■**Tip** If you've stored connection-string information in the ReportServer database, you must use the RSKEYMGMT.EXE utility to first extract the encryption key used. Without a copy of that key, any reports that rely on encrypted connection strings will fail. This isn't a huge deal if you have 30-50 reports, but I've worked with systems approaching 500 reports. Not having an encryption key to restore could be unpleasant in that scenario.

ReportServerTempDB

There's really no direct need to back up ReportServerTempDB, since it is intended to be a temporary database. However, if you've implemented some of the advanced report caching features with Reporting Services and have a fairly large deployment (more than 100 reports or more than 1,000 users), there could be a significant performance impact if ReportServerTempDB is effectively reset. There is an advantage to keeping a backup ready to return the Report Server to optimal performance as quickly as possible.

Databases in SUSPECT Status

Nothing instills more panic for a DBA than seeing a database in SUSPECT status. A database is placed in this status if SQL Server attempts but is unable to bring the database online, whether in ONLINE, SINGLE_USER, or RESTRICTED_USER mode. The SUSPECT status can be caused by one the following scenarios:

- One or more required data files are missing.

- One or more required data files are damaged.

- Recovery is not possible due to missing log files.

- Recovery is not possible due to damaged log files.

- Recovery is not possible due to a break in the LSN chain.

Essentially, SQL Server prevents you from accessing the database because it can't ensure consistent data. SUSPECT status is actually a good thing. It prevents you from proceeding with potentially inconsistent data. The operative word here is *potentially*. In the majority of the cases I've dealt with, the problem had nothing to do with inconsistent data, and a restore was not required. The single biggest issue with SUSPECT mode is that it generates panic and a "just get the system back up" mentality, without regard to data loss.

Usually, the true cause for data corruption (such as hardware failure or damaged disk drives) shows its ugly head well before a database moves into SUSPECT mode. If you're validating your backup files before writing them to a tape drive, you should also discover a problem before the database moves into SUSPECT status (if torn-page detection or checksum verification is enabled).

SQL Server 2005 and higher supports an emergency startup mode. This mode gives you yet another option for dealing with a database in SUSPECT status. Essentially, starting a database in emergency mode tells SQL Server to bring the server to an online status without attempting the recovery process. The database then remains in its damaged state.

While the database is still technically in its damaged state, you can at least detach it or extract the data from the database. However, you cannot guarantee the transactional consistency of the database.

Technically, the emergency mode feature did exist in previous versions of SQL Server, but you were forced to manually alter a system table in the master database in order to put a database into that mode. I've had the unfortunate pleasure of dealing with databases so damaged that starting in emergency mode was the only option; in every case, the reason it was the only option was because something was missed in the design of the backup and recovery scheme. Emergency mode should be a sign not only that there's a problem with your database, but that there's a problem with your process as well.

Restore and Disaster Categories

How do restore operations fit in with the disaster categories? I've split backup and recovery into two separate chapters, but you need to think about the ramifications of any disaster scenario both in terms of how you should back up your database and how you need to restore your database. When it comes to restoring, take the following factors into account:

- *Environmental*: Be prepared to restore to a completely new location in case of an environmental disaster. Be familiar with the methods to restore the master, move data file locations while restoring, and so on.

- *Hardware*: Hardware performance, whether it's a tape or disk drive, is as important to restore operations as it is to backup operations. The longer the process runs, the higher the likelihood of errors.

- *Media*: The quality of media plays a big role in restore operations. Poor quality tape or disk drives could result in the need to restore random damaged pages; this is not a scenario anyone wants.

- *Process*: Point-in-time restores, and the log-mark restore in particular, can be an excellent way to deal with process errors.

- *User*: Although point-in-time restores can bring you up to the point of a user error (assuming that point is known), all data after the user error is lost.

Caveats and Recommendations

The following items are some things to keep in mind now that you've read this chapter. Keep them in mind, and your next restore will (hopefully!) be smooth and uneventful.

- *Use checksum instead of torn-page detection*: Checksum validation is much more thorough than torn-page detection. Yes, torn-page detection is less of a resource drain, but it's a primitive technique for spotting corruption; it's possible to have a complete, yet damaged, page.

- *Always specify a recovery clause when performing a restore*: The default of bringing the database back online via recovery has tripped me up in the past. If you accidentally recover the database before restoring all the necessary files, you'll have to start the process over. If the full backup is of any significant size, this will result in a lot of downtime and frustration. Try to get in the habit of specifying the `WITH RECOVERY` clause even when you're ready to recover the database. Relying on default behavior can be costly.

- *Don't rush into a restore of any kind*: Stop. Breathe. Gather yourself before leaping into action. Map out a plan of action on a piece of scratch paper before starting anything (this is different than simply following the instructions of a prewritten disaster recovery plan). If possible, ask a colleague to double-check your work. DBAs, business users, or management almost always approach a restore situation with a sense of urgency. There is a fine line between urgency and panic; rushing to begin the restore process may create the momentum that carries you over that line.

- *Finding a database in* `SUSPECT` *status isn't the end of the world*: While a database in `SUSPECT` status could indicate a serious problem, it may just have a file in the wrong location.

- *Be careful with the* `SUSPECT_PAGE` *table and page-level restore*: That table only holds 1,000 rows, and it needs to be cleaned out manually. You may want to empty it on a regular basis. Also, keep in mind that the `SUSPECT_PAGE` table holds information for all databases on the instance.

Summary

I've explored many of the aspects of a restore process, from technical commands to the potential for errors. You've seen how to restore from full backups and from differential backups. You've seen how to restore to a specific point in time, how to mirror and stripe your backups, and much more. You have many options at your disposal when it comes to restoring a database and getting it back online again.

In the next chapter, I'll show you how you can have even more granular control over your backup and recovery strategy. You'll learn to back up and restore only specific files and filegroups. And if you're wondering why you'd care to do such a thing, you'll learn that, too.

CHAPTER 4

∎∎∎

Backing Up and Restoring Files and Filegroups

The concept of a filegroup has been in place since the introduction of SQL Server 7.0. Essentially, a filegroup is a construct to provide a logical storage location for an object when it is created. Thus, you can put different tables and indexes in separate filegroups to not only improve performance, but more important, to minimize backup and recovery times. As a database grows and performance and maintenance demands increase, the usage of filegroups becomes a necessity. New features within SQL Server 2005 leverage filegroups; some focus on performance, and some improve filegroup involvement in disaster recovery.

Even though the functionality has been available for years, few environments use specific filegroups either for performance or backup optimization. Whether a database is 1GB or 1TB, it's often with a single filegroup. True, databases often have multiple files, which can present some performance gain, but the benefits of a well-designed filegroup implementation can make the difference between a scalable system and a nonscalable system, both in terms of performance and *recoverability*.

While it's obvious that filegroups make sense for a 1TB database, it may seem that maintaining a filegroup scheme for a 1GB database creates more administrative work for very little gain. Filegroups do introduce additional administration, but they can provide surprising results, even for a relatively small database. For full-text search, SQL Server 2005 introduces new functionality that incorporates the backup of an external full-text catalog with the backup of a specific filegroup. That alone should make you reconsider the use of filegroups.

In this chapter, I'll review the benefits filegroups provide, how to back up and restore individual data files, how to back up and restore a filegroup, and new SQL Server 2005 improvements to filegroup functionality.

A Brief Review of Filegroups

As you've already seen, a database is made up of two or more files. At a minimum, it must include one primary data file (normally with an .mdf extension) and one transaction log file (.ldf). If more space is needed, you may add secondary data files to the database (.ndf is the standard file extension). A database also contains one or more filegroups, which contain one or more data files (.mdf and .ndf). Remember that while a database can have more than one .ldf file, log files are not associated with a specific filegroup but, rather, with each individual database.

Creating Filegroups

Unlike most database objects, there is no CREATE statement for filegroups, because they're part of the structure of a database. Filegroups and additional files are created either when a database is first built or later via an ALTER DATABASE statement.

When creating a database initially, you specify filegroups and specific files as subclauses to the CREATE DATABASE statement:

```
CREATE DATABASE AWSample
ON
PRIMARY(
NAME=AWSampleData,
FILENAME='D:\data\AWSData.MDF,
SIZE=2000,
FILEGROWTH=200),

FILEGROUP AWSampleData (
NAME=AWSampleData1,
FILENAME='D:\Data\AWSD1.NDF',
SIZE=2000
FILEGROWTH=200),

FILEGROUP AWSampleIndex(
NAME=AWSampleIndex1,
FILENAME='E:\Data\AWSI1.NDF,
SIZE=2000,
FILEGROWTH=200),

LOG ON (
NAME=AWSampleLog
FILENAME='F:\Data\AWSLog1.LDF',
SIZE=200,
FILEGROWTH=20)
```

This CREATE DATABASE statement creates the primary filegroup—the primary filegroup is named, aptly enough, PRIMARY—and two additional filegroups, each containing a single file initially. Notice from the names of the filegroups that the intent here is most likely to separate clustered and nonclustered indexes for performance purposes. Also note: *The log file has no direct link to any particular filegroup.*

■**Note** Each database must have a filegroup named PRIMARY that holds the .mdf file. That filegroup cannot be renamed or deleted.

If you want to add a third filegroup after the database is created, possibly to hold read-only data, you could use an ALTER DATABASE statement to do so:

```
ALTER DATABASE AWSample
ADD FILEGROUP AWSampleROData;
GO
```

This, of course, creates an empty filegroup. You still need to assign files to it:

```
ALTER DATABASE AWSample
ADD FILE (
NAME=AWSampleROData1,
FILENAME='D:\Data\AWSRO1.NDF',
SIZE=2000,
FILEGROWTH=200)
TO FILEGROUP AWSampleROData;
GO
```

The T-SQL commands to create a filegroup and assign specific files to that filegroup are simple enough, but if you're syntactically challenged like I am, you can create filegroups easily from SQL Server Management Studio, as shown in Figure 4-1. You can add more than one filegroup at a time, but you must hit the OK button—not the Add button—for the creation to take place.

Figure 4-1. *The SQL Server Management Studio interface for creating filegroups*

At this point, the filegroups have no files associated with them. Once you create the filegroups, you can associate new files with a specific filegroup using the Files page (which you get to from the "Select a page" menu on the left), as shown in Figure 4-2.

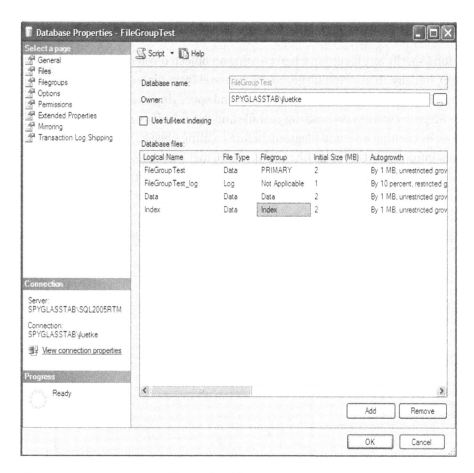

Figure 4-2. *Associating new files with a filegroup*

When adding a file to a filegroup, the Filegroup column shows only filegroups that you've created already. If you haven't saved the database with the new filegroups defined, they won't show up on this screen.

Notice that I'm using a naming scheme for both the filegroups and the files that indicates what a given filegroup contains and which filegroup a file belongs to. Examples in many sources, including BOL, label filegroups with no particular meaning (e.g., FG1 and FG2). For a relatively simple database, such meaningless naming would suffice. However, if you have a relatively complicated database design with numerous filegroups and files, that sort of naming scheme can create a challenging environment to support.

While two physical file names cannot be the same, it is possible to have filegroups under different databases with the same name. PRIMARY is a perfect example, because it exists in each database. I highly recommend naming each filegroup uniquely throughout an entire instance, particularly when working with a high number of databases on a single instance.

The Default Filegroup

If you don't specify any filegroup when creating an object, it will be placed on a default filegroup. Initially, this default filegroup will be the PRIMARY filegroup, but I highly recommend adding at least one additional filegroup and specifying it as the default. The PRIMARY filegroup will always hold the .mdf file and thus all of the system tables for the database. By creating a second filegroup before creating objects, you can separate the technical information for the database from the actual user data. That second filegroup is a better candidate for being the default group. Mixing actual, active data (meaning it is constantly updated) with the metadata contained in the .mdf file is a recipe for disaster.

SQL Server can have only one default filegroup per database. This may seem like an unnecessary thing to say, but the user interface implies otherwise, because it uses check boxes instead of radio buttons, as you can see in Figure 4-3.

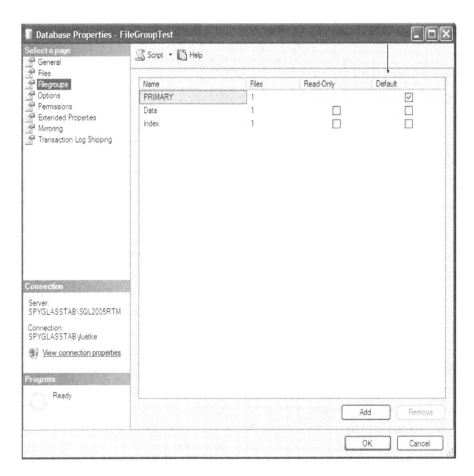

Figure 4-3. *You can only select one filegroup, so the default column in this interface should really be a collection of radio buttons.*

The default filegroup is associated with a database, so it makes sense that the T-SQL command to change it is ALTER DATABASE:

```
ALTER DATABASE AWSample
MODIFY FILEGROUP AWSampleData DEFAULT;
GO
```

I highly recommend creating at least one extra filegroup other than PRIMARY and changing it to have the DEFAULT property, as shown in the preceding code example. I also recommend avoiding the use of the DEFAULT property when creating objects.

Assigning Objects to Filegroups

When you create a table or an index, either you or SQL Server must assign that newly created object to a filegroup. If you specify a filegroup in your CREATE TABLE or CREATE INDEX statement, the object will be placed on the filegroup that you specify. Otherwise, SQL Server will place the object into the default filegroup. If you haven't created and specified a default filegroup other than PRIMARY, the newly created object will end up in the PRIMARY filegroup (which is generally not desirable). I do recommend that you use filegroups and specify a filegroup other than PRIMARY as the default.

Creating an Object in a Filegroup

To specify a filegroup, you simply add an ON clause to the end of the CREATE statement:

```
CREATE TABLE AWNotes(
[ID] INT,
[Notes] TEXT)
ON AWSampleData
```

In addition to placing tables and indexes on specific filegroups, you can specify a separate filegroup to hold any data for columns of type TEXT, NTEXT, or IMAGE. You set such a filegroup on a table-by-table basis. As you might expect, SQL Server uses the default filegroup for text and image data if no other filegroup is specified.

Assigning specific filegroups when creating a table with SQL Server Management Studio is not intuitive. The Properties window must be open when creating a table, as shown in Figure 4-4.

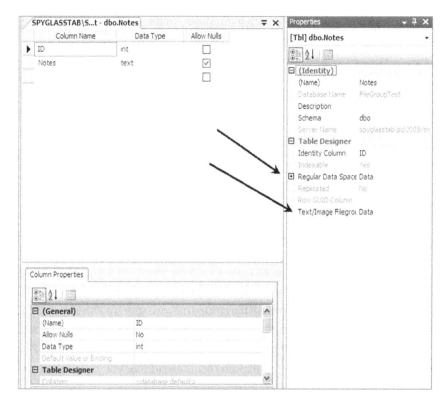

Figure 4-4. *You assign a table to filegroups from the Properties window. You can specify the filegroup for the table itself, plus a separate filegroup for* TEXT, NTEXT, *and* IMAGE *data.*

When creating indexes, the screen interface is similar, as you can see in Figure 4-5.

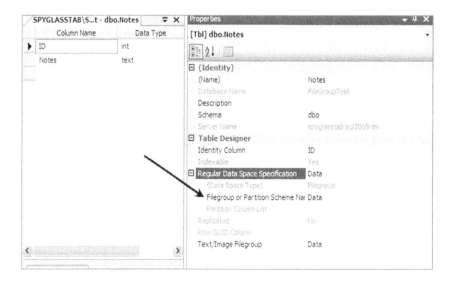

Figure 4-5. *Specifying a filegroup for indexes*

All in all, it pays to specify a filegroup for a table or an index when you create the object initially. Whenever possible, you should design your table and index layout across filegroups before building the actual database.

PLANNING FOR EXTREMES

When planning or designing a new database, someone will often say something like, "It's only going to be a 500MB database at maximum, so a single data file will do." These often turn out to be "famous last words." There was a time when someone declared, "No one will ever use more than 640K of physical memory." That statement led to an architecture design that limited memory for operating systems from DOS to Windows Millennium Edition (Me). Whoops.

I've run into many SQL Server databases in the 20-50GB range that started as Microsoft Access databases. When they were created, I'm sure someone decided that there would never be more than 50MB of data stored. As a result, these evolving database designs, both logical and physical, usually aren't built for any sort of scalability. I get involved because the performance of that 20GB database becomes unbearably slow.

When I have the luxury of working on a project from day one, I always stress planning for extremes. You say you currently have only 50 users? Plan for 50,000. You don't think that using filegroups will be necessary for either performance or recoverability enhancement? Build them anyway. I've never seen an operational database (that is, a database other than a data warehouse or other decision support database) that hasn't grown and evolved both in volume and functionality.

Using filegroups is a simple way to plan for extremes. Get in the habit of always specifying a filegroup when creating objects, even if you aren't using multiple filegroups. When the day arrives that you do, you'll save yourself from numerous headaches. If you aren't in the habit of explicitly specifying a filegroup, it can be easy to place objects where you don't want to. It can be especially frustrating if you don't catch the mistake immediately. Filegroups require a bit of up-front work, but the payoff in the long run can be significant.

Moving Objects to Different Filegroups

The easiest way to move objects is to update the property page for that table or index. However, moving objects en masse this way isn't possible—you'd need a T-SQL script for that. If you run a SQL Server Profiler trace while making such a change via SQL Server Management Studio, you'll see that SQL Server actually creates a second table on the new filegroup, inserts all of the existing data into that new table, drops the original table, and then changes the new table name to the original object name, as shown in Figure 4-6.

```
SQL:BatchStarting       CREATE TABLE dbo.Tmp_Notes   (   ID int NOT NULL IDENTITY (1, 1)...
SQL:BatchCompleted      CREATE TABLE dbo.Tmp_Notes   (   ID int NOT NULL IDENTITY (1, 1)...
SQL:BatchStarting       SET IDENTITY_INSERT dbo.Tmp_Notes ON
SQL:BatchCompleted      SET IDENTITY_INSERT dbo.Tmp_Notes ON
SQL:BatchStarting       IF EXISTS(SELECT * FROM dbo.Notes)    EXEC('INSERT INTO dbo.Tmp_...
SQL:BatchCompleted      IF EXISTS(SELECT * FROM dbo.Notes)    EXEC('INSERT INTO dbo.Tmp_...
SQL:BatchStarting       SET IDENTITY_INSERT dbo.Tmp_Notes OFF
SQL:BatchCompleted      SET IDENTITY_INSERT dbo.Tmp_Notes OFF
SQL:BatchStarting       DROP TABLE dbo.Notes
SQL:BatchCompleted      DROP TABLE dbo.Notes
SQL:BatchStarting       EXECUTE sp_rename N'dbo.Tmp_Notes', N'Notes', 'OBJECT'
SQL:BatchCompleted      EXECUTE sp_rename N'dbo.Tmp_Notes', N'Notes', 'OBJECT'
SQL:BatchStarting       CREATE NONCLUSTERED INDEX IX_Notes ON dbo.Notes   (   ID   ) WIT...
SQL:BatchCompleted      CREATE NONCLUSTERED INDEX IX_Notes ON dbo.Notes   (   ID   ) WIT...
```

Figure 4-6. *Example SQL Server Profiler output from tracing the movement of objects from one filegroup to another*

Luckily, the movement illustrated in Figure 4-6 is a set of logged actions, so if any one of the steps fails, the whole process will fail. That means that moving filegroups will cause the transaction log to grow suddenly. You need to move multiple objects in off-hours—all the more reason to create objects on appropriate filegroups from the start.

To move objects between filegroups, use an ALTER statement, such as ALTER TABLE or ALTER INDEX. The syntax requires you to drop the primary key constraint first; you'll need to add it back immediately after moving the table to the new filegroup. Here I'm simply moving a table called Notes from its current location (the PRIMARY filegroup—bad!) to the DATA filegroup:

```
ALTER TABLE dbo.Notes
drop constraint PK_Notes
WITH (MOVE TO DATA)
```

Oddly enough, the ALTER TABLE statement won't work if you have no primary key constraint to drop. At least that's how it behaves at the time of this writing. Still, this does allow for a way to script moving multiple objects between filegroups in one pass.

Filegroup Strategies

BOL states, "Most databases will work well with a single data file and a single transaction log file." Normally, I find BOL to offer the best documentation for any software product, period. In this case, I'd rather that sentence be stricken from the record. While it's true that databases can work well with a single data file and a single log file, it isn't true that this is the optimal configuration. If that were true, there'd be no reason to use filegroups at all.

While we're primarily interested in how filegroups play into a backup and restore strategy, they have other significant advantages, even for a relatively small database. I'll briefly discuss some of the other major benefits to filegroup usage before moving on to backup and restore implications.

■**Note** All of the scenarios in this section assume that each filegroup is on a separate I/O path. While there can be some benefit even when all filegroups are on the same data array, the intent is to be able to leverage multiple I/O paths. These scenarios also assume that both the transaction log for the database and tempdb reside on separate I/O paths. Yes, these are perfect-world configurations, but it's best to plan for extremes, then adjust your plan downward to what is reasonable to implement. I'll discuss I/O implications at length in Chapter 10.

Separating Clustered Indexes/Heaps from Nonclustered Indexes

For heavily used tables, separating the table from its nonclustered indexes can have a substantial performance impact. This is true not only for a DSS-type database, which is heavy with indexes, but also for an online transaction processing (OLTP) database that requires numerous nonclustered indexes. Normally with an OLTP database, the more indexes on a table, the poorer the performance, because insert, update, and delete are the more common operations. Each statement must update not only the table, but also every index. Nonclustered indexes tend to be fairly narrow, meaning a single index is built on one to four columns (of course, there are exceptions). If you separate a table's data and its nonclustered indexes into different filegroups, you can significantly reduce I/O requirements.

Separating Read-Only and Read/Write Tables

A filegroup has only two properties: default and read-only. From an I/O perspective, separating read-only operations from write operations can improve performance, assuming that you're placing them on separate filegroups placed on separate I/O paths.

Also, you may want to protect certain tables from changes. I've run into situations where DBAs have used two databases for a single application: one holding updateable information, and one holding read-only information (with the entire database set to read-only). This requires two different permission sets and more maintenance than is needed.

It's easy to underestimate the usefulness of a read-only filegroup. Of course, there's the possible performance gain. You could also use a read-only filegroup to protect specific tables from accidental or intentional changes. Plus, you only need to back it up after it is populated (more on that shortly).

Partitioning Tables

SQL Server 2005 Enterprise Edition provides new functionality called *partitioned tables*. The concept is similar to a partitioned view, but it's implemented on a much more focused level. Multiple filegroups are defined to hold horizontal slices of a table or index, and a partitioning scheme is defined to automatically place data on the appropriate filegroup. For example, when partitioning an order table, you could create a separate filegroup for each sales region and create a scheme to route data to the appropriate area. If well designed, the performance results will be impressive. Simply testing this feature with multiple USB drives acting as filegroups showed a visible impact on my humble laptop computer.

Isolating Specific Tables

You may need to protect specific tables or isolate seldom updated data. In SQL Server 6.5, you could back up and restore individual tables; when 7.0 came out, that feature was removed (probably because PSS was inundated with calls about databases going into SUSPECT status after a single table—transactionally inconsistent—was restored). The only way to back up specific tables post-SQL Server 6.5 is to place them on a separate filegroup to be backed up independently of a full backup.

You also may want to isolate specific tables for backup/restore purposes. This could be to move tables that rarely need to be backed up on separate filegroups, or to move tables that change often. As you'll see shortly, having a separate filegroup to handle a full-text index backup is a must. Yes, a full database backup now includes full-text indexes—you can start pondering whether this is a good or bad thing. I'll discuss the implications shortly.

Reducing Backup/Restore Time

Here's the main point of this entire chapter: you can back up individual files and filegroups to maintain a reasonable backup window. If your full database backup would take 22 hours to complete, you could instead back up individual files and filegroups each night of the week. Properly designed, this same technique can speed up the restore process as well. This takes us to the next section on the particulars of backing up and restoring files and filegroups.

■**Note** Numerous third-party products can significantly reduce backup/restore procedures by means of compression. These products are sound, and I both use and recommend many of them. However, I caution my clients (and myself) not to rely on them. What if pricing goes through the roof when there is market saturation? Also, using a third-party product means you've now introduced another application that may require bug fixes or security patches. Don't get me wrong, I love these products. However, when planning for disaster recovery, *always* plan for extremes, which should include not having the presence of third-party utilities.

Backing Up and Restoring Files

Even if you have a single filegroup, you can still back up its individual files. This allows you to spread out a complete backup over a longer time period, plus it significantly reduces restore time if a specific data file is damaged. While in Full Recovery or Bulk-Logged Recovery mode, individual files may be backed up without restriction. In Simple Recovery mode, only read-only files (implying a read-only database or read-only filegroup) may be backed up.

Backing up specific files does require more administrative work and detailed documentation—much more so than implementing filegroup backups. Also, keep in mind that you can place tables and indexes only on filegroups, not on specific files. One failed restore could leave the entire database unusable, whereas a failed filegroup restore may leave some of the database intact.

■**Caution** Although SQL Server 2005 and higher offers options for file and filegroup backup/restore while in Simple Recovery mode, suppress this bit of knowledge. I would never advocate the use of such a low-level approach for backing up a database in Simple Recovery mode. In every case where I've used it, the system required that approach because it was a high-transaction system that required minimal maintenance time. Constructing a complex file/filegroup backup/restore scheme while in Simple Recovery mode taunts the fates. Don't do it. Remember, the transaction log is your life!

Backing Up Database Files

Files are backed up with the usual BACKUP DATABASE command. You need to specify the database and each file to be backed up—for example:

```
BACKUP DATABASE AWSample
FILE='D:\Data\AWData2.NDF'
TO DISK = 'E:\BackupData\AWData1.BAK'
```

Rather than some examples that show multiple files listed, the payoff with file backups is to perform them file-by-file over a longer period of time. The illustrated backup is often called a *full-file backup*, because you can follow it up with differential file backups.

NEED FOR REALISTIC DATABASE FILE SIZES

Theoretically, a single database file can be as large as 16TB. However, I don't find this a statistic worth advertising. I would never even consider having a file of that size, whether it's a database file or a log file, at least not in the near future. Why? One word: portability.

Hopefully, you'll never have to worry about moving your backup files to a new location. But if you do have to, wouldn't you rather use a method that doesn't involve transmitting a multiterabyte file over the network or striping it amongst ten tape drives? I never create database files larger than the media I would use to move them. For tape drives, that would be 40-80GB. If my only method for moving is to burn files onto a DVD, it's 4GB. I've never had to resort to burning to a CD, but if I did, the maximum file size would be 650MB.

Storage technology is growing by leaps and bounds, and hopefully two to three years after writing this, portable storage will be able to effectively handle large data files. Until that time, I'm keeping a close eye on my file sizes.

If you're lucky enough to never have a disaster scenario and never have to restore from a backup or move data from one location to another, knock yourself out—fill that 16TB file.

Creating File-Specific Differential Backups

Once you back up an individual file, you can create differential backups of just that file. File differential backups can result in a fast backup (since only the pages that changed since the last full-file backup are recorded) as well as a fast restore. Keep in mind that the size of the file differential backups will continue to grow in size (assuming that additional data is added) until the full file is backed up again.

The following example creates a file differential backup of the file that I backed up in the previous section:

```
BACKUP DATABASE AWSample
    FILE='D\Data\AWData2.NDF'
WITH DIFFERENTIAL
TO DISK = 'E:\BackupData\AWData2_Diff.BAK'
```

Look at file backups and file differential backups as a sort of individual database backup scheme. The only thing to keep in mind is that files don't necessarily contain entire objects. Also, to avoid mass confusion and eventual insanity, use either file differential or database differential backups—not both.

Restoring Database Files

Assuming that a single file has been damaged, restoring it is similar to a standard restore process. Although it's possible to have file backups in Simple Recovery mode, I won't be exploring that scenario. I'm only going to cover Full Recovery and Bulk-Logged Recovery modes.

With SQL Server 2005 Enterprise Edition, you can do file restores online. All other editions require the database to be offline to perform the restore.

As it should always be in a restore situation, the first step is to back up the tail of the transaction log. The command is simply a BACKUP LOG statement:

```
BACKUP LOG AWSample
TO DISK='E:\BackupData\AWSample_TailLog.bak'
WITH NORECOVERY, NO TRUNCATE
```

From there, the restore process is similar to any other database restore. Be sure to specify NORECOVERY throughout the restore until you're sure you're finished. The following code walks through restoring a single data file:

```
RESTORE DATABASE AWSample
    FILE='D:\DATA\AWSData2.ndf'
FROM DISK='E:\DATA\AWSData2.bak'
WITH NORECOVERY
-- Continue to restore any application transaction logs
-- Apply the tail-log backup
RESTORE LOG AWSample
FROM DISK 'E:\BackupData\AWSample_TailLog.bak'
WITH NORECOVERY
-- I prefer to do recovery as a separate step
RESTORE DATABASE AWSample
WITH RECOVERY
```

As I mentioned in Chapter 3, I prefer to recover the database as a separate step. It's always a good idea to take a breath, look around, and stop to think, "Did I restore all of the files I needed to restore?" Once that database is recovered, any missed steps mean you have to start over.

Restoring Differential Backups

As you might have guessed, the process of restoring file differential backups is similar to that of restoring database differentials. Keep in mind that you must restore a file differential backup that corresponds to the specific full-file backup you're starting with.

The following code restores a single data file, much like the previous sample, but it also restores a file differential backup before applying transaction log backups:

```
RESTORE DATABASE AWSample
    FILE='D:\DATA\AWSData2.ndf'
FROM DISK='E:\DATA\AWSData2.bak'
WITH NORECOVERY
RESTORE DATABASE AWSample
    FILE='D:\Data\AWSData2.ndf'
FROM DISK = 'E:\Data\AWSData2_Diff.bak'
WITH NORECOVERY
-- Continue to restore any application transaction logs
-- Apply the tail-log backup
RESTORE LOG AWSample
FROM DISK 'E:\BackupData\AWSample_TailLog.bak'
WITH NORECOVERY
RESTORE DATABASE AWSample
WITH RECOVERY
```

File differentials, just like database differential backups, can dramatically increase the speed of the restore process. On the downside, file differential backups can make a backup/restore plan extremely complex (I'll discuss that further in Chapter 5).

Backing Up and Restoring Filegroups

File-based backup and restore gives you the most control over individual backup and restore time. However, since files don't necessarily hold entire objects, file-based backup and restore don't give you the greatest level of control over recoverability. That's where filegroups take over.

Tables and indexes are either explicitly or implicitly (via the DEFAULT property) assigned to a specific filegroup. This allows you to control what objects are backed up when and how often.

Backing Up a Filegroup

A filegroup backup is really just a shorthand T-SQL method for backing up all the files in that particular filegroup. The following example shows you how to back up the PRIMARY filegroup:

```
BACKUP DATABASE AWSample
    FILEGROUP='PRIMARY'
TO DISK = 'E:\BackupData\AWSFGPrimary.BAK'
```

If you look at the same command created through SSMS, you can see that selecting PRIMARY implies the backup of each individual file underneath it, as shown in Figure 4-7. In this example, PRIMARY actually has only two data files—the third file name shown is a reference to a full-text catalog that is assigned to that filegroup (more on full-text backup shortly).

Figure 4-7. *Backing up a filegroup is a shortcut to backing up all the files it contains.*

Restoring a Filegroup

Restoring a filegroup works the same way most restore operations do. You back up the tail-log, restore the filegroup (which really means restoring all the files in that filegroup), restore the tail-log, and recover the database—for example:

```
BACKUP LOG AWSample
TO DISK='E:\BackupData\AWSample_TailLog.bak'
WITH NORECOVERY, NO TRUNCATE
GO
-- Always back up the tail-log!
```

```
RESTORE DATABASE AWSample
    FILEGROUP='PRIMARY'
FROM DISK='E:\DATA\AWSFGPrimary.bak'
WITH NORECOVERY
-- Continue to restore any application transaction logs
-- Apply the tail-log backup
RESTORE LOG AWSample
FROM DISK 'E:\BackupData\AWSample_TailLog.bak'
WITH NORECOVERY
-- I prefer to do recovery as a separate step
RESTORE DATABASE AWSample
WITH RECOVERY
```

This example shows a basic filegroup recovery. Sometimes you may want to restore a single filegroup, but in most cases, you'll want to restore the entire database one piece at a time.

Performing Partial Backups and Restores

Although it does deal with filegroup backups, a *partial backup* is really more like a full backup. You perform a partial backup by specifying the keyword READ_WRITE_FILEGROUPS in your BACKUP DATABASE command:

```
BACKUP DATABASE Adventureworks
READ_WRITE_FILEGROUPS TO
DISK='C:\AWPartial.bak'
```

What's the point of a partial backup? Well, if you have filegroups that are read-only, they really only need to be backed up once, don't they? Plus, you don't really need to use the BACKUP DATABASE command to back them up—you could just stop SQL Server at some point and perform a file-based backup on those read-only files.

Let's say you have two tables: an Order table and an OrderHistory table. Order is 80MB in size, with another 70MB of nonclustered indexes on it. OrderHistory and its indexes amount to 2GB in size. You could perform a full backup amounting to a little more than 2GB in size, or, as shown in Figure 4-8, you could restructure the database so that Order, the indexes on Order, and OrderHistory are all on separate filegroups, with the OrderHistory table's filegroup marked as read-only.

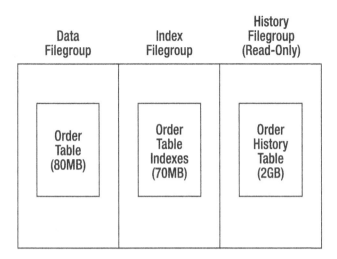

Figure 4-8. *An optimal filegroup configuration for using partial backups*

Doesn't it make more sense to only back up the filegroups used for current order data and indexes on an ongoing basis? Backing up the historical order data only once, instead of many times over, saves backup time and storage space.

To restore from a partial backup, the syntax is fairly intuitive when compared with the partial backup:

```
RESTORE DATABASE Adventureworks
READ_WRITE_FILEGROUPS
FROM DISK='C:\AWPartial.bak'
WITH PARTIAL, NORECOVERY
```

This RESTORE DATABASE command replaces only the read/write filegroups from the backup file (and since that's all you backed up with the partial backup, there isn't anything else to include). If you replace the missing read-only files, you can simply recover the database (remember how I prefer to recover the database as a separate step?):

```
RESTORE DATABASE Adventureworks
WITH RECOVERY
```

If you have to restore that read-only filegroup separately, you'll need to use a different technique. You'll still use the PARTIAL keyword, but you'll need to recover the database and put it online before restoring the read-only filegroup. Such a process is referred to as a *piecemeal restore*.

Performing Piecemeal Restores

With SQL Server 2000, you could do a sort of piecemeal restore, sometimes referred to as a *partial restore*. It had limitations, the biggest being that it was an offline operation. I never had the need to use it. Instead, I restored single filegroups that existed on separate I/O paths (so chances were only one would fail at any given time).

With SQL Server 2005 Enterprise Edition, you can do online piecemeal restores. After you restore the PRIMARY filegroup, you can bring individual filegroups online as you restore them. Users then have access to any objects assigned to online filegroups. This gives you a significant advantage to using filegroups just for the sake of recoverability.

I discussed this functionality while teaching a private SQL Server 2005 class and most of the students didn't see how it was useful. They'd ask, "What good is it to have access to only part of the database?" If you don't take this functionality into account when you construct your filegroups, it won't do you any good. But how about a database that has history tables, such as OrderHistory? By placing those seldom accessed tables on a separate filegroup, you can have the active tables up and running before the entire database is restored. If you take these things into account ahead of time, you can drastically increase the options available to you when designing a backup/recovery plan.

The command to indicate a piecemeal restore is PARTIAL. If you only want to bring the PRIMARY filegroup back online, you can simply follow your normal restore procedure but include the PARTIAL clause—for example:

```
-- Always backup the tail-log!
BACKUP LOG AWSample
TO DISK='E:\BackupData\AWSample_TailLog.bak'
WITH NORECOVERY, NO TRUNCATE
GO
RESTORE DATABASE AWSample
FILEGROUP='PRIMARY'
FROM DISK='E:\DATA\AWSFGPrimary.bak'
WITH PARTIAL, NORECOVERY
-- Continue to restore any application transaction logs
-- Apply the tail-log backup
RESTORE LOG AWSample
FROM DISK 'E:\BackupData\AWSample_TailLog.bak'
WITH NORECOVERY
-- I prefer to do recovery as a separate step
RESTORE DATABASE AWSample
WITH RECOVERY
```

At this point, the PRIMARY filegroup is online, while any remaining filegroups are offline with restore pending. Any objects contained in PRIMARY are now available for use. You can restore the remaining filegroups normally, since the PARTIAL clause indicates that the database is in a piecemeal restore process. Once you've restored all filegroups, SQL Server resets the PARTIAL flag.

If you've designed the physical and logical structure of the database properly, piecemeal restores can make the difference between being a hero and losing your job.

Backing Up and Restoring Full-Text Indexes

SQL Server 2005 includes added backup functionality: full-text indexes are associated with a specific filegroup in every database, as shown in Figure 4-9. When you back up that filegroup, the files associated with the full-text indexes are included.

Figure 4-9. *When creating a full-text catalog, you must assign it to a filegroup, even though the indexes themselves are stored externally.*

Technically, all of the full-text indexes are files contained outside of the database. To back up a full-text catalog in SQL Server 2000 and earlier, you had to stop the Microsoft Search service (which technically implements full-text searching), back up the files in the full-text directory, and restart Microsoft Search. Even so, if you didn't back up the database at the exact same time, the search may not have restored properly anyway.

Normally in the event of a failure, you would just repopulate full-text indexes from scratch. For many, that isn't a problem. I did, however, have one instance of a complete database failure. The restore of the database took only 90 minutes, but rebuilding the full-text catalog took almost ten hours. It turned out that the application depended almost entirely on full-text search, and I had to rebuild numerous indexes. In that scenario, having the full-text catalogs included in the full backup would have made a lot of executives happy.

The backup and restore process for a full-text index is no different than for a file, filegroup, or full backup/restore. You can back up and restore only the full-text indexes underlying the file (named in the pattern sysft_<<catalog_name>>), the filegroup that the catalog belongs to, or the entire database.

If you don't want to back up the full-text catalog, you'll have to do a filegroup backup and specify all files except the full-text catalog pseudofile. If you perform a full backup, the catalogs will get included automatically.

Files/Filegroups and Disaster Scenarios

File and filegroup backup/restore processing can greatly speed both backup operations and recovery scenarios. A piecemeal restore in particular can greatly speed the perception of a restored database in many—but not all—disaster situations. The following list provides some examples of when file and filegroup backups can and can't help:

- *Environmental*: An environmental failure ultimately means the restore of your entire database, so file or filegroup backup scenarios are usually of no help.

- *Hardware*: One of the key purposes of using filegroups is separating I/O, so using multiple RAID controllers, channels, or arrays to house separate files or filegroups can drastically reduce recovery time—that is, if you're lucky enough not to lose the hardware where the log backups reside.

- *Media*: As with hardware failures, using file or filegroup backups can drastically reduce the restore time if separate media groups are used. This caveat applies not only to on-disk backups but also to tape backups.

- *Process*: The restore process can be reduced if tables and indexes are strategically placed. For example, if you're updating a specific table, you could back up the filegroup that owns it, run the procedure, then restore the backup if the procedure fails.

- *User*: Again, if designed properly, you might be able to restore only the affected filegroup in the event of a user error. The user error still can end in data loss, but the impact may not be as great.

Caveats and Recommendations

Performing filegroup or file backup/restore operations can be fraught with missteps if you don't take care. In particular, the impact of having a backup of the PRIMARY filegroup is critical. Take special care on the following points:

- *Make sure you set the default filegroup*: If you use multiple filegroups, don't leave the PRIMARY filegroup as the default. The PRIMARY filegroup has to hold the .mdf file, which has metadata about the database structure. It's best to separate that from actual user data.

- *Transaction logs are your life*: This can't be said enough. To restore individual files or filegroups, a full transaction history is necessary.

- *Get in the habit of specifying the filegroup before creating the table*: Never create a table or index without the ON <<Filegroup_Name>> clause, even if you only have one filegroup (which, of course, would be PRIMARY). One of the keys to avoiding the mistake of placing objects on the wrong filegroup is to get yourself in the habit of using that ON clause. Trust me, it helps.

- *Be aware of a full-text backup*: Whether you want the full-text catalogs backed up or not, be aware of how a full-text backup works in SQL Server 2005. This also means understanding fully the impact of either backing up the catalogs (additional size and backup time) or not being able to restore them (impact to the applications using them).

Summary

You've seen how file and filegroup backups have the potential to either improve your backup/restore process, or, if implemented in an awkwardly complex manner, complicate it. File and filegroup restores can speed up the restore process or reduce the backup time required for large databases by spreading each backup across a longer period of time.

Including full-text catalogs in the SQL Server backup process adds another dimension to the requirements and restrictions on any given backup recovery plan. It can either be a benefit or another *gotcha*, depending on the environment.

I've now covered the tools used in a backup/recovery process. In the next chapter, I'll show you how you can put these various tools to use.

CHAPTER 5

∎∎∎

Creating a Backup/ Recovery Plan

Now that I've explained the options available to you to back up and restore a database, the next step is to put those features to use, combining them in a way to create a coherent, viable backup plan. Remember, I'm not talking about full disaster recovery planning. There are two methods to dealing with disaster: mitigating the risk of it occurring or the impact when it does occur and responding to the disaster. Backup and recovery is a function of disaster response.

When setting up a backup plan, you need to ask yourself some procedural questions. Where should I place the backup files? What naming convention should I use? Should I use single files or backup devices? These are questions that you, as the DBA, must ultimately answer. I discussed many of the issues surrounding these questions in Chapter 2, and I provided my biased opinion on how you should do things. However, everyone's environment is unique, and you'll ultimately have to decide how you should do things for yourself.

Some questions have a technical impact. How often should I back up the database? How much time can the system be down or impacted by running a backup? How much data loss is acceptable? In the event of a restore, how much downtime is acceptable? While the answers to these questions ultimately dictate the technical steps you'll need to take and which backup/recovery features you'll need to employ, only the business owners of the database application are qualified to answer them. Without those answers, any backup plan is potentially invalid.

Remember that backup is only half the puzzle. Don't forget that you also must define a plan for a recovery process. Don't stint on the recovery half of the puzzle. Backups are usually done at leisure, without any undue stress. Recovery, on the other hand, occurs when you're mostly likely to be under stress, and consequently when you most need a well-defined and clear plan of action.

There are various interpretations of backup/recovery plans (BRPs). Some view them as full disaster recovery plans; others see them as an internal IT function to define the steps necessary to back up and restore a database. Both interpretations have flaws.

True disaster recovery planning is a combination of an appropriate BRP along with techniques used to mitigate the risk of any given disaster. A BRP is only a piece of disaster recovery planning. One goal of disaster recovery planning should be that you'll never need the process of recovery. You can develop a bulletproof (OK, bullet-slowing) BRP, but your environment won't be better off if you're constantly invoking the BRP.

A system's business owners and IT staff must define both BRPs and mitigation techniques cooperatively. Business owners lack the technical knowledge of how to achieve the desired level of disaster recovery, while IT staff lack the appropriate business knowledge to determine an appropriate level of disaster recovery.

The misconceptions that a BRP is equivalent to a disaster recovery plan or that IT determines what BRP is used make for the most common and costly mistakes. In this chapter, I'll explain exactly what a backup/recovery plan entails, who is involved, and the constraints they face. Everyone wants to have no downtime and no data loss, but even approaching that level of protection can be a costly undertaking. I'll also look at the most common BRP scenarios.

Components of a Backup/Recovery Plan

On the surface, a BRP is deceptively simple to create because it has few high-level components. At a bare minimum, a BRP is composed of the following items:

- Documented data-protection requirements

- A documented daily/weekly/monthly backup scheme

- A documented restore process

- A documented testing and reevaluation plan

Seems straightforward, doesn't it? Think again. First, note that everything includes the word *documented*. It isn't enough to have a plan in place—it must be documented at some level. Raise your hand if you enjoy writing documentation. Something tells me that there aren't many of you with your hands up. Documentation is a time-consuming, boring (for most technical staff), and tedious task. When corners need to be cut on any activity, documentation is one of the first things to skimp on.

Second, consider *data-protection requirements*. Who determines those? It had better not be you. Without the involvement of the business staff, creating a backup/recovery plan could lead to the loss of a job. However, it's much more complicated than asking a manager for requirements; you have the responsibility as the technical expert to *make* the manager understand the implications of his choices. That isn't always an easy thing to do. If you talk in any sort of *tech-ese*, you won't be successful. You have to be clear, concise, and, most of all, able to explain things in a way that make senses to your audience. I'll discuss techniques that can help in Chapter 12.

Lastly, the prospect of testing and constant reevaluation might not sit too well with your manager. He has other things that need to be done, and you're the one who has to do them. By adding new tasks to his staff, you're endangering (at least from his perspective) other critical activities that he is ultimately responsible for. You're going to have to find a way to "sell" the backup/recovery plan to management. I'll explore techniques for doing this in Chapter 12 as well.

THE KEY TO DOCUMENTATION

Yes, most of us hate writing documentation. I know I do. It isn't a creative process like writing an e-mail, or in my immediate case, a book. Well-written documentation details every tedious step in a process. Have you ever purchased a "some assembly required" piece of furniture, or a child's bicycle? Is the included assembly documentation ever complete? I haven't seen many pieces of documentation that were complete. At some point, you end up winging it and just managing to get the thing put together. And why is it that there are always at least five nuts or bolts left over? The bottom line is that writing documentation is difficult for anyone. For those who can do it well, I salute you and urge your employer to give you a massive raise.

The problem for most of us is that we don't have an organized way to approaching documentation. Usually, we do it after we've already completed the activity, and much of the detail comes from memory. I know I've documented things that way, and I usually return to it five years later thinking to myself, "Whoever put this together clearly didn't know what they were . . . oh wait, *I* wrote this!"

It takes a great deal of discipline, but anyone can create useful documentation. The key is to break it down and follow a few simple rules:

- *Start simple*: There's no reason you need to document absolutely everything at once. An author doesn't try to write a novel in a single pass. When doing the documentation, people often hit a common problem for authors: writer's block. Instead, start with a high-level outline and build from there. Each level of the outline should have some reference to other documentation that is already available. For example, you could have a heading that says, "Restore from backup, but do not recover the database; refer to Books Online."

- *Document while doing*: Gather as much information as you can while you're actually doing the work. It can be notes on a scrap of paper or in a notebook, or better yet, screenshots slapped into a Word document—maybe even with a few notes! I've found that no matter how unorganized it is, documentation gathered during an activity is more useful than clean, organized documentation written two months later.

- *Don't write the documentation for yourself.* Even if you'll be the main consumer of the documentation, imagine you're writing it for someone else. Some colleagues insist that all documentation should be written so a ten-year-old could follow it. I personally think that's a little extreme (not that I think ten-year-olds lack the capacity to restore a database, but I would feel much more comfortable if someone with a little more IT experience does it). The problem with writing the documentation for yourself is that you'll assume certain steps—I guarantee it. Those small steps may throw someone else off completely.

- *Don't stop.* Never declare, "The documentation is finished." Never let a project manager have a separate step at the end of a project called "documentation." If documentation is included in a project plan, it should span the entire project, and then some. Writing documentation should be an iterative process. Even Books Online, arguably the best piece of documentation for any software product on the market, posts revisions now and then. Every time either you or a colleague use the documentation, examine it for errors or omissions and take notes. Then go back through and add what's missing.

Will these suggestions alleviate the agony of creating documentation? Of course not. However, they should help you create a much more useful document quicker and with fewer errors. When I remember to follow these rules, I always have better luck. Now if only I could remember to follow them every time.

Key Business Constraints for BRPs

The first step to creating a BRP is to define the data-protection requirements. Those requirements will ultimately be driven by external factors, and a compromise must be met. It doesn't matter how your organization works—whether each department has a separate budget for systems implementation, IT is given the complete budget for technology projects, or the entire company works on an internal economy. Each business unit has its own unique set of constraints that need to be met.

These four basic questions drive the constraints of a business unit:

- How much downtime is allowed for backup processes?

- How quickly must the system be restored?

- How much data loss is acceptable?

- How much will it cost?

■**Note** Get ready for the following answers to these questions: none, right away, none, and nothing. Have practical, nonconfrontational responses in your back pocket before you even start asking questions. Out of the hundreds of interviews I've conducted on this topic, only three business managers responded with different answers. Needless to say, I was speechless in each case.

The answers to these questions, while not quite mutually exclusive, almost always impact each other. A low amount of data loss might mean a slower restore time, whereas a fast restore time might increase the amount of processing time needed for backups. It is possible to obtain a relative balance between these constraints, but that usually means increased cost.

Time to Back Up

Even though backup operations are online, they still have a performance impact on a database. SQL Server 2005 improves on that speed by leveraging multiple processors whenever it can, but a heavily used database will most likely see some sort of performance hit when a backup occurs.

If the business requires optimal 24x7 performance, you'll need to take that into consideration when choosing your backup scheme. This does *not* mean that you'll necessarily need to restrict which backup methods you use; instead, it only indicates that you must take the performance impact of any single backup into account.

Ideally, you'll have some leeway when determining the optimal backup scheme. In many situations, the database is already in production, so experiments with backups could have serious repercussions. If the system is already in production, be sure to inform the appropriate business unit of a possible performance impact when you test a specific backup technique. That way, you can kill the individual backup if it has a significantly negative impact on the usability of the application.

■**Note** Be careful *who* you inform about a backup test. Informing all the end users might result in false positives: often when told that they might see a performance impact, users will *look* for the slightest change in performance. You may receive reports that it takes 20 seconds to do what normally takes 2 seconds, but the real increase may be only a second or two. This isn't a case of deliberate exaggeration; it's just a trick the mind can play on us. Instead, inform managers and supervisors to be on the lookout for reactions from staff. You still may get a false-positive report of significant degradation, but at least you won't be planting the seed that there could be performance issues.

Minimizing the time to back up usually involves frequent log backups and/or frequent file and filegroup backups. Also, consider examining the overall system load throughout the day, looking for regularly occurring low spots (perhaps right before and after a shift change, or during commute times for online commercial applications). Leverage those low spots to minimize impact.

Time to Restore

For most business units, a short time to restore is a critical requirement—sometimes the overriding requirement. A certain amount of data loss is acceptable just as long as the system doesn't remain down for any "perceptible" amount of time. That's the crux of the requirement: dealing with "perceptible" time.

It can be relatively common to have some sort of technical issue that has nothing to do with restoring a database, yet the perception may be that it's a database issue. Be prepared to do quick troubleshooting to eliminate the database as an issue, if it is indeed up and responding adequately. Run the same sort of queries on your local network as are executed by the application through the Internet or from a remote location. Is the performance acceptable? If so, then it's unlikely that the database has a problem at all, much less that it's down and needs to be restored.

When restoring, look to minimize the number of restore steps involved. Avoid restoring large numbers of (or large) log backups. A log restore essentially replays all of the transactions that occurred. A differential restore, on the other hand, simply replaces data changes that have occurred since the last full backup. Even a relatively large differential backup can restore in a reasonable amount of time. A file or filegroup restore can also speed things along, in some cases, depending on the specific nature of the disaster. If a disk-array failure holds a subset of data files, you can restore those files alone if you've backed them up separately.

The most important thing is to try to determine both what the best-case scenario and the worst-case scenario would be and present them to the appropriate business unit. Also, use the most conservative estimates you can, but base them on real tests.

Potential Data Loss

"It's all about availability." This mantra is in vogue these days, but if that were really the case, you wouldn't need to ask how much data loss is acceptable. For a large online retailer, which is worse? Losing 30 minutes' worth of data or being down for 30 minutes? I would argue the former. That data lost is unidentifiable. The company could have no record of an order ever being placed for customers who have order numbers and possibly even billed credit cards. Those customers could be lost for good, and they'd probably influence others to avoid the retailer.

The one key to minimizing data loss is frequent transaction log backups. Without a complete string of log backups, restoring to a point in time is impossible. Storing copies of log backups in multiple locations is also a good idea, either by copying them directly via a job step or by leveraging the `MIRROR TO` backup clause. Again, you must present a best-case/worst-case scenario to the business unit, using real test data and remaining as conservative as possible.

Cost

Cost is a critical constraint that's often overlooked or at least ignored until it becomes visible. People often equate cost to price: how much money is this going to take? If you take this approach, things can spiral out of control. If you focus solely on price, you'll dramatically underestimate the effort involved.

To truly represent cost instead of price, you must factor in more than monetary requirements. How much staff time will be required? Is there any training required? How much will it cost to create the documentation? A number of factors are difficult to place an exact price tag on, but at the very least, you must be sure to consider them in your planning process.

■**Note** Backup/recovery plans are rarely price justifiable, at least not in terms of immediate return on investment, and a full disaster recovery plan certainly isn't. Linking price to cost places executive buy-in to any such activity in jeopardy.

There is a distinct difference between price and cost. Price always breaks down into dollar amounts. Cost can include abstract items such as time required by staff, training, and consulting time. Yes, you could convert all of these things to a price tag, but often there are implications that are difficult to relate in terms of dollar amounts.

When discussing cost at the executive level, terms such as *total cost of ownership* (*TCO*) and *return on investment* (*ROI*) come up. Avoid these buzzwords, as they tend to spiral your BRP out of control. Instead, stick with specific types of cost. Don't tie your cost to a dollar amount, at least initially. That can end an initiative before it even starts.

Cost can be represented in terms of time, knowledge, availability, risks, and deadlines—anything that affects the activity under discussion. It's especially important to stress non-price-related costs when discussing potential BRPs with the business owners of the database. The following are a few examples of abstract costs.

Hardware Cost

Yes, there is an obvious price tag to hardware, but consider everything that is involved in selecting hardware. Do you have a preferred vendor? If not, it's time to look at your options and consider the best price vs. performance vs. quality. Do you have a hardware expert on staff to do that research? To perform a thorough job, that staff member may need to invest a significant amount of time. He might not have time to perform his other tasks, or his daily tasks might prevent him from doing a thorough job and/or completing the research in a timely manner.

There's also the cost of maintaining the hardware. Is it a piece of hardware your staff is familiar with? If not, more research and training will be involved. This may create undue stress on your in-house hardware expert and create the risk of losing him to another company. Hiring is a pricey and costly undertaking as well.

Another thing to consider when choosing hardware is the vendor. Notice that I labeled the shopping process as price vs. performance vs. quality. *Never* leave quality out of the equation. You can easily get high-performing hardware at bargain-basement pricing, but how stable is the hardware? What is the company's support like? Worse yet, is there an imminent risk of that company going out of business anytime soon?

Software Cost

Again, yes, there is a price tag associated with any specific software. For the purposes of this book, I'm assuming that you have only the features of SQL Server 2005 available (remember, plan for the worst). A number of vendors provide backup-enhancing products or backup products designed to centralize all backup operations, from Active Directory backups to SQL Server database backups. These products will absolutely have a price tag. Most scenarios come with two price tags: the initial purchase and a maintenance fee, which is usually required for support and upgrades. The former is a one-time purchase; the latter is usually a yearly fee at 5-20% of the cost of the initial product.

The same nonquantifiable costs that occur when selecting hardware apply when selecting software purchases as well. How well is the product supported? Is the company at risk of disappearing? What is the learning curve for using the project? Is formal training required?

Consulting Cost

Consulting is yet another item with an inevitable price tag, but hiring consultants is often a necessity to get a BRP or disaster recovery undertaking off the ground. Too many companies are running on a shoestring budget, and the on-site staff members have difficulty just keeping their heads above water, much less pursuing a proactive initiative.

Choosing a consulting company can be (and really should be) a time-consuming process, unless you already have a consultant whom you're comfortable with. Each consulting company has a specific rate. Furthermore, a company can either bill hourly or offer fixed-fee billing for a specific set of deliverables. However, when leveraging an external consulting firm, monetary costs may be just the tip of the iceberg.

If you're already using a consulting organization you're familiar and comfortable with, chances are you won't have too many additional items to deal with. Mutually beneficial relationships have a way of managing themselves. However, if you've just selected a firm from a Request for Proposal (RFP) process and chosen based on price and the perceived ability to complete the necessary task, you may have a lot of additional work (read: cost) ahead of you.

Even if you have a consulting vendor you've worked with before and trust, you should always take the time to do due diligence to verify that the vendor can perform the work you require. If this is a new business relationship, this verification process should be much more thorough (remember, expect the worst). You should check references, verify résumés (where applicable), and conduct some sort of technical interview. Once you do that, you'll need to deal with the ongoing management of both the work being done and the business relationship itself, such as invoicing procedures, regular status assessments, and so on. Ultimately, all of these things could require a great deal of time, not just from a management, but also from your technical staff as they help assess the progress of any work being done.

Tip Beware anyone offering a turnkey solution. I have nothing against consulting firms; in fact, I have my own. I do, however, believe that consulting services or staff augmentation should always play the role of augmenting in-house staff and capabilities. If a consulting firm builds a complete solution for you, you'll be dependent on that consulting firm to maintain that solution. Usually even the most thorough documentation won't suffice when it comes to maintaining anything in which your staff had no involvement.

Maintenance Cost

Maintenance is a truly abstract cost and usually one that is never considered—that is, until its effects are felt. The range of costs that could be categorized as maintenance is quite broad. Even when considering maintenance only from a business point of view, there are a wide variety of possible activities and costs that could be termed as "maintenance."

Consider application patches: at first glance, application of a patch seems like a technical cost of time required for testing and application. If done properly, though, application patches require testing time from members of the business unit itself. They're the only ones who have the necessary background to determine if the patch has fixed existing bugs or created new ones. Unfortunately, thorough testing by the appropriate business unit is often sacrificed for lack of time.

An example more applicable to the topic at hand would be the review of an existing BRP. I've argued previously that disaster recovery planning, including individual backup/recovery schemes, should not be considered as a project that you need to complete but rather as an ongoing job role. I've also argued that when creating a backup/recovery plan, technical staff should never be the ones to establish requirements such as acceptable data loss, restore time, or service interruption when backing up the system. If you follow these recommendations and review the existing BRP regularly, you'll need to perform at least a portion of the review with the business unit. This requires someone's time. As it's often said, time is money. It can become painfully apparent how true that saying is once you experience frequent requests for time.

Key Technical Constraints for BRPs

Just as each business unit may have its own unique constraints when developing a backup/recovery plan, different areas of IT (such as the network, the server, and application development) can also create constraints on the backup and restore methods available for use.

Ideally, you should try to identify the technical constraints before discussing the constraints of the business unit. It's much easier to convince the business unit that a given approach is technically impossible if you come to the table with information in hand. Even if you're able to identify technical constraints before exploring business constraints, you should always review technical constraints after identifying the needs of the business unit as well (technical ➤ business ➤ technical).

THE "PLOP" FACTOR

The sound of a large stack of papers hitting a table (plop!) can be a powerful negotiating tool. As I'll discuss in Chapter 12, the pragmatics of actually creating a disaster recovery plan should force interaction between different areas of the business. Depending on your particular work environment, this could be complicated by competition for resources, office politics, or personal agendas. I wish that this weren't the case, but unfortunately it's a reality I see day in and day out.

To effectively convey a need or constraint, you need to come to any discussion prepared. Even if you never use it, bringing documentation that supports your position will aid you in presenting your case effectively. In fact, going to such a meeting without documentation will play against you. Not bringing documentation may cause others to see you as generally unprepared and having not thought out your specific needs.

While the "plop" factor is extremely important, *never* bring unrelated documentation or "pad" the amount of documentation you have. Yes, often it won't be reviewed, but if it is and it's clear that you've exaggerated the amount of documentation you have, your cause is dead. It isn't particularly helpful in your career either.

The primary technical constraints are

- Hardware capabilities

- Personnel availability

- Portability

- Cost

Hardware Capabilities

There seems to be a growing trend to consolidate hardware wherever possible. While consolidation seems prudent to keep hardware and maintenance costs down, it does present challenges when designing a backup/recovery plan. I've established that hardware is one of the primary disaster categories. Consolidating processes, even backup/recovery ones, can add significant risk in terms of greater fallout from hardware disasters.

All too often, hardware is approved and purchased before any attempt is made at identifying the actual hardware requirements—the "blank check" temptation. I can't emphasize enough what a bad idea this is. First, you're taking advantage of your colleagues; even if you're in a highly political work environment, this will ultimately find a way to boomerang back to you. Second, while it may seem like you're able to purchase way more capacity than you need—whether it's additional storage area network (SAN) storage, a tape array, or tape loader—you may ultimately find that you underestimated what you needed. You're making the purchase before you even know what your requirements are, remember? While the idea of openly allocated money for hardware purchases is seductive, don't be enthralled before identifying your requirements.

Legitimate hardware constraints from a technical perspective usually fall in the area of capacity:

- Do you have tape drives available for use?

- Do you have enough tapes to maintain a thorough backup history?

- Do you have sufficient disk space for TO DISK backups?

- Do you have enough disk space to perform mirrored backups of the transaction log?

Be deliberately conservative with estimations. If money is allocated toward hardware, make sure that it will be a significant amount of time before you'll need to request additional funds.

DISK IS CHEAP

Lately, whenever I discuss the need for concise database design or the importance of maximizing disk utilization, a common response to my recommendations is simply "Disk is cheap." It's true; the cost of storage continues to drop as capacity continues to rise. However, working under the assumption that this trend will continue violates one of my basic principles of disaster recovery planning: assume the worst.

I remember one of my first computer-upgrade purchases. It was two 4MB DIMMs (i.e., memory cards) to increase my server's memory to a whopping 8MB. A month before I placed the order, the price per DIMM was around $300. Shortly before I placed the order, a factory somewhere (Taiwan, I think) burned down, and the price per DIMM nearly doubled. The moral of this story is that you never know what could happen that might change the market price of disk storage. A key manufacturer could go out of business, or solar flares could become a daily occurrence, endangering magnetic media world-wide. Never assume that current costs will continue. I'm writing this in 2007, and US gas prices are a prime example. Does this principle border on the paranoid level? Of course. But that doesn't mean that I'm wrong about disk space possibly growing in cost. Absolutely not.

Personnel Availability

Most IT organizations are doing all they can to keep their heads above water, much less focus on proactive activities. Creating thorough backup/recovery plans is a textbook example of proactive work. Often a backup schedule is just slapped together, with little regard for the needs of the business, and recovery is dealt with only if a disaster situation occurs.

In almost every case, the problem is not that design, planning, and testing are seen as unnecessary, but it's just that no one has time to do these things. Hiring additional staff is usually difficult, and the cost of hiring consultants can be difficult to justify for this type of work.

The lack of qualified technical personnel time impacts how detailed or complex any BRP can be. Never create a plan that's beyond what the staff can handle. Be aware of how much time will be available before even beginning the backup/recovery planning process.

Portability

Any BRP has to include where the backups will ultimately be placed. From a technical standpoint, the size of the database and the methods used to perform the backup may be a major roadblock to maintaining flexibility regarding where the backups will ultimately be placed.

If you don't break down the backup process into smaller steps, transporting a large database via tape may require striping the data across multiple tapes. You need to store those tapes as a consistent set. If you're employing a third-party data-archival service to manage tapes, you'll need some assurance that they'll maintain that integrity. Verifying third-party compliance takes someone's time, which, as you've already seen, may not be available in the first place.

Cost

As with business-driven cost, technical cost doesn't necessarily equate to a price tag (or at least you should avoid trying to apply a price tag if there is anything unclear about the factors feeding into the cost). Rather, technical cost is a combination of direct costs, time commitments from staff, and indirect complications that arise from ongoing activities.

Training

Whether through formal classroom training, online training, or self-study, multiple staff members need to understand not only the backup/recovery plan but also the technology that drives it. Consider the technology that SQL Server 2005 entails:

- *Storage devices*: Understanding storage can be as simple as knowing how to load a tape into a tape drive or a group of tapes into an autoloader to as complex as understanding the configuration of your SAN environment. Some of you may be thinking, "The server staff handles that. It isn't my responsibility." Well, what if they aren't there? You don't need to be an expert at any of these things, but you must have a basic understanding.

- *Third-party backup products*: Large organizations tend to use a centralized backup design, where all backups—whether a file system, e-mail, or database backups— are stored and managed in a centralized location. Again, you may view this as the responsibility of a different department in your organization, but in my opinion, it's irresponsible of a DBA to not have at least a basic understanding of how that software functions.

A number of other areas could require training as well. Some may be as simple as a process detail, but none should be ignored when estimating the impact of implementing a backup/recovery plan.

Initial Design

Creating a backup and recovery plan requires time for performing discovery, such as determining business and technology constraints, as well as considering multiple approaches to finding an optimal design. The query optimizer does it in SQL Server—why shouldn't you as a DBA?

Here's the question: how much time should you put into exploring alternate approaches? From a managerial point of view, being presented with more than one option is almost always preferable to being presented with *the* solution. Always come to the table with at least two options. Not only will it help legitimize a selected approach, but you just may think of new constraints or possibilities that hadn't occurred to you.

Ongoing Testing and Design Review

Often sacrificed at the altar because "we don't have time to do this," testing and continual review of the backup/recovery plan is perhaps the most important item *not* to sacrifice. Very few systems are static; they're constantly evolving in both design and usage. As a result, backup/recovery needs may change. And changes to business requirements can also create new technical constraints, again leading to the need to change backup and recovery plans. You need to review your BRP periodically to ensure that its design remains valid given the business and technical requirements and constraints.

Testing a recovery process can be the most feared task of any DBA. If the database is relatively small (less than 50GB or so), testing by restoring to a development database is straightforward. However, when it comes to larger databases where available disk space plays a role, even establishing a valid testing process can be an excruciating process. Again, testing is often one of those items that isn't seen as urgent, or the resources necessary to do testing are few and far between. An untested process is a substantial risk. Even if it's only once a year, always test a restore to ensure reliability.

Tip I was once called into an organization to assist in the restore of a mid-sized SQL database. I was told that the IT department had complete backups, including differentials and incrementals. That immediately concerned me—there is no incremental backup within SQL Server. It turned out they were using an open file option with their standard backup product, which let them back up files even though those files were open, which almost never works for any transaction database. We couldn't get a restore of the database without setting off SUSPECT mode. In the end, we had to create a new database and use the emergency startup mode for the database to extract as much data as possible. Had they tested their restore process *just once*, they could have prevented the entire problem.

Maintenance and Troubleshooting

Even once you design, test, and automate the plan, you'll still need to perform maintenance or spend time troubleshooting unexpected behavior (automated does not mean
automatic). Problems will still arise even with a perfectly designed BRP created and
tested by a guru-level DBA. Ultimately, everything is created by humans, and, as we
know, to err is human. Any automated system simply does what a human tells it to do,
often without regard to the consequences.

Some issues are unforeseeable and have no place (directly) in human error. In
World War II, pilots blamed odd hardware malfunctions on "gremlins." The technology
world is no different. Systems have become so complex that it's practically impossible
to identify the exact state of any system at a specific point in time. Although executives
hate this type of answer, "things just happen" is a legitimate explanation to an issue in
some circumstances.

Also, beware of anyone presenting a turn-key solution. Some may claim that their
product or design needs no maintenance and will work flawlessly once configured correctly. This is rarely true. Maintenance and troubleshooting time should always be
included as a cost to any undertaking involving technology.

SQL Agent

I've examined business and technical constraints and presented a more abstract view of
backup/recovery plans. Now it's time to switch gears and talk about the technical specifics of implementing a plan. Automation is the first issue to look at.

For the purposes of this book, I'm assuming that you'll do all scheduling via the SQL
Agent service. However, any number of scheduling applications could execute T-SQL
scripts to achieve the same results. I'm going to focus on SQL Agent because it's already
incorporated into SQL Server, most of us are already familiar with it, and it includes
enhanced functionality when it comes to configuring automated SQL Server activities.
The 2005 version of SQL Agent includes even more functionality.

I'll digress a bit and focus on SQL Agent itself. This may seem out of place in a book
focused on disaster recovery, but the SQL Agent service executes most automated activities, so it's important to be aware of the new benefits that the 2005 version brings, as well
as potential pitfalls.

Job Schedules

In SQL Server 2005, the GUI no longer displays a button for creating a schedule when creating a backup. That doesn't mean you can't schedule the backup through the GUI, though. The ubiquitous Script button at the top left of every screen in Management Studio includes a "Script to Job" option.

One of the more infuriating aspects of previous versions of SQL Server was that whenever you created a schedule for a SQL Agent job, a new row was created in `sysjobschedules`, even if the schedule was *identical* to a previously created one. Constantly re-creating the same schedule caused needless work and increased the possibility of human error. I've even run into some situations where clients give schedules names such as "M-F 4am" rather than more useful and descriptive names such as "Daily Backup."

Reporting Services for SQL Server 2000 introduced the idea of a shared schedule. However, in SQL Server 2000, you actually implemented a shared schedule via the application rather than through the SQL Agent itself. SQL Agent 2005 now has built-in support for shared schedules.

The shared schedule concept has both positives and negatives. It simplifies scheduling and reduces the likelihood of human error, but if overused, backup jobs can queue up behind each other, or you could overload the server capacity by running everything at once. Be sure to assess the impact of any shared schedules.

Jobs and Job Steps

When you define a schedule, you must have a job to execute. Many novice DBAs mistakenly assume that only one action may be executed. Actually, a number of job steps can be executed, each with a precedence defined to control the overall order in which the steps execute. Figure 5-1 illustrates a job step in which the success action is to continue on to the next step in the overall job.

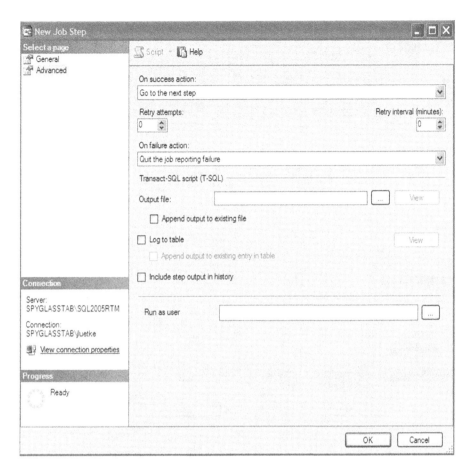

Figure 5-1. *In the Advanced section, you have control over what happens when a job step is successful and over what happens when it fails.*

In Figure 5-2, you can see that you can rearrange multiple job stops or specify a specific starting step. There's a reason for that ability, which I'll talk about next.

Figure 5-2. *SQL Agent provides you with basic workflow capabilities in that you can specify success and failure actions for each job step.*

You might be wondering why it's important to a backup recovery plan to be able to rearrange the steps in a backup job. Prior to SQL Server 2005, there was no MIRROR TO clause for the backup commands. It's a welcome addition, but there are still limitations. As you've seen, if you're backing up to a tape device, the manufacturer, make, and model—even the firmware version—should be exactly the same. If you back up to a disk device, you'll have more flexibility, but what if you need to have a copy of the transaction log FTP'd to a remote server, just in case? Having the ability to add a second job step to copy the transaction log to a remote location after the backup has completed increases your data protection immensely.

Job Step Tokens

SQL Agent offers *job tokens*—a great feature I rarely see used. Essentially, these system functions act as variables only when they appear in job steps. The variables can be extremely useful when defining job steps. Here are a few of the available tokens:

- Current date (DATE)

- Current time (TIME)

- Message number (A-ERR)

- Message text (A-MSG)

- Server name (A-SVR)

- Instance name (INST)

- Database name (A-DBN)

These tokens aren't new to SQL Server 2005, but their syntax has changed with the addition of Service Pack 1 (SP1) for SQL Server 2005. Previously, you simply placed these tokens into square brackets in the job step text:

```
BACKUP DATABASE AdventureWorks TO DISK='E:\backupdata\aw[DATE][TIME].bak'
```

With SQL Server 2005 SP1, you now also enclose job-step tokens in parentheses preceded by a $ within an ESCAPE_NONE macro:

```
BACKUP DATABASE AdventureWorks TO
DISK='E:\backupdata\aw$[(ESCAPE_NONE(DATE))][$(ESCAPE_NONE((TIME))].bak'
```

I use tokens quite a bit, which is a bit odd for me since they aren't for the syntactically challenged (and that would definitely be me). They're case-sensitive, and any misspelling causes the job step to fail. For detailed information on the use of tokens, search for "token" in the Books Online index.

Agent Proxies

One issue with previous versions of SQL Server was limiting the security context used when executing an unattended job. Remember that a job can take on a number of execution forms, such as a T-SQL statement, an operating system command, or even an ActiveX script. Most users can create a job in at least one of those forms, so there needs to be a way to limit what they can do. With T-SQL, having the proper security on the database is sufficient, but for an operating system command or an ActiveX script, the number of items to secure can be daunting to manage.

Both SQL Server 7.0 and 2000 provided the ability to limit the execution of command-shell scripts and ActiveX scripts to administrators only. It also provided a proxy account that you could use to limit the security context if you did allow that execution. In SQL Server 7.0, that account was a fixed account, meaning that it had a fixed account name, but in SQL Server 2000, the administrator could select which account was to act as the proxy.

SQL Server 2005 presents a wide range of proxy categories. Within those categories, you can create multiple proxy accounts and select which one you want to use for any given job step, as shown in Figure 5-3.

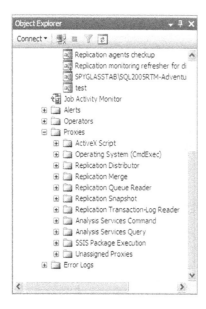

Figure 5-3. *SQL Server 2005's proxy categories—a major improvement over the single-proxy account made available by SQL Server 7.0 and 2000*

If you don't specify a proxy account, the job will run under the SQL Agent account, as shown in Figure 5-4. Be careful how much power you give SQL Agent in the first place (no domain administrators, please).

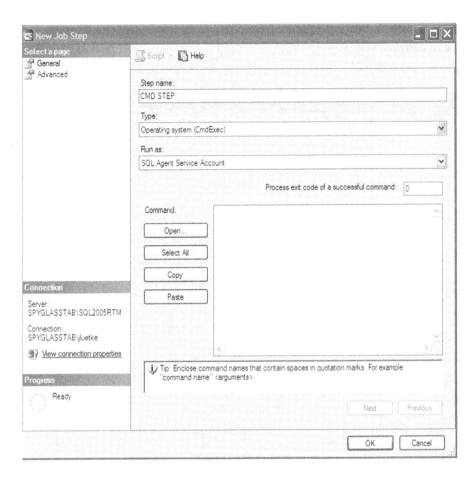

Figure 5-4. *Without a proxy defined, the job step runs as the SQL Agent service account.*

Be sure to take time to fully understand the proxy system. For large organizations, you can use it to delegate certain management functions. Wouldn't it be nice for someone else to have the responsibility of keeping an eye on replication?

If you want to use a proxy account, the process is a little more complicated (and thus, a bit more secure) than you might imagine. Proxies get assigned both a *credential*, which is an external account to use (corresponding to an Active Directory user and group), and *principles*, which are the users that will act as the credential if they attempt to use this proxy.

First you need to create a credential, which is the main security menu for the instance (see Figure 5-5).

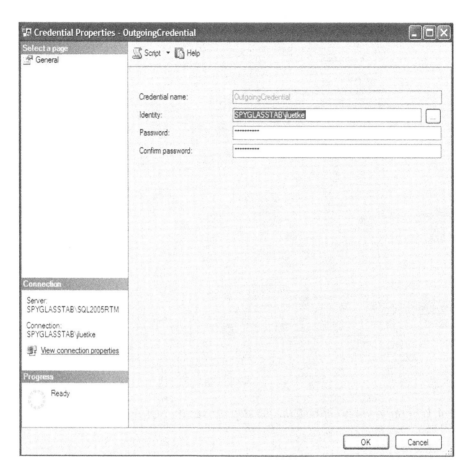

Figure 5-5. *This credential, named* OutgoingCredential, *has its own password, but will act as my local user account if invoked.*

Now when you create a proxy account, you have a credential to select, as shown in Figure 5-6. OutgoingCredential ensures that anyone using CMDExecProxy will have the security context of SPYGLASSTAB\jluetke, plus they'll only have access to the operating system (CmdExec) subsystem.

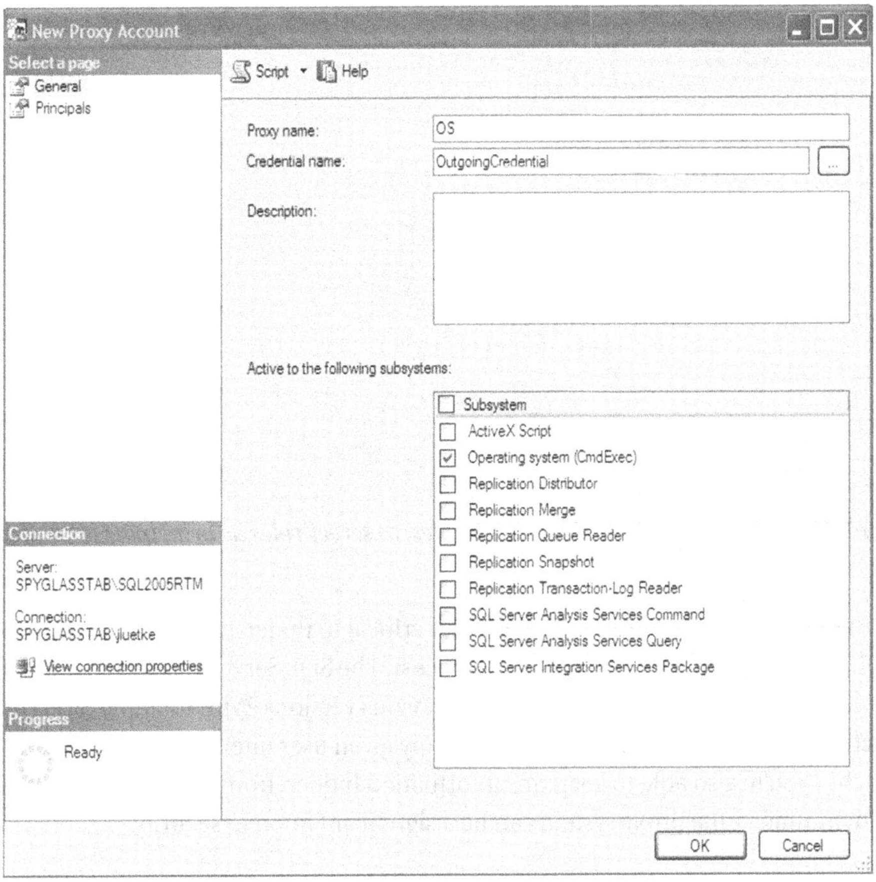

Figure 5-6. *Now you can assign a credential to the new proxy* CMDExecProxy.

Finally, you need to force users to use the proxy account. You do this by assigning principles to the proxy, as shown in Figure 5-7. If any of these users or roles create a job step calling a command-line job, they'll execute it under the security context of SPYGLASSTAB\jluetke.

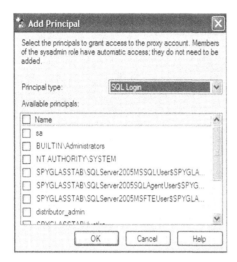

Figure 5-7. *You can assign SQL logins, MSDB roles, or server roles as principals for a proxy.*

Is this all a bit confusing? Yes. However, it's critical to understand if you're going to use SQL Agent as your backup scheduling process. The SQL Server 2005 proxy system is immensely more complex and flexible than previous versions. With multiple levels of abstraction, you're not only in control of how any given user interacts with the operating system, but you're also able to keep this information hidden from standard users. In a large environment, the proxy system can be a significant boon to security.

Alerts

SQL Agent has always had the ability to fire alerts given various conditions. This hasn't changed under SQL Server 2005. You can create an alert based on a SQL Server error message, a user-defined error message (the message ID must be greater than 50,000), a SQL Server performance event, or a Windows Management Instrumentation (WMI) event.

Of course, you can also set an alert notification for any specific job step, which is what we're most interested in. You can have it notify an operator, and this is where things change from previous versions. SQL Agent still offers the same three notification methods: e-mail, pager, and network messages via the net send command. The big change is with e-mail notification: SQL Agent no longer uses SQL Mail, but Database Mail instead. The latter is SMTP-based, stateless, and significantly more reliable than SQL Mail ever was. For those of you who've used SQL Mail, you know exactly what I mean. For those of you who haven't, you're lucky.

■Tip Be wary of relying on net send as a notification method. It makes use of the Messenger service, which many administrators have disabled by default. A bug allowed users to leverage the Messenger service to compromise a PC. Even though the bug has been corrected, paranoia often wins over in these situations, and the Messenger service remains disabled (I see paranoia as a good thing).

Prior to SQL Server 2005, the mail-notification method, SQL Mail, presented all sorts of issues. It was MAPI-based, which meant it was constantly checking for new mail. If there was some hiccup in communication between it and the MAPI-compliant mail server, SQL Mail would cease to work, forcing you to stop and start the "service" (it was called a service, but was really just an extended stored procedure). Also, you needed to have a MAPI-based e-mail client *installed* on the server. Also, if that client was anything other than Microsoft Outlook (Outlook Express didn't count), it probably had issues.

SQL Mail is still available (in SQL Server Management Studio, it's under Management ➤ Legacy—how fitting), but the primary mail-notification system is Database Mail, which is SMTP-based and completely stateless. It doesn't need an SMTP server to be installed on SQL Server, and it needs only one (or more, since it supports a fail-safe address) IP address to send the message. I had been using an extended stored procedure SMTP-based mailer for the SQL Server 2000 databases I worked with, so having Database Mail included in the product is invaluable.

USING A MASTER JOB SERVER

SQL Agent has long had the ability to use a single server to control all the jobs on your network. SQL Agent in SQL Server 2005 is no exception. I've used this functionality many times. It can be a real time-saver, and it avoids the need to purchase a third-party schedule-management package. Once target servers are configured to use a master job server, they frequently check that master server for new jobs to download. This makes for a clean way to push out common scripts or code, maintenance tasks, and so on. The jobs themselves, although defined on the master server, are executed on the target server. You can also set up target server groups to filter which servers get which jobs.

That being said, the target server cannot change the configuration of a job. The frequent checking for new schedules can put a bit of a load on the master job server in a large environment, but in those cases, that SQL Server instance wouldn't be doing much other than centralizing jobs.

One word of caution: you may want to use the master job server as a way to push out scripts that create local jobs on the target servers. I've had a few bad experiences with certain types of jobs in this configuration under SQL Server 7.0 and 2000. I haven't seen anything unusual with SQL Server 2005, though.

Base BRPs

As I mentioned previously, disaster recovery planning of any kind, including basic backup/restore schemes, should be an iterative process. The first step in designing a backup/recovery plan should be coming up with a basic, bare-bones, meets-the-requirements approach and then enhancing it from that point on. I'll start with a generic template that contains required steps regardless of the specific business or technical needs and constraints. From there, I'll examine common business and technical scenarios to which you can apply the general template. When discussing approaches to common scenarios, I'll include samples for three arbitrary categories of database sizes: small (less than 50GB), medium (greater than 50GB and less than 500GB), and large (greater than 500GB). Given the size of the databases, an approach to dealing with any specific scenario may change or be completely untenable.

A General Template

While backup/restore planning is always specific to each individual situation, you should always use a general set of rules—templates, if you will—as a starting point. Every backup/recovery plan should contain the following:

- A documented schedule for backing up system databases

- Documentation for restoring system databases

- A list of requirements or goals to achieve

- A description of a potential approach

  - Backup types and schedule

  - Naming standards

  - Restore scenario

  - Handling out-of-sequence backups

- An identification of risks involved in the plan

I prefer to back up system databases at least once a week. Given their small size, you might decide to do so nightly. Of course, if you've made specific changes, you should back up the applicable system database right away. For example, adding jobs should prompt a backup of MSDB, and changes to the instance configuration should prompt a backup of the master database. Be sure to have at least one copy of the resource database on hand. If you apply a new service pack, the resource database will be changed, so you should make a new backup of it immediately. Rather than repeat information in each sample scenario for system databases (both the schedule and the restore documentation), I'll assume you've already established system database backup schemes.

One other quick point: none of these scenarios or templates are mutually exclusive. It's possible that you're looking to minimize your backup window while minimizing data loss. The key is to be clear about why you're selecting a particular backup scheme and understand how it affects other backup/restore scenarios that you may also want to achieve.

Scenario: Short Backup Window

Time is a luxury. Common base BRPs focus on minimizing the time required for a particular part of the plan. In a perfect world, backups would happen instantaneously, disasters would never occur, and DBAs would be treated like kings. As we all know, this is far from a perfect world. Trying to minimize the time required to perform a backup can end up being quite complex.

Requirements

In this scenario, there is only a short period of time where you can make backups without interrupting other tasks or impacting user experience. Other maintenance work can also limit the backup window. The bottom line is that *all* backup procedures need to occur as quickly as possible.

Potential Approach

One of the biggest technical restraints that affect this scenario is the size of your database. For a medium or large database (greater than 50GB), a single, full backup can be prohibitive in terms of time; once the terabyte range is hit, it is all but impossible.

For smaller databases (less than 50GB), completing a single full backup is usually possible. The real question is: how often can you perform that full backup? Nightly? Weekly? Monthly? Given the best-case scenario of a nightly full backup, a backup scheme would look something like this:

- Full backup Sunday at 6 p.m.

- Log backups every 15-30 minutes

Something this simple could become more complex if a full backup were available only weekly or monthly.

> **Note** I'm leaving differential backups out of this scenario, because as the day, week, or month progresses, the size of a differential backup, as well as the time required to perform it, will increase steadily. Remember your primary goal here is to minimize backup time, not restore time.

For medium to large databases (greater than 50GB), a single full backup is almost impossible. At this point, filegroup and file-based backups are essential. This implies that you're using multiple files and, hopefully, multiple filegroups. It's hard to imagine having databases in the terabyte size where filegroups aren't involved, but believe it or not, I've seen it.

The advantage to using filegroups is twofold. First, a filegroup backup essentially acts as a shortcut to backing up the individual files it contains (less backup code to write). Second, it allows you to be selective in what you back up. That means less data to back up, which means a faster backup.

As an example, assume you have a sizeable database (around 500GB) that you need to back up as quickly as possible. Your primary reason for backing up is data protection, not data availability. You can separate all of the nonclustered indexes onto a separate filegroup so you can isolate it in your primary backup plan.

The resulting design could consist of three filegroups: one named PRIMARY (holding only the .mdf file), another for data (.ndf files holding data tables only), and one for indexes (.ndf files holding only nonclustered indexes). Your backup scheme would look something like this:

- PRIMARY filegroup (Sunday at 10 p.m.)

- Data filegroup (Monday through Friday at 10 p.m.)

- Index filegroup (just once)

- Log backup (Monday through Friday, every four hours)

You aren't continually backing up index data; that filegroup is only backed up once so that you have a complete set of backups. You could even shortcut that step if you want to—more on that shortly. Yes, it will take longer until the database functions effectively, but what you care about is a short backup time and protecting the data.

A CASE FOR SIMPLE RECOVERY MODE

I've often heard the edict, "No production database should be in Simple Recovery mode." I've read this in books, magazines, and on web sites. I've listened to colleagues give presentations extolling the vices of Simple Recovery mode and the virtues of Full Recovery mode. I've seen consultants chastise customers for not being able to fully recover a database to the point of failure. I've read "standards" documents at organizations that internally forbid the use of Simple Recovery mode. Even the model database—the template for every new database created—is set to Full Recovery. I've even lived by this credo for a time.

I now disagree with my historical self.

A common question on various SQL Server forums is, "My transaction log is huge! What do I do?" Managing transaction log growth and effectively sizing your database can be difficult tasks, especially for a database with unpredictable usage patterns.

Inherent Risks

Focusing on keeping the backup time down almost always results in either longer restore times or a potential loss of data. By keeping the driving force on the speed of the backup, you risk downplaying the impact on a restore situation. Another odd but accurate way of putting it: you risk failing to recognize your risks.

With any BRP that emphasizes a specific need with regard to either backup or restore, you must take extra care in assessing the impact on the entire plan. With a fast backup-based approach, be sure that all parties involved, including technical and business owners alike, are fully aware of the risks.

Tip Documenting and discussing risk is the most important aspect of a backup/recovery plan (or a full disaster recovery plan). Every time I've seen some sort of backup/recovery plan fail, it's usually a valid failure, meaning that the plan worked as intended. However, the impact of that failure—the risk—was never fully discussed with the appropriate people.

Always list risks in ranges from worst case to best case, being conservative (or in my case, slightly paranoid) when making estimates. In backup/recovery situations, it's particularly important to set expectations low. Table 5-1 shows what a risk breakdown might look like for a fast backup scenario.

Table 5-1. *Risk Breakdown for a Fast-Backup Scenario*

Risk	Worst-Case Impact	Best-Case Impact
Data loss	Data lost to the last full backup	Data lost only at the point of failure
Restore time	Last successful full backup plus all transaction log restores	Current full backup and no more than a day's worth of transaction logs
Perceived downtime	Dependent on restore time	Dependent on restore time

Scenario: Fast Restore Required

SQL Server 2005 places a great deal of focus on high availability. Essentially, availability is the business driver behind a need for minimal restore time. Any system that is critical to conducting business probably falls under this category, and systems needing as close to 24x7 availability as possible are quickly changing from the exception to the norm. However, the fast-restore scenario encompasses more than 24x7 systems.

A system that is needed only three hours a day can be just as critical in its availability as one that must be up continuously. A fast restore doesn't mean a need for five nines of uptime; it means a need to return a database to functioning status as quickly as possible. High-availability techniques are intended to keep a database functional continuously. It's extremely important to differentiate between the need for fast recovery and the need for high availability. They are not synonymous. Many a backup recovery plan design has been muddled by confusing high availability and fast restore.

Requirements

The database should have as little perceived downtime as possible. Note that the key here is *perceived* downtime, not actual, physical downtime. From an end-user (and executive) perspective, it only matters that the database is unusable. Why it is unusable is irrelevant. Save any discussion for the real source of the problem until *after* the issue is resolved.

You also must define and document the time period each day (or each week, etc.) during which it is critical that the database be operational. As mentioned previously, this scenario applies to more than 24x7 uptime requirements. Imagine a system that creates shipping manifests for the morning load of delivery trucks. Downtime in the afternoon may affect no one. Downtime while the manifests are being generated may result in, at best, customer dissatisfaction with late deliveries. It could result in a quantifiable monetary loss if the deliveries aren't made at all.

Potential Approach

Frequent, short backups are generally the key to ensuring that a fast restore is possible. The use of frequent differential backups is a must. This assumes that the database is small- to medium-sized (up to about 150GB maximum). The full restore operation should really be the only truly lengthy operation, and it should be reasonably predictable (the size increases at a steady rate). Without using file or filegroup backups, large databases aren't applicable in this scenario, as the full backup time will be prohibitive.

The critical elements in the approach I'm describing are the number of backups in between full backups and the use of differential backups. Yes, you could perform a full backup nightly and transaction logs every 30 minutes, but restoring a transaction log is a relatively slow process; the transactions are literally replayed.

By using frequent differential backups, you ensure that a minimal amount of files are required to return the database to operational status. You should continue to have frequent full backups (nightly is a minimum); otherwise, the size of each differential backup will continue to grow to a potentially unwieldy size. You should time log backups so that no more than one or two, plus the backup of the log's tail, are required for restore. Here's a possible schedule:

- Full backup nightly (starting at 10 p.m.)

- Hourly differential backups during active usage periods (perhaps 7 a.m. to 7 p.m.)

- Hourly transaction log backups, at 30 minutes past the hour during active system usage

If data loss is acceptable, you could perform a full backup nightly and differential backups every 30 minutes while leaving the database in Simple Recovery mode. This eliminates the need for the possible backup of the log's tail as well as any transaction log backups. If fast restore is truly the requirement, some level of data loss might be acceptable.

IMPERSONATION AND BACKUP OPTIMIZATION

SQL Server 2005 allows impersonation from one database to another on the same server via the TRUSTWORTHY database property, the AUTHENTICATE permission, and the EXECUTE AS clause. Essentially, you can allow a user from one database to interact with another (local) database without explicitly adding that user and giving her object or schema rights. I've taught this topic many times, but for a long time I had difficulty coming up with a realistic business scenario in which to use it. Now I have one.

When you need a quick restore, it may be beneficial to create a separate database just for the purposes of backup and restore. You could then use impersonation to integrate it with the primary database, yet back it up and restore it with a completely separate approach. This way, you could effectively partition a system into two separate databases with completely different restore and availability needs.

Yes, you could achieve the same sort of functionality using filegroup backups. And yes, there is potentially a major issue with database design and maintaining transactional consistency between the two databases. However, in the example of a manifest-creation system, you could restore that "sub-database" without disrupting the larger system. Even a single filegroup restore has some impact on a large database, as transaction logs must be restored to achieve transactional consistency.

The use of impersonation as I've described is an intriguing idea worth consideration in certain system configurations. For example, you might have a fully contained subsystem that you can back up and restore independently of the rest of the system. In the event of data loss, you must be able to re-create records in the subsystem with little or no impact on consistency. In the example of the manifest system, perhaps a routine in the larger system can re-create shipping information based on sales orders.

The impersonation technique clearly should be the exception and not the norm, and as with everything else, it would require significant testing before you could give it a stamp of approval in a production situation. Still, I wouldn't be surprised to find myself using this technique in the future.

Inherent Risks

The drive to have the database restored as quickly as possible often places excessive stress on a DBA. Have you ever had the CEO of your company stand and look over your shoulder as you work? The more stress you face, the faster you try to work, and the more likely it is that you'll make a mistake. To minimize the likelihood of stress-related errors, respond to the "looking over your shoulder" syndrome by having another set of (technical) eyes watch what you're doing.

Given the proposed backup scheme (in Full Recovery mode), Table 5-2 shows what the risk matrix would look like.

Table 5-2. *Risk Breakdown for a Fast-Restore Scenario*

Risk	Worst-Case Impact	Best-Case Impact
Data loss	Data lost to the last good full backup and the associated differential backups	Data lost since the last transaction log backup
Restore time	Mistakes made during restore require multiple attempts at a full backup restore	The time of a full backup restore, one differential restore, and a tail-log restore
Perceived downtime	Restore time plus an application reconfiguration required	Restore time only

Scenario: Minimal Loss Desired

Data means everything. Minimal data loss is usually mutually exclusive with the fastest restore time possible.

Note SQL Server 2005 is marketed as having "Always On Technologies." It's true that there are some fantastic improvements in the areas of high availability (some of which I'll cover in the next half of the book), but that focus draws attention away from the backup/restore scenario in which minimal data loss is the goal. In my book, backup/recovery comes first, then high availability. Unless a client specifically indicates that *x* amount of data loss is acceptable, I assume that zero data loss is the goal.

Requirements

When a database is critical to the day-to-day financial success of the company, it definitely has a need for minimal data loss. Any database that must retain a continuous log of transactions (a bank, perhaps) cannot tolerate data loss. The database needs to return to a functional state as quickly as possible. Any interruptions caused by backup operations—however important those backups may be—take second seat to data protection.

Potential Approach

Transaction log backups are *the* key toward minimizing data loss. Lose a single file, and you're looking for a new job. Yes, you still need that full backup, and differential backups certainly help restore times, but that isn't your main objective. Your main objective is no data loss. Period.

The nice thing about setting up this type of backup/recovery plan is that it doesn't much matter what the size of the database is. It could be 50MB, or it could be 50EB (exabytes—in other words, 50,000,000GB). You have to protect the transaction logs at all costs.

If minimal data loss is the need, you have to focus on protecting your backups as much as possible. Yes, you can do things like physically protect backup tapes and such, but that isn't part of the backup/recovery plan. You have to incorporate some level of protection into your plan, such as taking advantage of the new MIRROR TO clause. The following is one potential approach to take:

- Full backup weekly, with five weeks' worth kept on file

- Log backups every 30 minutes, mirrored to four devices, and stored for ten weeks

Depending on the size of the database, you could include file/filegroup backups, differentials, and so on, but your main goal is to have a solid base to restore the database from (the full backup) and a complete history of activity that can be replayed on the database (the log files).

You should also consider a formal policy prohibiting the use of creating any backups outside of the normal backup scheme for the purposes of refreshing a test database. The WITH COPY_ONLY clause prevents differentials from becoming obsolete, but you need an official policy to enforce its usage.

Inherent Risks

Having multiple copies of different types of backups on multiple media formats is guaranteed to be an administrative nightmare. Without a documented system of cataloging backups and a staff member to ensure that the cataloging is done correctly, the risk of losing a single tape or file (or just misplacing it) goes up.

Without an equally effective naming scheme, restore operations could become confusing. You certainly don't want to waste time trying to figure out which files you need to restore from tape. Proper naming and cataloging in this scenario means the difference between success and failure.

■**Caution** Some excellent third-party backup suites integrate large volumes of data from multiple sources and catalog it automatically. They can be an excellent investment in a large environment, but be careful in these situations. There is a tendency for the administrator of that system (it requires a dedicated administrator) to take ownership, explicitly or implicitly, of the entire backup/restore process. You cannot let that happen. The backup administrator should be in control of the process but not the *design* of the process, or the ownership.

Table 5-3 shows the risks inherent to the "minimize data loss" scenario.

Table 5-3. *Risk Breakdown for a Minimal-Loss Scenario*

Risk	Worst-Case Impact	Best-Case Impact
Data loss	No data lost since the last good full/log backup combination	Zero data lost
Restore time	Could include an old full restore and weeks' worth of log restores	Current full restore, all logs since the full restore, and the tail-log restore
Perceived downtime	Dependent on the number of log restores	Dependent on the number of log restores

Scenario: Flexible Portability

Storing a copy of the data off-site is critical (just ask the city of New Orleans after the hurricane season of 2005). However, sometimes storing data off-site isn't as easy as it sounds. Some backups might not fit on to a single tape, or perhaps tape backup is unavailable, and burning a copy of the backup to a DVD is your only option. In any event, your backup/recovery plan must provide for a regular move to off-site storage.

Requirements

If your system exists in an environment that has a relatively high probability of disaster (most notably environmental disasters), off-site storage of backups is a must. The backups must be able to fit on some sort of portable media (transmitting over the network is not an option yet), and no discrete piece of the backup should be striped across multiple physical devices.

Potential Approach

File and filegroup backups are almost certainly required here. No single backup file should exceed the capacity of a single storage device. For small- to medium-sized databases (less than 500GB), you can achieve this by aligning disk file sizes with your storage medium. For the sake of example, let's say your tape drives can only handle a single 40GB file. If that's the case, each data file should not exceed 40GB.

For large databases (greater than 500GB), this scenario of flexible, portable storage presents some real challenges. You could use an external hard disk device as your storage medium and back up files together in 1TB chunks. Or, you could stick with the single-file method on tape drives, but it would take a lot of tapes and a long time to achieve a full backup.

Note There are certainly hardware methods to deal with a large database. Tape arrays provide larger amounts of storage, although they do stripe the backup from a hardware standpoint. You can also use a bit-based backup over a network from SAN to SAN. I'll discuss some of these technologies in Chapter 10. For now, though, you should consider options such as these *after* you've defined the base requirements and a base plan. Never jump to a solution before you've clearly defined the problem.

You definitely need to create filegroup backups and perhaps even move to the partial backup/piecemeal restore. Let's assume that 40GB is your maximum portability size. For all sizes of databases, the plan would look something like this:

- PRIMARY filegroup the first Sunday of every month at 10 p.m.

- Single file backup nightly at 10 p.m.

- Transaction log backups every 30 minutes

As with most backup/restore plans, transaction logs are the key. In this case, if you lose a single data file, you could restore only that file plus all the transaction logs since that file was created to ensure transactional consistency.

Inherent Risks

Because of the complexity of the backup plan (lots of file backups spread over multiple days), this scenario runs the risk of logistical issues. As with the previous scenario in which minimal data loss was the goal, proper naming conventions and cataloging are a must.

Another key risk is the off-site storage. Where is it? Is it environmentally protected? Is it secure? Keeping the backup tapes at someone's house is definitely a start and better than nothing, but that has plenty of risks in and of itself. I once had a client whose two-year-old tried to jam a backup tape in a VCR.

Table 5-4 shows the risks inherent in this scenario.

Table 5-4. *Risk Breakdown for a Flexible-Portability Scenario*

Risk	Worst-Case Impact	Best-Case Impact
Data loss	Possibly months' worth of data	Almost zero data loss
Restore time	A restore over every data file and all of the log files	A single file restore, plus log files
Perceived downtime	The length of a complete restore	If the data file is in a filegroup that's accessed infrequently, possibly zero perceived downtime

Scenario: Specific Tables Only

In SQL Server 6.5, you could back up and restore a single table. Once SQL Server 7.0 came out, that functionality was removed. My guess is that PSS took one too many calls about the restore of a single table destroying referential integrity. I dealt with that very issue myself many times.

Versions 7.0 and beyond now include the ability to back up and restore filegroups. You can place specific objects on specific filegroups. If you want to back up only one table, create a filegroup for it and you're all set.

Note Third-party utilities allow table-level restore. However, while they may prove useful, don't rely on them when planning. Assume you have only the native SQL Server tools to use.

Requirements

Perhaps you don't need to back up the entire database; you might be able to re-create it from seed data. Maybe you only need the Order and Order Detail tables. In that case, you can create a filegroup called Order_FG and place those two tables on it. Since those are the only tables receiving incoming data, that's all you need to back up.

Potential Approach

You should include the PRIMARY filegroup any time you decide to use filegroup backups (remember, it contains information about the database itself). The approach is simple and is laid out in the following list of backups to be taken:

- PRIMARY filegroup backup every Sunday at 10 a.m.

- Order_FG filegroup backup every night at 10 p.m.

- Transaction log backups every 30 minutes

You still need all of the transaction logs to ensure consistency. Actually, if you're ever in doubt, back up the transaction logs on a frequent basis.

Inherent Risks

When you choose to restore only specific tables, be sure that the approach you're choosing is really necessary. It should be rare and applicable only in very specific situations. Continually question whether it is sufficient to restore just a few tables, even if your testing at first appears successful. To determine whether it's valid to restore specific tables, someone needs intimate knowledge of the database structure *and* of the application design itself. Personally, I would avoid the approach of restoring specific tables described in this scenario, but I do acknowledge that it can be useful at times. Table 5-5 shows the risks to prepare for.

Table 5-5. *Risk Breakdown for a Specific-Tables-Only Scenario*

Risk	Worst-Case Impact	Best-Case Impact
Data loss	All `Order` and `Order Detail` information	Zero data loss
Restore time	Dependent on the number of transaction log restores required	Dependent on the number of transaction log restores required
Perceived downtime	If a full database reconstruction is necessary, could be much longer than just restoring data (due to the need to load seed information and such)	If portions of the database are usable without these two tables, possible to have partial availability

Scenario: Large Full-Text Catalogs

Since full-text catalogs are now included with a full backup, you may need to separate the backup of the database and the backup of the full-text catalogs. The inclusion of full-text catalogs in full backups is new behavior in SQL Server 2005, and business units need to be aware of it.

Requirements

The application in question relies heavily on full-text indexes, so ensuring that they're backed up is critical. In fact, the bulk of the data used by the application is the full-text catalogs, so without them, the system would be unusable.

Potential Approach

By default, the full-text catalog has its own file. All you need to do is a specific file backup. Because the full-text data is actually stored externally to the database, you don't even need transaction log backups. You might, for example, schedule the following single task:

• Nightly backup of all full-text catalog files at 10 p.m.

That's it. It's extremely simple, but being a new feature to 2005, it should be clearly spelled out as a possible backup/recovery approach.

Inherent Risks

Table 5-6 shows the risks inherent in a scenario that backs up large, full-text catalogs.

Table 5-6. *Risk Breakdown for a Full-Text-Catalog Scenario*

Risk	Worst-Case Impact	Best-Case Impact
Data loss	None really, since these indexes aren't permanent data	None really, since these indexes aren't permanent data
Restore time	Depends entirely on the size of the indexes	Depends entirely on the size of the indexes
Perceived downtime	Could be unavailable until the indexes are restored, if the application relies on them 100%	Could appear partially available if the application has some functionality without the indexes

As with the previous scenario, this should be an extremely rare situation. Backing up full-text catalogs was the only backup need for one of my clients, yet SQL Server 2000 was the only platform they had. To perform their backup, they had to shut down the Microsoft Search service, back up all of the external index files, and restart the service.

Another thing to consider is that you'll need to rely on external systems to back up the full-text index files at an operating-system level (often by using a backup agent capable of backing up open files). The full-text indexes are tightly coupled with the data they're built from. If there is change to the database, simply restoring an old copy of the index files won't work—you'll have to rebuild the indexes completely.

Initial and Periodic Testing

The most important piece of any backup and recovery plan is testing. Of course, after you've designed the plan, you should thoroughly test both the impact of the backup process and the success of the restore process. That means that restoring a single backup is not sufficient. You should test it in as real-world a scenario as possible. If backups run during periods of production use, you should test them. If a restore scenario requires you to retrieve a backup file from a tape library, you should test that also.

Yes, *test* is a four-letter word. No one likes to do it. I sure don't.

The point of testing is not simply to see if things work. A well-thought-out testing plan should provide much more information than just success or failure. Performing a test provides a mountain of information, in particular when the test fails. The best way to learn is by making mistakes. Isn't it better to make those mistakes during a test run than during a real disaster scenario? Consider these questions while performing a test:

- Why did it work?

- Why did it fail?

- How long did the process take?

- Were there any delays, and if so, why?

Another item that no one wants to hear: testing is a continual process. How often should you review and test? Definitely not more frequently than quarterly, unless you're actively experiencing problems with the plan. You should test at least once a year, and preferably every six months, assuming things are running smoothly.

Continual review and testing is not just a go-through-the-motions task. It's your opportunity to learn and enhance. Document what works and what doesn't. Document restore times, and compare them to previous tests to extrapolate future restore times. The possibilities for insights via testing are endless.

Enhancing Basic Scenarios

Once you've chosen a basic plan, you should review it at a later date to see if there are ways to further minimize risks and guarantee that the requirements are met. As you might expect, the plan you'll end up needing in the real world won't fit one of the templates neatly. Building a plan is a constant struggle between uptime, backup requirements, and potential data loss. Politically, it can be a nightmare to get anyone to agree on a single approach. (I'll discuss how to achieve political success in disaster recovery in Chapter 12.)

You can speed up single database backups with the use of filegroup backups. File and filegroup backups could include file differential backups to increase restore time. If full-text search is used but not critical, removing its associated file from the backup routine can speed things up significantly.

Using filegroups to separate data files and indexes can speed the backup of the actual data. It won't necessarily improve restore times, but you can arrange filegroups in very creative ways to improve the backup or restore process.

The partial backup/piecemeal restore routine, with strategically configured filegroups, allows you to bring the database online as each piece is being restored.

There are a number of creative ways to improve on these basic scenarios. Always keep this one thing in mind: start with a simple plan, and then improve it. Never look for the final solution in the first step.

Caveats and Recommendations

This chapter has covered in detail the essential aspects of creating a sound plan for backup and recovery of a database. As you might expect, the planning process is fraught with pitfalls. Keep the following in mind as you plan for your own databases, and you'll likely avoid those pitfalls:

- *Be conservative*: One of the biggest mistakes you can make when designing a backup/recovery plan is to set expectations too high. Always be conservative with estimates, risk assessments, and the like. Nothing will kill your career faster than overpromising and underdelivering. (Hint: Don't mention that you're being conservative. It defeats the purpose completely.)

- *Be paranoid*: Nothing makes for a better backup/recovery plan than a paranoid mind. Assume the worst. Assume things won't work as planned; this help generates the drive to test regularly. Assume you'll be fired if the plan fails. However, don't have a defeatist ("This will never work") or nihilist ("Oh, what's the point?") attitude. Only the truly paranoid need apply.

- *Be diligent*: Remember that a backup/recovery plan isn't just a function of the DBA; the business unit has the final say (if it can pay for it) and equal responsibility. Always keep the business in mind. The point of backup and recovery is not the protection of the database, but the protection of the business processes it supports. It's also critical to set expectations appropriately. No one likes surprises, especially not upper management.

- *Be vigilant*: Test, test, and test again. Review plans with business partners to ensure they still apply (especially if there's a change in management). There will be times where you'll have to convince people to participate, but you're the last line of defense for the data. Act that way. *Think* that way.

Summary

This is the last chapter concerning backup and recovery in isolation. BRPs are primarily a response technique. True disaster recovery is the combination of preparing a response and mitigating the risk of the disaster in the first place.

In the next four chapters, I'll discuss technologies that help you mitigate the effects of various disaster scenarios. Some of those technologies are quite simple, while others are complex and have some hidden sand traps that will surprise you if you aren't prepared.

CHAPTER 6

■■■

Maintaining a Warm Standby Server via Log Shipping

Until now, I've been focusing on response techniques for dealing with the aftermath of a disaster. In this and the next three chapters, I'll focus on techniques for mitigating disaster risks. Of course, each technique presents its own disaster scenario in which you must reset the mitigation solution. I'll cover these situations, but I'll focus more on how the technology helps minimize the likelihood or impact of any given disaster scenario. The first stop is log shipping.

Environmental disasters are the least likely to occur, but they tend to be the most difficult to recover from, much less prepare for. In many ways, log shipping is the ultimate in environmental disaster mitigation. It's cost-effective, relatively easy to use, and stable.

The practice of log shipping is used to keep a warm standby server available in case the primary server fails. The method is literally to copy log backups from the primary server to the secondary server where you then restore them. In addition to serving as warm backups, these standby databases can also be accessed by clients as read-only databases if necessary.

Some people find log shipping to be archaic, unsafe, or require too much manual intervention, making it an unviable mitigation approach. I fundamentally disagree. Yes, there is a manual aspect to the process. Yes, there is a guarantee of a certain amount of data loss. And yes, log shipping in one form or another has existed for more than a decade. None of these arguments specifically demonstrates that it isn't an effective tool when it comes to disaster mitigation. It may not be as "sexy" as some of the newer technologies, but log shipping still gets the job done.

In this chapter, I'll explore log shipping in general and show you how to automate it with SQL Server 2005. In addition to configuration, I'll discuss the actions required during a failure and explain how to reset the entire configuration back to its original state (which isn't always a straightforward task).

Log Shipping vs. Replication

While talking with colleagues or giving presentations on disaster recovery, the subject of replication in the context of establishing a standby server inevitably comes up. Many believe that replication instead of log shipping should be used for establishing a standby server. Since I don't have a chapter in this book called "Replication," I obviously don't agree.

There is a legitimate argument here, though. I concede the following points about using replication to create a standby server:

- *Faster data transfer*: In general, the process of getting data from point A to point B is faster when you use replication, because it is direct communication. Log shipping takes time to back up the log, copy it to the standby server, and restore it.

- *Less potential data loss*: Depending on the type and the configuration, replication could theoretically prevent data loss altogether. Log shipping guarantees some amount of loss of data. Of course, if the log backup includes no changes to the data or structure of the database, nothing is lost.

- *Multiple, active standby servers*: Log shipping provides for multiple standby servers, but these servers can be used as read-only reporting databases at best. With replication, the other standby servers are fully accessible.

It is this final point about accessible standby servers that begins my counterargument. If you need to have fully accessible multiple servers (meaning available for insert, update, and delete operations), then you have a distributed system. Data is being submitted or altered from multiple points. So what exactly is the object of disaster recovery? Each individual node, or the entire distributed system?

The primary purpose of replication is to supply pieces of information to or from a centralized location. More exactly, a replication topology is more like a distributed database. Any other uses of replication (and there are a lot of creative uses) are for secondary purposes only.

Note SQL Server 2005 introduces a new type of replication: peer-to-peer. Normally, replication topologies follow a publisher/distributor/subscriber model. In the peer-to-peer model, every server involved is essentially both a publisher and a subscriber. There is, of course, a latency issue as the individual nodes sync themselves, but this could be a possibility to consider as a mitigation technique. There's also a point of diminishing return by adding too many nodes—the replication overhead becomes too complicated and costly. I've spent a lot of time with replication, and until I put peer-to-peer through the wringer so to speak, I'm not going to endorse it.

Replication also incurs significant overhead, both in resources required and administration and maintenance. It's a relatively complex technology, meaning there are more points of possible failure than with log shipping. Without a doubt, it has improved significantly with every major release of SQL Server and every subsequent service pack. However, it was never intended for use in disaster mitigation by establishing a standby server.

You may remain unconvinced, but I stand fast in my point of view. In any event, to truly cover replication would require another 150-200 pages. Replication is a technology and a topic for another time and place.

Benefits of Log Shipping

I often find myself arguing the case for using log shipping (usually as opposed to some sort of replication technique). Database mirroring (which I'll cover in depth in Chapter 8) presents another alternative to log shipping—some of my colleagues say a far superior alternative. While I think database mirroring is a great technology, log shipping is more appropriate in many business scenarios.

For some systems, you might simply need to move data to a remote location. The need to protect against data loss is critical, but you achieve zero data loss by reentering some data if you have to. Missing 15 or 30 minutes' worth of transactions isn't the end of the world. Losing the entire system is. Environmental disasters are the prime candidates for causing complete system loss.

Log shipping is an excellent mitigation technique for environmental, hardware, or media-related disasters. It's superior to many other techniques because it requires no information about the state of any other system (with one exception, which I'll get to when I discuss architecture), it has no limitations to the number of servers acting as standby databases, it has almost no resource overhead on the primary server, and you can actually use the standby servers for read-only access. Let's look at each of these benefits in detail.

Log Shipping Is Stateless

Mitigation techniques such as clustering and mirroring require a constant connection between the primary and secondary servers to establish the state of each system. A constant, repetitive conversation is occurring:

Primary server: Are you OK?

Secondary server: Yup, how about you?

Primary server: I'm fine. Are you still OK?

Secondary server: I said yes. Don't nag.

Monitoring server: All right, you two. Let's see some ID and a current status!

Primary server: Primary here. I'm OK.

Secondary server: Secondary here. I'm OK, too.

Monitoring server: OK, I'll check back in 30 seconds.

Secondary server: Boy is that guy annoying.

Primary server: Hey secondary, are you OK?

Ad infinitum.

If having some sort of automated failover is required, this type of communication is a necessity. However, it adds a small resource drain on all participants, plus any disruption in the conversation can result in a false indication of system failure.

Log shipping avoids both resource requirements and false-positive system failures. Neither the primary server nor the secondary servers need to know if the other even exists, much less what its status is. A monitoring server may be involved in a log-shipping scenario, but it too doesn't care so much about the state of the servers. Instead, it cares about the success or failure of the jobs that facilitate log shipping in the first place. Plus, primary and secondary servers have no need to answer annoying requests for status from a monitoring server.

STATELESS VS. COUPLED SYSTEMS

When systems work together, they either *want to know* the state of the other system (whether it's online or offline), *need to know*, or *couldn't care less*. In large-scale system design, the terms are *loosely coupled* vs. *tightly coupled*. Nobody talks about *uncoupled* systems, because that implies that they aren't a part of a distributed application framework—uncoupled systems are stand-alone systems.

Log shipping is almost an uncoupled system, but one piece of information is crucial to it functioning properly (teaser: more on that coming up). Clustering, on the other hand, which I'll examine in the next chapter, is a textbook case of a tightly coupled system. Other mitigation techniques in this book fall somewhere in between.

Why are state and tightly coupled vs. loosely coupled systems important when it comes to disaster recovery? When designing any type of distributed system, it is critical to understand when a tightly coupled system is appropriate and when a loosely coupled system is advantageous. Tightly coupled systems require that you consider different issues in disaster recovery planning than do loosely coupled systems. Identifying tightly vs. loosely coupled design is critical in establishing the appropriate disaster recovery approach.

Multiple Standby Databases Are Possible

Theoretically, there's no limit to the number of standby databases you can maintain. However, from a practical standpoint, having more than four or so reduces the likelihood that you'll be able to properly monitor the process of maintaining those standbys. Remember, you can set all the alerts you want, but that doesn't guarantee that an automated process is automatic.

Savor this for a moment: there is no theoretical limit to the number of standby servers you can have. How many other mitigation technologies can make a boast like that? Not a one. Of course, each standby server adds administrative overhead, and you want to limit the number for sake of sanity.

No Location Boundaries Exist

Because no constant nagging notification of server state is required, it is possible to have standby servers all over the world. If we ever colonize Mars and have a network connection to that planet, we could even place a standby log-shipping server there. Yes, network latency has an effect on the entire process, but it does not *stop* the shipping from occurring. Let's say you have a primary server in Chicago, a standby in New York, and another standby in Shanghai. The server in Shanghai is likely to be slightly behind the server in New York, but the logs will eventually get shipped.

Even with network latency factors, the lack of location boundaries is a huge benefit. You could have a standby server on every continent (yes, even Antarctica). Is there any surer way to mitigate environmental disaster?

Low Resource Overhead Is Incurred

Without getting too deep into the specifics yet, you can enable log shipping by creating a log backup job on the primary server (log shipping works in Full Recovery and Bulk-Logged Recovery modes only) and placing those backup files in a location accessible over a network. On the secondary server, you restore a full backup of the databases but leave it in standby mode, ready for log restores. You then create a job to pick up the primary server's transaction logs, copy them locally, and then restore them while leaving the database in a standby mode.

The primary server requires almost no additional overhead. You should already be backing up transaction logs, and the secondary servers initiate the file copy. That puts a slight load on the primary server's networking resources in general, but not on SQL Server directly.

Standby Databases Are Accessible

Another great feature of log shipping is that you can place the standby servers in standby recovery mode. While in this mode, a standby database is able to restore additional transaction log backups. Also, you can access it as a read-only database. Using log shipping in this manner is a great way to create reporting databases that have near to real-time data, especially if you have reporting needs for the same data in different physical locations.

Drawbacks of Log Shipping

Does log shipping sound too good to be true? It is. Like everything else, it has its limitations. Some of these limitations are major, which is why log shipping is often overlooked for more robust solutions.

Data Loss

By design, log shipping almost guarantees data loss if the primary server is lost. How much is lost depends on how often the transaction log is backed up on the primary server, how often the secondary servers check for new transaction logs, how long it takes to copy the transaction log file over the network, and how long it takes to restore it. You could configure log shipping to back up the log on the main machine, copy it over the network, and restore it every five minutes, or you could configure log shipping to execute every two hours. If data is continually being entered into the main system, you're guaranteed to have a certain amount of lost data. Depending on the frequency of the log shipping, as well as the activity on the primary database, it's likely that there will be data loss. The upside is that you should at least know exactly how much data you've lost.

■**Note** Data loss is often not so large a problem as you might think. In many environments, there is already a means in place to identify and reenter lost data. So long as the amount of data to be reentered is minimal, the price of reentering it might be far lower than the cost of ensuring that no loss at all occurs. In short, it is sometimes cheaper to accept the risk of having to reenter some data than to design a system in which re-entry is never needed.

Network Latency

Because you know you're going to lose some amount of data, you decide to have frequent backups and transfers across the network. However, doing so can actually have the opposite of the intended effect. If the standby servers are separated by a significant distance, a large number of small network packets might slow the overall network traffic. This isn't because you don't have enough bandwidth, but rather because there are so many routers and switches in between point A and point B that they become saturated with processing incoming network packets (the transaction logs). Such saturation is a rare occurrence, but it's an issue many DBAs miss.

BANDWIDTH VS. LATENCY

Bandwidth and latency are two completely different issues, yet many people have a tendency to focus on bandwidth alone or, worse yet, lump the two into a single category.

Bandwidth is the amount of potential data that can be sent simultaneously. If you think of data being transmitted in terms of traffic, a low-bandwidth connection would be a single-lane, one-way road, and a high-bandwidth connection would be a ten-lane highway. Bottlenecks due to low bandwidth are becoming a rare occurrence. The types of activities that could saturate bandwidth and affect performance are massive data transfers or too many systems performing sizeable network transfers at once. Bandwidth is currently (at the time of this writing) measured in megabits per second (Mbps). A home DSL connection might provide a download speed of 1.5 Mbps. This is not a measure of speed; this is a measure of how much data can be transferred simultaneously. High numbers are best when referring to bandwidth. One other caveat with bandwidth is that there can be separate download bandwidth and upload bandwidth. Downloading a large file might occur quickly, but uploading to another location might take significantly longer.

Sticking with the traffic analogy, latency occurs when you have stop signs or traffic lights on the highway. A ten-lane highway won't help much if there's a stoplight every two miles. In technical terms, every network packet must pass through a number of switches, routers, and firewalls to get from point A to point B. Each time it stops, the packet must be disassembled, reviewed, and reassembled before it can be passed on to the next destination. Latency is currently (at this writing) measured in milliseconds; the smaller the number, the better.

Latency is the more common issue with networks. Rarely have I encountered networking issues caused by bandwidth problems. In fact, bandwidth issues seem to occur only at night during batch-processing operations. The problem with latency is that it can be difficult to troubleshoot, and worse yet, there's often nothing you can do to directly improve the situation. If your network provider has your traffic consistently going through eight to ten *hops* (the network equivalent to a stop sign), your options for lowering that number will be limited and expensive.

Understanding the difference between bandwidth and latency can save you significant time when discussing performance issues and networking. I'll spend more time discussing the impact of both bandwidth and latency in Chapter 10.

Potential Limit to Database Size

When I'm defending log shipping, people often argue, "It just won't work for VLDBs." There's some validity to that statement, but only during setup or a reset. Log shipping requires a full backup from which to start, so sizeable databases are difficult to transfer over to a secondary server. From that point on, the only size consideration is how large the transaction logs are. You should be backing up the transaction logs frequently, so size shouldn't be an issue.

Of course, this does assume that you have capacity on your standby servers to handle a sizeable database. Keep in mind that for every standby server, you're storing a complete copy of the database.

Failover

Failover and failback (which I'll discuss next) are the true limitations to log shipping. When something goes wrong and you need to fail over to the standby server, roll up your sleeves—that failover is a manual process. I'll cover the exact process shortly, but the main point here is that failover is manual. That means you need to have a failover plan that's ready and that you've tested. As you'll see shortly, a failover plan can actually be quite complex, depending on your environment and requirements.

Failback

With log shipping, the only thing requiring more manual time than a failover event is a failback event—that is, resetting the topology back to its original configuration. You literally have to re-create the topology. There is no simple switch that allows you to revert back to the primary server. Remember, during a failover, the standby server is now actively running transactions. Unless absolutely no data changes occurred since the standby server was made the primary server, you'll have to create a backup of the new primary server, move it to the standby server (the old primary server), and reconfigure the entire thing. If absolutely no changes occurred during the failover situation, failback might be a bit easier to manage by using a local backup on the original primary server. Experience has taught me that having no changed data is a rare or nonexistent scenario.

Log-Shipping Architecture

Whether you're configuring a log-shipping plan manually or using an automated technique via SQL Server, the basic architecture of the process is the same. As you'll soon see, the log-shipping architecture is far more flexible than many realize. It will also become apparent that log shipping is an optimistic mitigation technique. Although it protects data well, it doesn't help you recover from a disaster scenario without the application of a little elbow grease.

Basic Architecture

The initial configuration of a log-shipping scenario is actually simple. Designate one server as the primary and another as the standby. Copy a full backup of the database from the primary server to the standby server and restore that database without recovering it. (You remember the default RESTORE clause is WITH RECOVERY, correct? Be sure to specify that you don't want that recovery.) Create a location on the network (a file share or FTP site, for example) that's accessible by both the primary and standby servers. Figure 6-1 illustrates what you should have after following these steps.

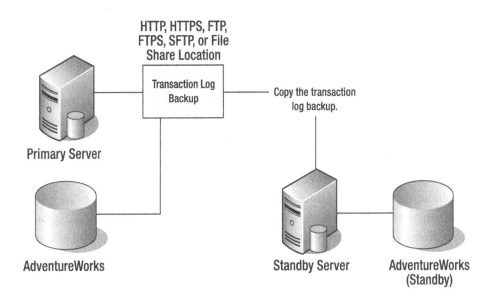

Figure 6-1. *A simple standby database scenario*

The standby server then picks up the transaction log from the central location, copies it locally, and restores it (but leaves the database in an *unrecovered* state). This process repeats until a failure or a break in the LSN chain occurs—for example, if someone accidentally deletes a log backup before it's restored.

Note that there must be an equivalent and uninterrupted LSN chain on the primary and secondary servers. You can create separate full backups, file/filegroup backups, and differential backups. A transaction log backup truncates committed transactions from the active log, which means you may only maintain one transaction log backup chain.

The instant you create a new log backup on the primary server that doesn't get placed in the central log backup location, log shipping ceases to function.

Tip You can maintain multiple log backups and deploy log shipping by using either the `MIRROR TO` clause, which makes copies to locations other than the log shipping pickup point, or the `WITH COPY_ONLY` clause, which tells SQL Server not to reset the LSN chain.

Multiple Standby Servers

One of the often overlooked benefits of log shipping is that there is no limit to the number of standby servers for one primary server. You could have standby servers all over the world, mitigating some of the worst environmental disasters imaginable, which we've unfortunately seen in the last few years with Hurricanes Katrina and Rita and the massive tsunami in the Indian Ocean. Log shipping is a loosely coupled technology, giving it the unique ability to use multiple standby servers. Figure 6-2 shows a multiserver, log-shipping deployment.

Imagine the level of low-cost data protection you can achieve by using multiple standby servers in multiple locations. No fancy, expensive geo-locating SANs are required. The network infrastructure is already there, and you can secure the transfer of data with existing protocols, such as HTTP over Secure Sockets Layer (SSL), known as HTTPS; File Transfer Protocol over SSL (FTPS); and Secure File Transfer Protocol (SFTP).

If something fails on the primary server, you're most likely to lose data. Each standby server might be at a different state, so it could take awhile to find the most likely candidate to perform a failover if necessary. However, quick failover and zero data loss are not the main goals of log shipping. The primary purpose of a log-shipping topology is to protect data.

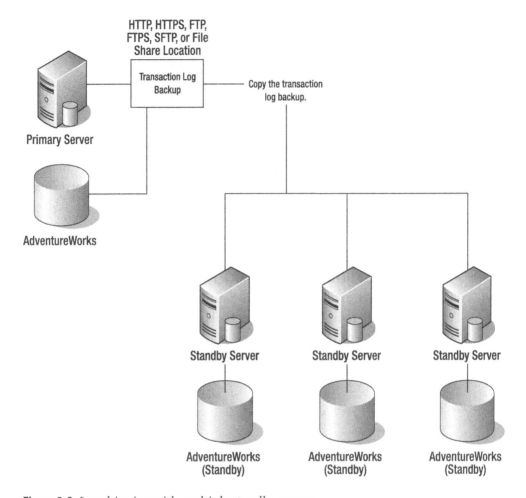

Figure 6-2. *Log shipping with multiple standby servers*

Configuring Log Shipping

Contrary to popular belief, no specific tool is required to create a log-shipping scenario. SQL Server 2000 Enterprise Edition and SQL Server 2005 Workgroup through Enterprise Editions are nice enough to automate that process for you, but if you really want to set everything up yourself, you can. If you want an automated method, a simple search on the Web produces many homegrown scripts that people have used.

Some prefer to have SQL Server handle all of the log-shipping process. If you have SQL Server 2000, you'll have to purchase the Enterprise Edition for all servers involved (that pretty much shoots the multiple-standby-server topology out of the water). SQL Server 2005, however, supports automated log shipping for every version except SQL Server 2005 Express Edition. For those with limited financial resources, log shipping in

SQL Server 2005 becomes an even more attractive data-protection technique. For those with limited financial resources using SQL Server 2000, it's probably best to use a manual log-shipping scenario.

Manual Log Shipping

To use log shipping, you don't need any additional software, tools, or built-in functionality. Ultimately, all you need are two or more servers, a central location they can both access, and scheduled jobs to back up the transaction log on the primary server and restore the log (without recovery) on the standby server.

Let's look at each step in detail:

1. *Create a central location for each server to use*: This can be a network share that both can use, or a network share for one server and an FTP server for another that ultimately resolve to the same physical location. It's very flexible; the only requirement is that both must be able to access it. Figure 6-3 shows the file-sharing dialog, which you can access by simply right-clicking on the folder.

Figure 6-3. *Using a file share for log backups assumes that all SQL Servers involved in log shipping are in the same Windows domain structure.*

If your standby server isn't on your local network and in the same Windows domain, or is on a completely different networking environment entirely (such as Unix or an NFS-based system), you'll need to access the primary server log backups either directly from an HTTP or HTTPS site or from an FTP or FTPS/SFTP site. Figure 6-4 shows the dialog you'll see when using Internet Information Services (IIS), Microsoft's built-in Web server, to create an HTTP(S) site. You could easily do the same with any non-Microsoft Web server as well.

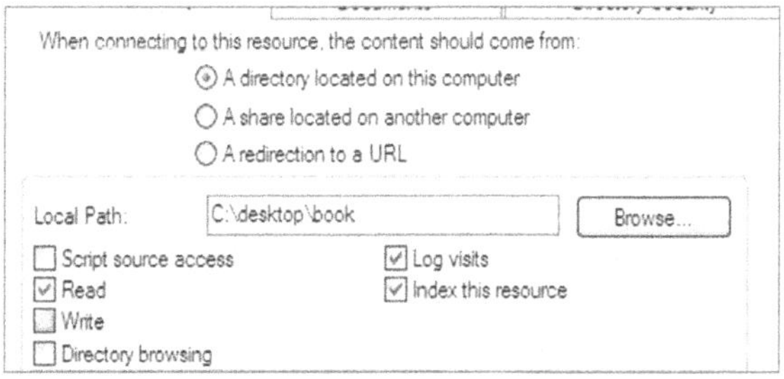

Figure 6-4. *You could expose your log backup location as an HTTP/HTTPS site.*

FTP is slightly different. By default, Windows FTP will not be included when installing IIS, so you need to install Windows FTP explicitly. Once you've installed Windows FTP, simply create a site and then expose folders with various permissions underneath them. Figure 6-5 shows an FTP site exposed within the IIS management tool (available under Administrative Tools ➤ Control Panel).

■**Caution** Network administrators are often hesitant to install FTP without a sound business need. Be sure to have business buy-in before installing FTP. Also, leverage an existing FTP installation rather than request an FTP site dedicated to just your standby server scenario.

Figure 6-6 shows the dialog involved in setting permissions to the actual FTP site. Many administrators want to place additional NTFS security on the folder. The folder structure might be beneath an existing, company-wide FTP structure.

■**Note** SFTP is based on SSH for security, and FTPS is based on SSL certificates. The FTP server with IIS 6 doesn't support either protocol. If you're limited to IIS 6's FTP service, you need to use a third-party product to encrypt a data transfer directly over FTP. (You can encrypt or secure a data transfer indirectly, but that would add another chapter to this book.) Later versions of IIS should support FTPS, but not necessarily SFTP.

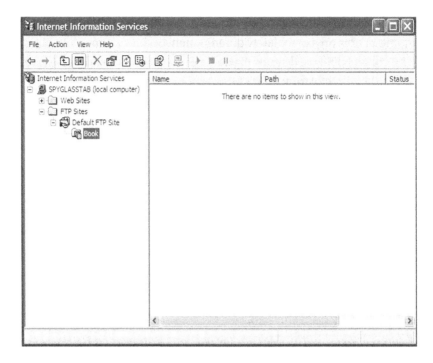

Figure 6-5. *As you can see, FTP is distinct from the actual Web server; you can run FTP and not run IIS.*

Figure 6-6. *An FTP Virtual Directory almost always points to a local directory.*

2. *Create a log backup job on the primary server:* Simply create a log backup scheme that writes to the shared location. If the shared location is hosted on the primary server, simply write to that directory. If it exists on another server (which would probably be the case for FTP, SFTP, or FTPS), create a second step to the SQL Agent job that copies the current log backup to the appropriate server. Do *not* back up directly to a network location.

3. *Create a restore job on the secondary server:* The job needs to copy the log backup from the shared location to the local server and restore the backup. Do not recover the database.

That's it. Once set up, each step follows in sequence again and again and again— you get the picture. The process continues as long as needed. You need to use some sort of naming scheme so that the secondary server knows which log backup to restore (but not recover). SQL Agent tokens, covered in the previous chapter, are a great way to automate this.

Note Some of my colleagues tend to question the sense in configuring log shipping manually if it's available as an automated technique. They have a valid point. However, I feel that going through the process of manually configuring a log-shipping scenario is critical to becoming a true DBA. Why? Indicated as a guiding principle earlier in the book, one of my personal mantras is to assume the worst. Don't expect an automated process to be your only technique. What if there's a bug in the software? Are you willing to wait until the next service pack? If you're able to create it, you'll understand how it works. If you understand how it works, you're more likely to be able to troubleshoot problems effectively with an automated process. Manually configuring log shipping is not that complicated.

I could go into the exact details of manual configuration, but SQL Server 2005 has a solid, automated process already in place. My reason for reviewing manual configuration is to give you a basic understanding of exactly what occurs during log shipping. As you can see, it's far from complicated.

Log Shipping in SQL Server 2000

If you have SQL Server Enterprise Edition, you can use SQL Server Maintenance Plans to automate the log-shipping configuration. I was never a big fan of that approach, since I'm not a big fan of Maintenance Plans under SQL Server 2000 (its functionality is just compiled into a single program, `sqlmaint.exe`).

If you have SQL Server Enterprise Edition and you want to have it configure log shipping automatically, you simply have to enable the check box for it on the first screen of Database Maintenance Plan Wizard, as shown in Figure 6-7.

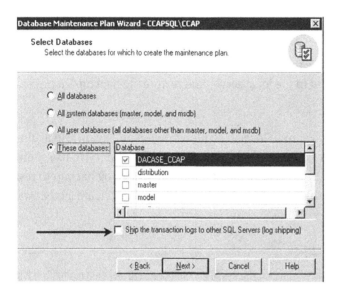

Figure 6-7. *The check box lets you enable the log-shipping configuration dialogs.*

From that point on, configuring log shipping in SQL Server 2000 is almost identical to configuring it in SQL Server 2005, so I'll focus on SQL Server 2005 in the rest of this chapter.

Log Shipping in SQL Server 2005

If you aren't keen on manually configuring log shipping and don't happen to have the Enterprise Edition of SQL Server 2000, SQL Server 2005 is the answer to your log-shipping dreams. (OK, maybe I'm the only one who has that dream. Have I mentioned that I'm a geek?)

The main change from SQL Server 2000 to SQL Server 2005 with respect to log shipping is that everything in SQL Server 2005 is carried out via stored procedures rather than called by some black-box .exe. That makes me very happy. In SQL Server 2005, you implement log shipping with actual stored procedures that you can look at and see exactly what they're doing. This goes for all of the activity on the primary server, the secondary servers, and, if you're using one, the monitoring server.

Enabling log shipping begins at the primary server. You can either go to Management Studio to view the properties of the database you want to "ship," or you can right-click on the database in question and then go to Tasks ➤ Ship Transaction Logs, as shown in Figure 6-8.

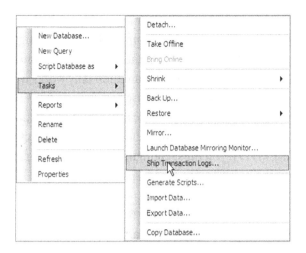

Figure 6-8. *You can access the log-shipping interface by right-clicking on the nonsystem database.*

Whether you go directly to the properties of the database or use the right-click menu, you're taken to the same screen, shown in Figure 6-9.

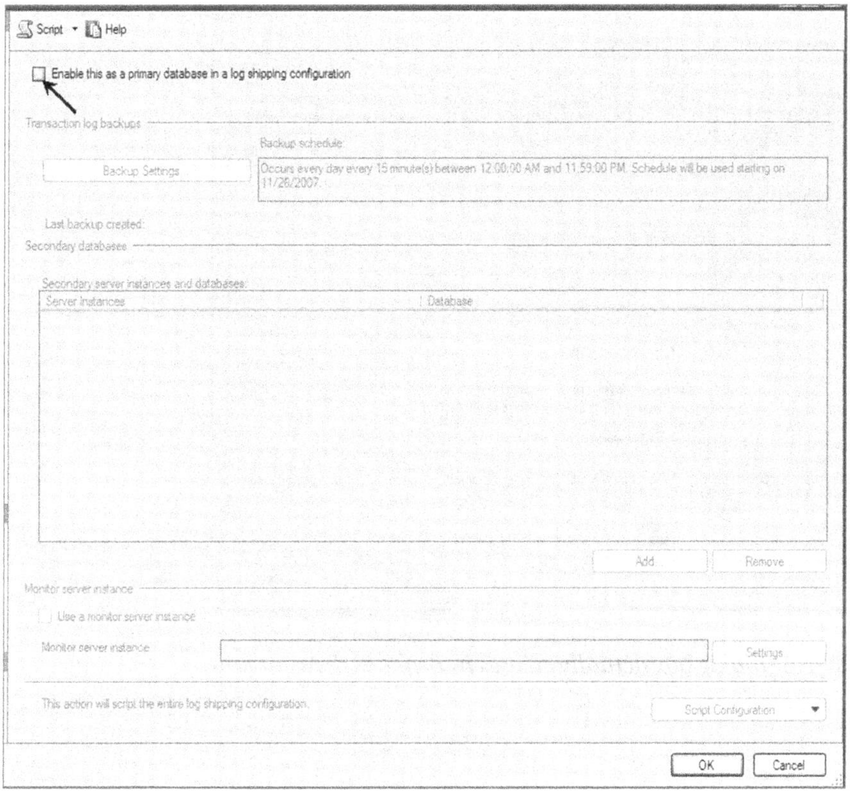

Figure 6-9. *Here you can see the log-shipping database in its disabled state. Note that you start the configuration process from what is to be the primary database.*

Of course, the Enable check box won't be checked when you start. Once you do check that box, the Backup Settings button will become available. From the Backup Settings screen, you can designate a central backup location that both the primary and standby servers can access. SQL Server 2005's built-in log-shipping automation only works with file shares, not with FTP or HTTP. That means that in order to use SQL Server 2005's built-in log shipping, the primary, secondary, and monitoring servers must be on the same Active Directory domain or be within trusted domains within the same Active Directory forest. If you need or want to use FTP or HTTP, you must configure the log shipping manually. Don't worry if some of this sounds a bit Greek to you: I'll spend more time on networking issues in Chapter 10.

The primary server uses the local location shown in Figure 6-10 as the location for transaction log backup files. This local location should be the same location used by the network share. Even though both ultimately point to the same location, the secondary servers use the network share location, while the primary server uses the local path.

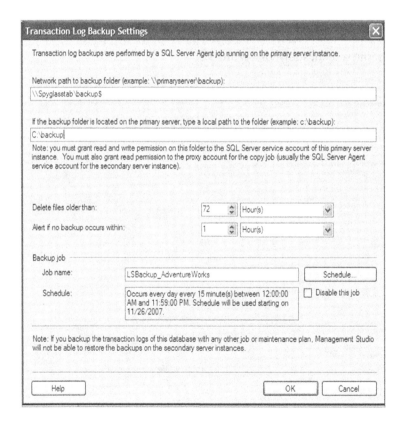

Figure 6-10. *This dialog box actually creates multiple SQL Agent jobs.*

■**Tip** Whenever you need to set up a network share, make it a hidden share by appending $ to the name. If a share is flagged as hidden, no one can browse the network to find it. To access it, you must type it in explicitly. The share and the directory underneath it should both be secure, so you don't need to do this from a security standpoint, but rather simply to keep people from accidentally opening the share and poking around. (Even administrators accidentally delete things.) However, make sure you don't use one of the hidden administrative shares, such as C$, D$, or E$, because they require administrator access. If you care at all about security, avoid these shares at all costs. If you have a solid network/server staff, they won't let you use those hidden administrative shares anyway.

On the Transaction Log Backup Settings screen, you also set a retention time (the default is 72 hours) and an alert time (the default is one hour). You'll probably want to change these, as your backup location will double as the primary backup location for your transaction logs. Would you only want to keep three days' worth of transaction logs for your primary database? I wouldn't. You also won't be able to have a separate log backup process running; if you do, you'll end up breaking the LSN chain for log shipping.

Note that the default transaction log backup time is every 15 minutes. That's a pretty safe default, but you may need more or require less due to resources. Remember, this number is going to dictate how much data you lose in the event of a failure.

When using the log-shipping configuration tool, you specify one or more secondary servers by launching the tool from the primary server and not from each of the secondary servers. You don't need to configure each individual secondary server when using the automated method of log shipping supplied by SQL Server (a nice improvement over earlier versions). After you've enabled the primary server and specified a backup job, file, and network share locations, simply hit Add on the main screen, as shown in Figure 6-11.

A number of steps are involved when you add a secondary server. First, you need to initialize the secondary server. This means you need to take a backup of the primary server and restore (but not recover) it on the secondary server in preparation for log shipping. As shown in Figure 6-12, you have three discrete options when it comes to getting a copy of the database over to the secondary server.

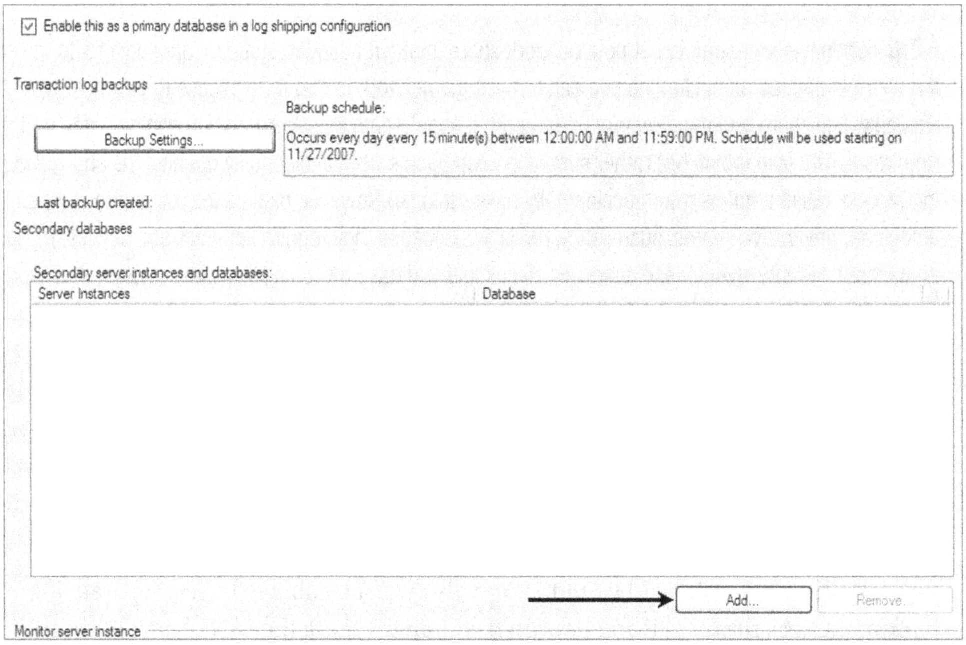

Figure 6-11. *You can add a new secondary server from the primary log-shipping server.*

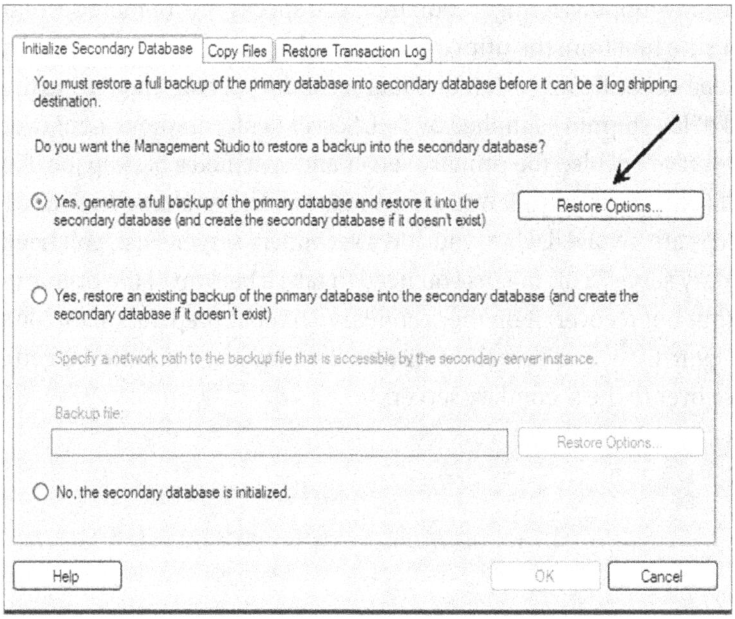

Figure 6-12. *Options when copying a database to a secondary server*

The first option is to generate a new full backup and restore it on the secondary server. If you choose this option, you must specify the location of the data files and the log files (as indicated by the arrow in Figure 6-12). You do this using the Restore Options dialog box shown in Figure 6-13. The result of specifying the data and log-file directories is the functional equivalent of restoring a database using the WITH MOVE clause.

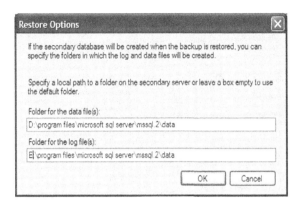

Figure 6-13. *Be sure you have enough disk space available for the secondary log-shipping database.*

The second option for restoring a backup is almost identical to the first option. It allows you to use an existing backup in the network location of your choice. One warning if you use this option: be sure you have an uninterrupted string of transaction log backups corresponding to the backup file you choose to use. Typically you would use this option for large databases in which the time required for creating a new backup file would creep into production usage hours.

The final option in Figure 6-12 assumes that you've already restored the backup with the NO RECOVERY clause on the secondary server. Typically, you'd use this option if the backup file has to traverse a long distance or is just too large to copy over the network in a reasonable amount of time. Usually backup tapes are transported to the secondary site, and the database is restored by hand.

The next step in automating log shipping is to copy the transaction log backups to the secondary servers. As you can see in Figure 6-14, you need to choose a destination folder that will be a local drive reference *on the secondary server*. You don't need to specify where the files are copied from: you already did that when you specified the backup options when you chose a network location for the backup files. The initial step of specifying that network location for the backup files is done precisely for the purpose of making it easy for each secondary server to locate a new transaction log backup to copy.

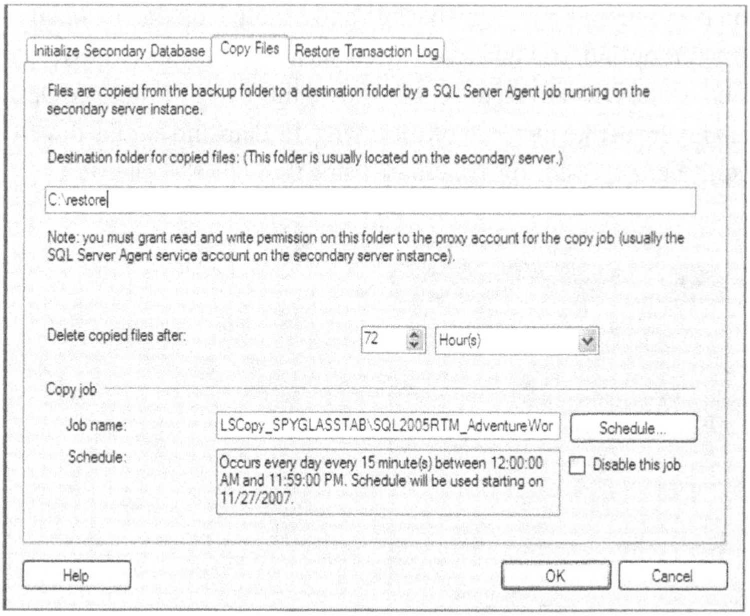

Figure 6-14. *The transaction log backups are copied to the secondary server from the primary server.*

Finally, you need to choose among the ongoing transaction restore options. The first option is to specify "No recovery mode" or "Standby mode." In most cases, you should choose "No recovery mode" because it renders the database on the secondary server unusable.

It's possible to have the secondary database available as read-only. To do this, choose the "Standby mode" option. It seems like you should always use this option, because in standby mode, the secondary server is available for reporting purposes and such. However, there is a significant drawback when using this mode.

As you can see in Figure 6-15, when you choose the "Standby mode" option, you can also choose to "Disconnect users in the database when restoring backups." This means users will be forcibly disconnected when a transaction log is being restored. If left unchecked, the transaction log restore will simply fail and wait for the next scheduled restore attempt before loading it. If you're frequently backing up transaction logs at the primary server (which you're probably doing to minimize the possible data latency between the primary and secondary servers) and you check the "Disconnect users" option, users of the secondary database will have a frustrating experience when running reports. Plan carefully before choosing the "Standby mode" option. It can be useful, but you should probably change the frequency of your restore operations to coincide with the downtime of the secondary database.

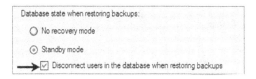

Figure 6-15. *When you check the "Disconnect users" option, users are forcibly kicked from the secondary database when a transaction log restore occurs. Standby isn't nice enough to wait for executives to finish running a report.*

The benefit of automated log shipping is that you can repeat it for additional servers. For instance, if you happen to have a server a few cities away and can afford to back up, copy, and restore transaction logs on a more frequent basis, you can add that distance server as another secondary node. If you have a direct but slow network connection to Guam, you can set the frequency of the backup and restore SQL Agent jobs to a much slower frequency so that the network can keep up properly with the backup and restore jobs.

After going through all of the setup for the primary and secondary servers, be sure to script out the log-shipping creation process, as shown in Figure 6-16. Once you finish configuring a log-shipping scenario, SQL Server attempts to generate that scenario in one go. If that generation fails, you'll have to correct the problem and restart manually. If you don't have a creation script to modify (perhaps a directory was named incorrectly or NTFS permissions weren't set), you must start over from scratch. Starting over isn't the end of the world if you're trying to configure only a single secondary server, but starting over can be a huge waste of time when configuring multiple secondary servers, each with different configurations. In any event, a script of the log-shipping topology creation is a good thing to have on hand.

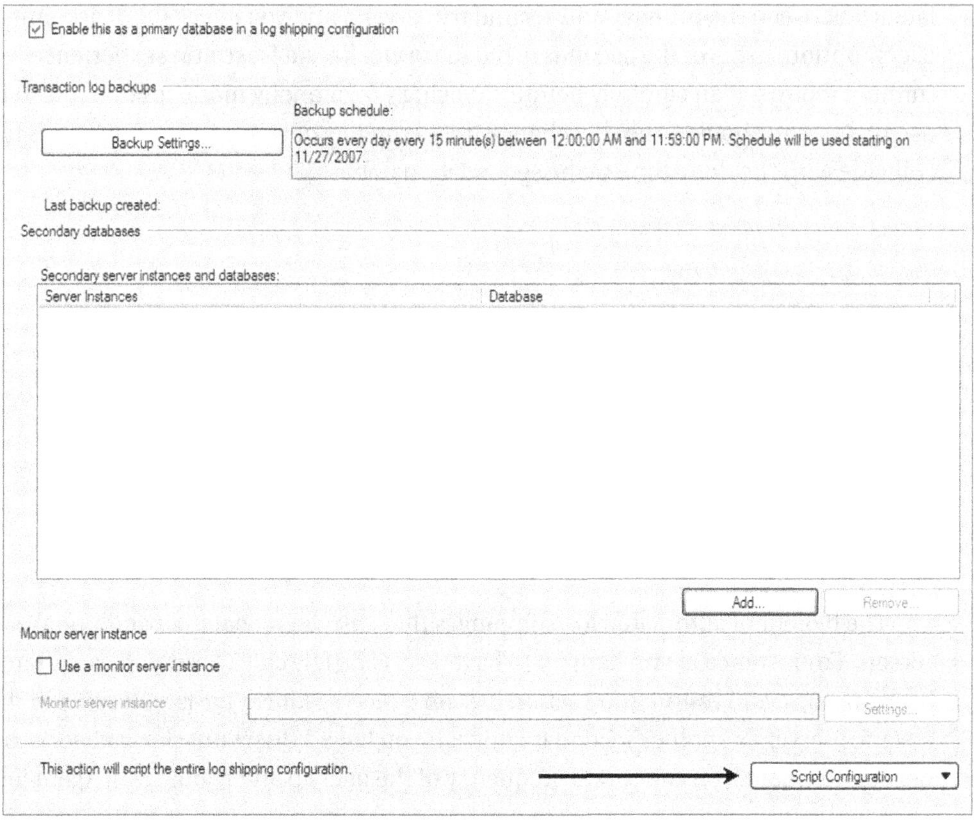

Figure 6-16. *The Script Configuration button scripts out the entire log-shipping configuration for both primary and all secondary servers.*

Dealing with Failover to a Secondary Server

Does log shipping sound too good to be true so far? Well, there's a catch—actually, two catches. The first is the process of failover, and the second is the process of failback. Let's discuss failover first. It isn't an automatic process, and there are multiple ways to perform it. That means documenting what technique you're going to use (ack!) and practicing that procedure thoroughly (double ack!).

Log shipping is a bit optimistic when it comes to failover. In other words, it assumes that failover will never occur. Fast failover is more of a high-availability goal than it is disaster recovery. The primary purpose of log shipping is the protection of data from local disaster. Don't rely on log shipping if your primary need is one of quick failover. Database mirroring, covered in Chapter 8, is much better suited for that purpose.

If you do use log shipping as a failover solution, you must incorporate a number of fixed steps into the entire log-shipping solution. You must be prepared for a failover, which requires manual intervention. You also need to be prepared for a variable step: client redirection. You can achieve failover and client redirection in a number of different ways, none of which are particularly graceful.

Step 1: Identify Database State

First, you must decide if the primary server or database is damaged to the point where failover is even necessary. You may want to avoid failover completely if the time required to fail over to a standby server is relatively close to the time required to repair the primary server, *and* the amount of acceptable data loss on the primary server is equal to or less than what would be lost by failing over to a standby server.

Note the *and* condition—both items must apply. If, for some reason, you could bring the primary server back online quickly but at the cost of losing a significant amount of data, you should begin the failover process.

If you decide failover is necessary, take the time to examine what happened to the primary server and what you might still be able to retrieve from it. Are you able to perform a tail-log backup? Can you still copy existing transaction log backups to the secondary server and restore them to the standby database? Rushing into a restore process could result in needless data loss.

Step 2: Restore Any Remaining Log Backups

It's possible that you still have log backups and perhaps even a tail-log backup that you can restore. Before applying these log backups, be clear on what the disaster is. If it's a process or user disaster, applying the transaction logs before failing over might just propagate the same disaster to the secondary server.

■**Tip** Do *not* recover the database after you restore all of the available logs. Keep that as a separate step. I've wasted countless time recovering a database before all backups had been restored. Get in the habit of taking a deep breath, looking around for any stray log backups laying around, restoring those backups into the proper location, and *then* recovering the database.

Step 3: Recover the Standby Database

Once you're confident that all transaction log backups that can be restored are restored to the standby server, it's time to recover the standby database. As you saw in Chapter 3, the command is simple:

```
RESTORE DATABASE AdventureWorks
WITH RECOVERY
```

You don't need to specify files to restore or any other options. Just specify the database name and the WITH RECOVERY clause. Once you do this, the standby database is online, available for read/write operations and ready to become the new principal database.

■**Note** Remember, if you fail to specify a `WITH` clause, the default is to get the `WITH RECOVERY` behavior. While restoring transaction logs, be sure to explicitly indicate `WITH NO RECOVERY`. Once the database goes through its recovery process, no additional transaction logs can be restored! If this hasn't sunk in by now, go back to Chapter 3 (do not pass Go; do not collect $200).

Step 4: Copy Dependent Items

Copying dependent items is a commonly missed or underestimated step in the failover process. A number of items could have been added to the primary server after the secondary server was established—for example, new database logins or external applications or services. However, those items won't have been propagated to the secondary server.

By far, the most common dependent item is a SQL Server login, whether it's via Windows authentication or SQL authentication. As users are added to the primary database, they will, of course, get restored on the secondary database. However, the logins associated with those database users will not be moved. This will most likely result in a dreaded orphaned user scenario in which the login and database users are out of sync. Rather than spend another three to four pages explaining the entire orphaned user scenario and how to work around it, I suggest simply firing up BOL and looking through the index or doing a search for "orphaned users."

■**Note** If you're using Windows authentication for your SQL Server instances and they reside on the same domain, the orphaned user scenario shouldn't affect you.

Step 5: Redirect Clients to the New Primary Server

BOL indicates that you simply need to redirect clients to the new primary instance. That's easier said than done, and there isn't an automated technique for doing so. Again, it really isn't intended to be a failover mechanism, but more of a data-protection technique. When it comes to redirecting clients, you have a number of techniques at your disposal. I'm only going to discuss the ones most commonly used.

Change DSNs on Client Machines

One technique for redirecting clients to the new primary server is to change the Data Source Names (DSNs) on all your client machines to point to what used to be the secondary server. However, if you have Windows-based applications that use a local DSN, this is *not* the technique to use. Changing local DSNs would require visiting every client machine and updating that machine's DSN entry to point to the secondary server—not an efficient approach.

You could always deploy a registry update to make the change via Active Directory, which would definitely increase the efficiency of the process. However, the users would have to log off and back in in order for the Group Policy Object (GPO) to process the registry update. Again, the approach isn't all that efficient. Plus, what happens to those handfuls of people who don't receive the directive to log out and back in? What if the registry update fails for some unknown reason? Those users get left out, and the result will most likely be an angry help desk and a significant amount of support work—again, not very efficient.

If your client machine is a middle tier through which all real clients get routed, then changing the client DSN can be a feasible technique. For a single server acting as the middle tier (whether it's an application server or a Web server), changing that server's DSN will work nicely with little interruption to the end client. Even if you have a farm of servers acting as one, it's still easier to update a farm than every single client. However, you must be diligent in your process and in your documentation; updating a server farm and missing a single server can create the same support nightmare that a misbehaving registry update can cause.

THE CONFUSION OF CONFIGURING A DSN

One of my biggest pet peeves with all products is terminology, or more precisely, outdated or misleading terminology. For example, look at the number of features that use the term *snapshot* in SQL Server 2005: snapshot isolation, database snapshots, snapshot replication, Snapshot Agent. These kinds of less-than-distinct naming conventions lead to more confusion with clients than I care to deal with.

My biggest terminology annoyance is the name of the icon within the administrative tools for configuring DSNs: *Data Sources (ODBC)*. It still appears that way with Windows XP and Windows Server 2003. I often have to dispel the assumption that whenever you add something, you're using ODBC. Not true. You're creating a DSN for some sort of database connection. It could be ODBC. It could be ODBC for OLE DB. It could be the Oracle OLE DB driver for Oracle. It could be SQL Server Native Client (lovingly termed SNAC). Whatever database networking clients are installed on that machine will show up when creating a DSN. Rarely will they actual go through an ODBC layer.

Rename the Server and Change the IP Address

If you have no middle-tier application layer, the simplest method for manual failover is to rename the standby server, change its IP address to what you've been using for the principal server, and reboot. (Be sure not to reboot the principal server without changing its IP address to something else.) As I said, it's a simple procedure, but it's not always the best.

OCKHAM'S RUSTY RAZOR

Long ago, William of Ockham, a philosopher/scientist (at the time, they were synonymous), came up with what is now a well-defended principle in both modern philosophy and science. It basically says, "The simplest explanation tends to be the correct one." I always argued against that mantra—usually unsuccessfully. (Yes, I was a philosophy geek in college. I even started in the PhD program, further cementing my name in the annals of geekdom.) However, I am fully convinced that in the IS/IT world, Ockham's razor is a dangerous idea.

The simplest explanation can only be correct if you have accounted for all factors in the equation. In a disaster scenario (heck, in any technical scenario), how often is that the case? DBAs often choose the simple solution because they can execute it quickly. The problem is that they don't take some time to consider all the factors or possible issues involved. If Ockham were alive, I'd send him an e-mail that just says, "THHHHHHHPT."

When using the rename/IP-change technique, you better be sure to change the internal name of the SQL Server itself. SQL Server 2000 and 2005 will continue to run almost everything without changing that internal server name. However, certain functions, such as replication, will display odd behavior. (I won't elaborate on the exact behaviors I've encountered, because this is supposed to be a book, not a four-volume epic tale.)

Changing the name is simple, and I suggest always adding the process to any disaster recovery documentation:

```
Sp_dropserver <<oldservername>>
Sp_addserver <<newservername>>, 'local'
```

Note Be sure to reverse all of this once the primary server is restored; otherwise, you'll have a name-resolution conflict on the network between the restored primary server and the secondary server that is now acting as the primary.

It's important to get the 'local' clause in when you add the new server name. The reason you have to drop the old server name is because it has been flagged as local. To verify the name change, simply check the results of SELECT @@SERVERNAME; it should show the new name.

If this method of renaming a server to make it the new primary server seems a bit out of date, that's because it is. SQL Server 2005 should be able to handle this itself, shouldn't it? The need for that internal server really should be obsolete, given all of the new features available. The problem is that there are still a lot of backward compatibility issues for Microsoft to consider when putting out new releases of the product. I could attempt to analyze every possible dependency on the internal @@SERVERNAME property, but I only have one lifetime. It's much safer to just assume the worst. Hey, I've said that before, haven't I?

Another potential problem with the server-name/IP-change technique is one of IP routing. I won't even pretend to be an expert on network internals, but I am beyond the neophyte role. Your firewalls may be open to the proper IP address, but it may take some time before that IP address is associated with the new machine. Routers and switches cache IP-to-MAC address tables. Depending on the size of your internal network, or if you're going over the Internet, there may be an unexpected and indefinable delay.

Redirect DNS

The most complicated technique for redirecting clients to the new primary server is to actually change the DNS name for the principal server so that it resolves to the IP address of the standby server. Again, as with the name/IP-address change, unexpected and indefinable delays can occur as the IP address gets propagated to all DNS servers. If the clients and server are on a small internal network with its own DNS server, there will be no discernable delay. If the network involved is a large wide area network (or, in the worst case, the Internet), it could take some time for all of the DNS servers to be updated.

Note I'm deliberately being a bit vague about the steps required for changing the DNS name for a number of reasons. First, different DNS servers are out there, and the process can vary from server to server. Second, unless you know exactly what you're doing, you could be doing more harm than good. Leave the process of changing DNS name resolution to your network staff. If you have no network staff, have an external consulting firm come in to your company and validate the technique you're going to use. Trust me: it's worth the small monetary investment to have someone else look over your work.

Dealing with Failback to the Primary Server

Now I've come to failback, the second major problem with log shipping. Resetting the log-shipping scenario back to its original configuration amounts to essentially re-creating the entire topology from scratch (you've been documenting, haven't you?). If the secondary server is in a position, both from a hardware and location perspective, to act as the primary server, great; you can simply switch roles. The secondary will become the primary, and the primary will become the secondary. Chances are you'll have an uninterrupted LSN chain already in place, so you won't need to have a large database restore.

However, my experience tells me that believing the secondary server can become the primary server is a fantasy. In most cases, secondary servers are either performing another function in the first place or have minimal resources to support the database and application using it for a long period of time. Why? Since log shipping is primarily focused on mitigating environmental disasters, the likelihood of it ever being invoked is small. What's the likelihood that a tornado will wipe out your data center, or that flooding will engulf the data center? The probability is pretty low, and if it isn't, you should reconsider where you keep your data center.

Usually, cost and politics require that you use only existing SQL Servers, which are primary for some other database, as secondary servers in log-shipping scenarios. Rarely will management pony up the money to buy servers dedicated for use only when failover occurs. This means you must use the painful method of failback when the primary server has been restored, which is simply to start over from scratch.

Monitoring Your Log-Shipping Environment

One of the more problematic tasks with any automated process is establishing an effective monitoring technique. SQL Server 2005's automated log-shipping system includes the option of having a dedicated monitoring server. SQL Server doesn't supply an actual interactive monitoring tool. The monitoring server, which you can specify by selecting a specific instance on the main log-shipping configuration dialog, simply runs periodic jobs to collect history information and sends out alerts, as you can see in Figure 6-17.

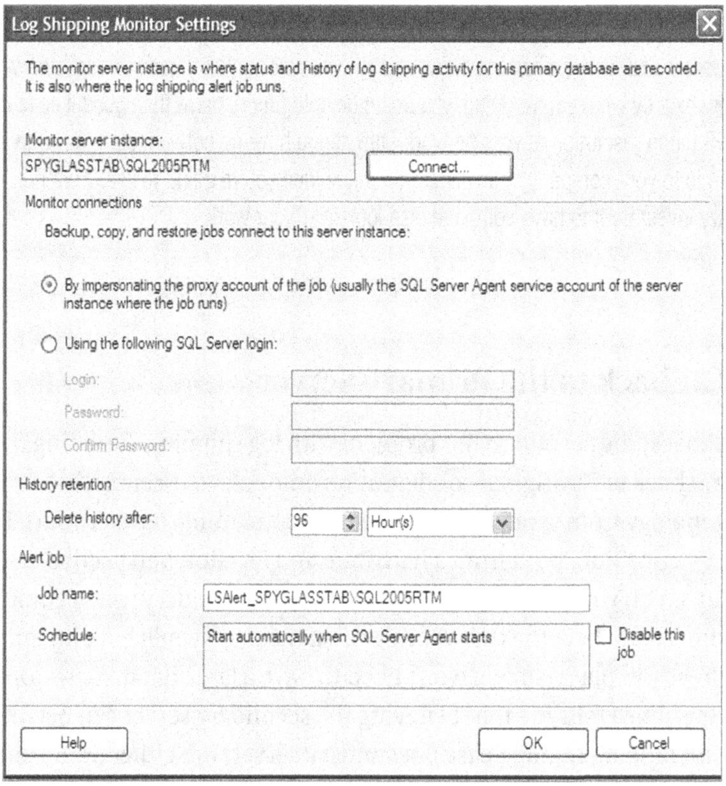

Figure 6-17. *Creating a log-shipping monitoring instance*

Notice that the job schedule is set to start automatically when SQL Agent starts. This might seem odd until you see the stored procedure that is executed (`msdb.dbo.sp_add_log_shipping_monitoring_jobs`). This stored procedure simply adds the required jobs to gather backup history information from the primary and secondary databases. Later, that data shows up on the Transaction Log Shipping Status report. You can run this report by right-clicking on the SQL Server instance, selecting Reports, and then selecting the Transaction Log Shipping Status report.

What are you really monitoring? The success and failure of backup and restore SQL Agent jobs. Are there other ways to monitor this? Of course. You could easily set the primary and secondary servers to forward their alerts and copy their `msdb.dbo.backuphistory` table information to a server. Essentially, that's what the automated method is doing.

At times, you may need to use a manual method for log shipping—for example, when communicating via FTP to a server not on your domain. Just because you use a manual method doesn't mean that you cannot monitor the progress of the log-shipping process. You can easily set up some alerts and copy the history tables by hand.

Log Shipping and Disaster Categories

How does log shipping help in terms of the five disaster categories? Well, it certainly should help by getting a copy of your data off to remote location and minimizing the impact of environmental disasters. However, it presents a problem for systems that require high availability due to the length of time required for failover and failback.

Here's how log shipping affects each disaster scenario:

- *Environmental*: Log shipping is one of the few mitigation techniques that focuses on protecting data against environmental disasters. The first goal of log shipping is to get that data onto another server. Granted, the failover process isn't instantaneous, and data loss is essentially guaranteed. It has its drawbacks, but log shipping is an excellent solution to mitigating environmental disasters.

- *Hardware*: The same holds true for hardware errors. Again, you'll lose some data, but at least you'll know exactly how much data is lost.

- *Media*: This is the dangerous category, not because of data loss or downtime, but because of the failover process itself. A media disaster may turn out to have a straightforward and relatively quick resolution. Jumping to invoke a secondary server during a media disaster could be a mistake, resulting in more time and data loss than simply waiting to repair the primary server.

- *Process*: There is a real danger in relying on log shipping to mitigate process errors. It can be effective, if and only if the error is detected before the shipped log backup has been restored. In a configuration where the log-shipping interval is quite frequent, it is unlikely this will be the case.

- *User*: As with process errors, log shipping is only effective if the user error is identified before the shipped log backup has been restored. The likelihood of this being the case is almost completely dependent on the process involved in the notification of a user error.

Caveats and Recommendations

If I had to make a single recommendation, it would be to ensure that you have a failover/failback plan in place and to practice that plan on a regular basis. If you're lucky, you'll never need to fail over, but as the Boy Scouts say, "Be prepared."

Keep these tips in mind when using log shipping:

- *Avoid using any replication method as a disaster-mitigation technique*: Yes, this is me on a soapbox, but I really believe this. (I'll gladly argue it over a cup of coffee.) While log shipping resembles replication as far as architecture, it has a level of overhead and complexity that worries me. I question its effectiveness as a mitigation technique.

- *Don't forget to monitor*: Automated does not mean automatic. Log shipping is so straightforward to set up, it can be easy to overlook some sort of monitoring technique, whether it's the built-in jobs provided in SQL Server 2005 or alerts. If you're using a manual log-shipping configuration, remember that it isn't much more work to set up a few alerts or have jobs to copy tables.

- *Don't create separate log backups*: Plan on the location of the log-shipping backups to be the primary location of your actual log backups (or treat it as an exact mirror). If you create a log backup and neglect to copy it to the log-shipping backup location, you'll invalidate your topology. Unfortunately, achieving the goal of using one location for both primary and log backups requires tight control from a process perspective over the SQL Server. Often, too many people have their hand in the SQL cookie jar.

- *Be prepared for failover and failback*: Walk through your failover and failback processes, document them, test them, rinse, and repeat. Did I mention document? A failover event is rare, so it's critical that you remain diligent when it comes to preparation. Again, I've experienced firsthand the results of complacency. I cannot stress preparation enough.

- *Don't forget that you can use those secondary databases for reporting purposes*: While not strictly a disaster recovery tie-in, reporting is another selling point for log shipping. You can create copies in remote offices that you can use for reporting purposes.

Summary

Log shipping is a simple, low-cost means of achieving off-site database redundancy. Recovery is a manual process, but with thorough documentation and practice, you can configure recovery and redirect operations surprisingly quickly.

Sadly (for me), log shipping isn't used nearly enough. I've dealt with tornadoes and flooding, and a simple log-shipping configuration could have been the difference between staying in business and filing for bankruptcy. I really do recommend considering log shipping in your overall strategy.

Of course, there are drawbacks. Failover and failback can both be a real pain if they aren't practiced, documented processes. Data loss is almost a certainty, but unlike in other scenarios, the amount of data loss is fully identifiable. One mitigation technique that focuses on losing as little data as possible is database clustering, which is next on the list.

CHAPTER 7

■■■

Clustering

Clustering is the use of two or more servers connected to a single copy of data. If one node fails, another takes its place. On the surface, it's that simple.

Whereas log shipping focuses on moving a copy of the data to a remote location, clustering seeks to ensure that the entire database instance will be available in the event of a hardware failure. It requires no complex steps in the event of a failure and no need to redirect clients manually to the standby server.

Instead of focusing on installation and configuration, I'll point out spots where errors or missteps often occur. I won't provide step-by-step setup instructions or show a number of screenshots that walk you through the process; that just isn't what this book is about. Plenty of excellent books and articles out there deal with high availability and clustering. I have no intention of reinventing the wheel; instead, I prefer to point out how to repair a flat.

What interests me about clustering is how it fits into the overall disaster recovery picture. While clustering certainly isn't in the foreground of that picture, it's still in the frame. Clustering provides strong protection, specifically against hardware disasters involving the physical server itself.

Clustering Basics

The first thing you need to understand about clustering is that it isn't a SQL Server–specific technology. The operating system carries out the actual clustering configuration, internal workings, and workload. Clustering was a bit awkward in Windows NT 4.0, improved tremendously in Windows 2000, and has become even more stable and robust in Windows Server 2003. At the time of this writing, the next version of Windows Server is still in design phases, but I expect steady improvements toward usability and stability.

Another key aspect to clustering is that it is extremely tightly bound to the hardware on which it resides. You can't simply pick any two servers and set up clustering (well, you could try, but it certainly wouldn't be fun or advance your career). Many vendors go so far as to sell hardware packages designed precisely for clustering.

A number of services can be clustered. Microsoft Exchange Server supports clustering; you can also use clustering to support a file server. However, it's important to understand that all clustering operations sit on top of Microsoft Cluster Server (MSCS). With earlier versions of MSCS, the installation and the actual clustering functions didn't work so well. With each progressive version, things have become simpler and more robust, both with clustering itself and with SQL Server's use of clustering.

Clustering Architecture

Any cluster architecture has three base requirements: two identical servers and some sort of shared storage between them. The shared storage is usually either an external SCSI cabinet or a SAN. Both servers have a network card for outside access (that is, for users accessing the cluster), and in the best-case scenario, a second network card dedicated to internal communications between the two servers, as shown in Figure 7-1.

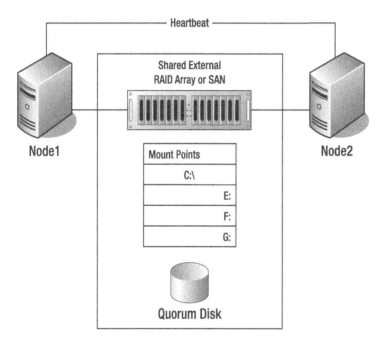

Figure 7-1. *A minimal clustering configuration*

The main goal of a clustered architecture is for one server to take over all operations if the other server should fail. Two basic mechanisms help to accomplish this goal: the quorum database (explained shortly) and the ongoing network heartbeat between the nodes. Windows Server 2003 and SQL Server 2005 also provide a more granular means of failover: *mount points*.

"SHARED" STORAGE

A number of devices can qualify as "shared" storage, including a network share, network-attached storage (NAS), a SAN, or an external SCSI disk array. I've even encountered shared storage as a virtual drive shared by two virtual servers on the same physical server (more on hardware virtualization in Chapter 10).

For the purposes of Windows clustering, the only valid forms of shared storage are either a SAN or an external SCSI cabinet. You can get clustering to work in other configurations, but given how sensitive clustering is when it comes to hardware, using any other technique would bring a world of pain.

Keep in mind that Windows clustering also uses nonshared storage; each server must have its own local hard drive. It can be easy to accidentally place data that should be shared onto a local drive instead.

Cluster Resources

Since clustering centers on multiple server nodes controlling specific disk resources, you must usually configure numerous cluster resources. Ultimately, all cluster resources, no matter how minor, have a dependency on a specific disk resource and a specific IP address, but a failover doesn't imply a problem with disk storage.

All too often, clustering is used only to mitigate hardware disasters, but cluster resources can be used in a number of creative ways to protect against process and user disasters as well. In addition to the server itself, you can configure the following resource types for failover in a cluster:

- Drive partitions

- IP addresses

- Network names

- Network shares

- Print spoolers

- IIS

- SMTP

- FTP

- Custom applications and services

As you can see, clustering can do much more than protect SQL Server from hardware failure. Your applications may have dependencies on services other than SQL Server. Clever uses of clustering, such as having a custom application run a batch file of some sort that the clustering service interprets as a failure, can be a creative way to easily gain programmatic control over failover. Some failovers are catastrophic, while others may simply be the result of a deliberate test or a patch installation. Configuring a custom application can be most useful when dealing with the latter group of failovers.

For example, say you have an older, unsupported server-based application that you'd like to run on your server environment (presumably to take advantage of newer, faster hardware). The only problem is that in the event of a failover, it won't attempt to shut itself down. This could result in data damage or lost data. With a simple batch file, you could detect when a clustered service stops and request the legacy application to shut down in whatever language it may understand.

Quorum

Derived from Latin, the word *quorum* goes back to the days of the Romans and refers to a meeting in which various issues were discussed. Usually each topic included a vote to establish a plan of action. A 100% majority was not required for a vote to pass but, rather, a majority of those participating in the quorum. Often, a quorum would either accidentally or deliberately exclude key individuals when a vote was expected—hmm, sounds like politics today.

With Windows clustering, a quorum refers to an area of disk storage where all nodes participating in the cluster can come to meet to decide on who controls what resources (in a very nonpolitical manner, contrary to our ancient Roman friends). In technical terms, a quorum is an area of storage on a shared disk, accessible by all servers involved in this particular instance of clustering. The quorum is usually referred to as the *quorum database. Do not take this to mean that the quorum is a SQL Server database!* It is a proprietary storage structure used by Windows to house quorum data—for example, node x owns resource 1, node y owns resource 2, and so on. Without a quorum database, there can be no clustering.

With a two-node configuration, the function of the quorum is quite simple. Only one node can own a specific disk resource, so each node must be in agreement about which resources each is controlling. This information is retained in memory when both nodes are running, but it is also written to the quorum. Why? Let's say a node physically fails. As soon as the operational node sees that the failed node isn't participating in the quorum, it checks the quorum to determine if another node has control over disk resources that it would normally control. Depending on the configuration, the operational node could regain control of those resources automatically, or could regain control only in the event of administrative intervention.

The quorum also holds configuration information pertaining to the cluster itself, such as resources, failover and failback settings, and so on. The quorum is the critical element to a cluster configuration. The quorum should always be on an isolated disk partition. That way, if some sort of damage occurs to the quorum, it won't affect your SQL Server data, Exchange data, or file-system data—in other words, the data for the clustered service. Getting the cluster back up and running can be a completely different story. I'll discuss some of the utilities to reduce the impact of a lost quorum a little later in the chapter.

Heartbeat

A constant *heartbeat*, or communication, occurs between all nodes of the cluster. This communication is separate from any communication with the quorum. The role of the heartbeat is simply to help each node determine whether the other node(s) are functional. If the heartbeat is lost for a particular node, the clustering software will interrogate the quorum to determine which surviving node should take ownership of resources from the lost node.

Therein lies the rub with the heartbeat mechanism: any network disruption with the heartbeat communication can initiate some sort of failover. Three to five years ago, this was a real concern. Today, networks (and those that manage them) have come a long way. It's less likely that network failure will be a problem unless there is a hardware issue with the network card. Still, it can occur, particularly in a poorly configured environment. Network cards and routers run at different speeds (such as 10Mbps, 100Mbps, and 1000Mbps) and in different modes (half duplex and full duplex). If the network cards and any other network devices aren't configured to dynamically establish the proper speed and mode for optimal communication, heartbeat interruptions can occur. This can happen with cheap equipment or with quality equipment that has a slight defect.

A heartbeat interruption can be extremely difficult to diagnose, often causing DBAs to hard-code speed and duplex mode settings or temporarily remove a node from a cluster. If your servers are failing over randomly, a heartbeat interruption could be the cause.

Mount Points

New to SQL Server 2005 clustering are mount points. Actually, mount points existed in Windows Server 2000 but were not supported for clustering. Windows Server 2003 and SQL Server 2005 mount points are finally supported for SQL Server features.

Mount points are far more common in Unix-based systems; in Windows, a mount point refers to the area of a disk drive that is bound to a drive letter. (Yes, I know this definition isn't exactly right, but it's close enough for discussion purposes.)

Each drive letter has to have a base drive letter and directory location, but this base location can be bound to any point on the disk. Imagine you have a C: partition on a RAID 10 array. You could create additional partitions that are simply locations on C:, as shown in Table 7-1.

Table 7-1. *Drive Letters Bound to Various Mount Points on a Single Disk*

Drive Letter	Points To
E:	`C:\Exchange`
F:	`C:\SQL2005`
G:	`C:\UserData`

Each drive acts as if it were a completely separate drive partition as far as both the user and the clustering service are concerned.

Previously, a disk failover had to be performed at the RAID array level. For example, say you had a number of items set up as clustered resources, including network shares. If a SQL Server instance failed, it would have failed over the disk array that it used. If you had any other resources on that disk, they would have failed over too. An instance could fail for any number of reasons that didn't involve the disk subsystem. Since the array sizes would be so large, management would usually want to leverage that space for additional functions other than SQL, such as file shares. I worked with one client who used the same data array to house both data for a SQL Server instance and the home directories for each user's Windows login. The SQL Server instance failed, and so did every home directory, causing a momentary but highly visible disruption in end-user operation. Needless to say, the CEO wasn't happy that none of the drives mapped when the users logged in. To make matters worse, the failure occurred at 7:55 a.m., just as everyone was starting their day.

By using mount points, only the individual drive letters fail over, not the entire array. The client I just mentioned wouldn't have a reason to mix the SQL data with the home directories, and therefore, wouldn't have had to deal with an angry CEO. Mount points provide granularity for controlling clustered disk resources previously unavailable to the SQL Server DBA.

CLUSTER-ABLE VS. CLUSTER-AWARE

Simply clustering two or more servers together doesn't guarantee that when one node fails, everything will resume on a second node. Some applications and services are designed to detect a failover event generated by the cluster service, while others are not. Applications or services that have no direct interface with information presented by the cluster service must use alternate means of responding to a failure.

To detect cluster events such as a failover, applications and services must be *cluster-aware*. They don't necessarily appear as cluster resources that you can configure for failover, but they have the ability to listen to the cluster service and react accordingly, if programmed properly. They respond to shutdown requests from the cluster service first and foremost, because a failure event could be caused by something that allowed the cluster service to shut down programs cleanly before taking itself offline.

If a program or service can be configured as a cluster resource, it is considered *cluster-able*. A cluster-aware program simply listens to the cluster service; a cluster-able program *interacts* with the cluster service. You can configure cluster-able services as cluster resources, which have individual settings that indicate how they react during cluster events. For example, you can set how often a resource polls the active node to see if its counterpart is running, or whether the resource should attempt to fail back automatically if its home node comes online again.

While there is a generic resource type for use with custom applications, you can code a program or service to be either cluster-aware (just able to listen to cluster events and react) or cluster-able (able to interact directly with the cluster itself). If you're developing an application to run in a cluster environment, keep this in mind. (Explaining how to code the service is well beyond the scope of this book.) If a third-party vendor says that his application works with a cluster, clarify whether he means cluster-aware or cluster-able. If the vendor doesn't understand the request for clarification or doesn't know the answer, it might be wise to consider a different product.

SQL Server Clustering

Failover clustering is a feature provided by the operating system. SQL Server itself does nothing in regard to clustering other than ease the installation process. SQL Server is a cluster-able process that you can configure as a cluster resource—no different than a file share or an IP address.

SQL Server 2005 has dramatically improved its support of Windows clustering. The best news of all: the Standard Edition supports two-node clustering, a significant licensing savings for many environments. While SQL Server 2000 Enterprise Edition was limited to the number of nodes it could support, SQL Server 2005 supports all of the nodes supported by the operating system. If the operating system has an eight-node cluster, you can install SQL Server 2005 on each node. If, in some future service pack, more than an eight-node cluster is supported, SQL Server 2005 would theoretically be able to use more than eight nodes.

Keep in mind that when I say, "SQL Server supports clustering," it's a bit of a loaded statement. What do I mean by "SQL Server," exactly? A lot of services could be installed—which ones am I talking about? Table 7-2 lists which services are cluster-able and which are cluster-aware.

Table 7-2. *Cluster-able and Cluster-aware Services in SQL Server*

Service	Cluster-able	Cluster-aware
Database engine	Yes	Yes
Analysis Services	Yes (new)	Yes (new)
SQL Agent	Yes	Yes
Full-text search	Yes (new)	Yes (new)
SQL Mail	No	No
Database Mail	No	Yes
Reporting Services	No	Yes*
SSIS	No	Yes*
Notification Services	No	Yes
SQL Server Browser	No	Yes

Relies on exterior resources, which may not respond well in a failover situation

Another extremely nice improvement is that you may now install Analysis Services as a clustered instance. This is a critical step given that business intelligence receives such a high level of marketing with the release of SQL Server 2005. The idea is that business intelligence (not the technology, per se) should be a business-critical activity; I agree.

Custom Utilities/Applications

Plenty of applications that are not cluster-aware will continue to run in the event of a failover. Remember, a failover event doesn't necessarily mean that a node is physically failing. It could mean that someone shut down a service without using the cluster service to do so. A custom, cluster-*unaware* application could continue to run on the failed node and start automatically on another node. This could be potentially catastrophic.

I worked with a client who had a custom Java application that sent data to a business partner via an early form of a Web service. It ran on a SQL Server that had centralized data. When we upgraded that SQL Server to run in a clustered configuration, we had to manually set up the Java application on each node (it was cluster-*unaware)*. The application was initiated by a scheduled SQL Agent job. Everything worked fine until someone (OK, it was me) shut down the SQL Agent on the active node without using the cluster service. This cascaded into a complete failover, which started SQL Agent on another node, which in turn started the Java application on another node. We now had two instances of that Java application sending duplicate records. IT staff on the business partner's end worked with the data sent as best it could, but our data, which incidentally got replicated all over the place after it was transmitted and consequently received back, was an *unknown* amount of garbage. And *that* resulted in a manual cleanup that impacted us for weeks. Needless to say, the configuration has been corrected since then, but this is an example of how clustering is not the high-availability answer to everything.

For applications that are cluster-unaware, you must create manual compensation steps to include the cluster-unaware applications in the entire clustering solution. In the previous example, our solution was to have a simple batch job that fired whenever a new instance of the Java application started. The role of this batch job was to see if an instance of the Java application was running on the other server participating in the cluster. The batch job was included in SQL Agent and set to fire whenever SQL Agent started. If SQL Server failed over (and not the entire node), SQL Agent needed to fail over as well (it relied on the MSDB database). Thus, SQL Agent would start on the secondary node, firing the batch job. Sounds like a lot of work for a simple issue, doesn't it? It was. That's why including cluster-unaware applications in a clustered environment is frowned upon (personally, I consider the practice scowled upon).

Sample Clustering Configurations

Even though clustering provides some level of hardware redundancy, there are a variety of possible configurations. Different configurations do have some impact on the level of protection, but you're still just dealing with hardware protection.

Active/Passive

When restricted to having just two nodes, the active/passive configuration is my preferred configuration. Everything runs on the first node, while the second node does nothing but sit idly by waiting for a failover, as shown in Figure 7-2. You're assured that the passive node has all of the available resources to resume operation; you don't need to worry about juggling memory or CPU utilization.

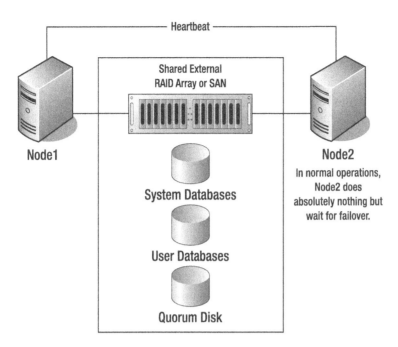

Figure 7-2. *An active/passive cluster configuration*

The drawback to this situation is that the second node is essentially wasted hardware. If everything runs smoothly, the only time that second node will ever be used is when you install a service pack or need to reboot the active node due to some sort of maintenance.

You also risk that the passive node will sit unused. Often hardware issues only crop up when the server is under constant use. A good example is the RAID/SAN controller. You'll only see problems with an I/O controller when it's under heavy use. If you never run SQL Server for any period of time on the passive node, you won't be able to tell if the hardware is defective. To deal with this risk, you can reverse the roles of the active and passive nodes for a few weeks at a time during testing and sometimes for a brief time while in production. In doing that, you're likely to discover a defect in hardware.

Note If the hardware does have some minor manufacturing defect, it usually fails within the first 30 days. It's best to have the hardware running continually for at least two weeks before moving to production. *Never* purchase hardware and put it immediately into production unless it's to replace an existing piece of equipment that failed.

Active/Active

The active/active configuration is by far the most common implementation of Windows clustering that I've encountered. Even though there is no double licensing cost for SQL Server in an active/passive environment, management is rarely comfortable with the thought of a hardware investment that "does nothing" (apparently providing redundancy has no value). Thus, both servers are used, each hosting its own SQL Server instance.

Running in active/active mode adds complexity to the configuration of each individual node, as well as to the individual hardware requirements, as you can see in Figure 7-3. Each node must have sufficient hardware to run both instances of SQL Server. You also must configure that hardware (by setting the maximum memory, CPU affinity, and so on) so that in the event of a failover, the second SQL Server instance won't collide with the first. Most clients I've worked with will accept a certain level of performance degradation, but keep in mind that a hardware failure might last for a period of days or weeks while the replacement equipment is being acquired and configured. Will your users be willing to accept poor performance for a long period of time?

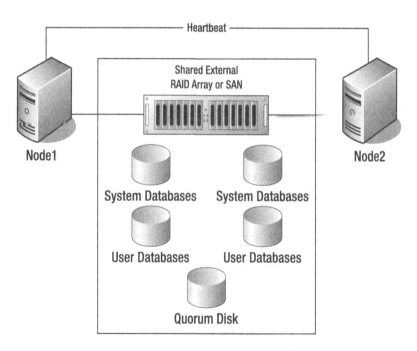

Figure 7-3. *An active/active cluster configuration*

THE N+1 PRINCIPLE

The primary goal of clustering is to reduce the risk and impact of any single node failing. An active/active configuration is an effective means of maximizing hardware investments, but it doesn't necessarily significantly reduce the impact of a failed node. While it does reduce the risk imposed by having a system completely unavailable, there is the possibility for significant performance degradation, which in turn can be as disruptive as complete unavailability.

The standard recommendation in any high-availability/scalability scenario is to work from a simple N+1 formula, where N represents the number of servers required for satisfactory performance, and 1 represents an unused, standby node. If you follow this recommended formula, losing a single server should have no direct impact on performance. Should scalability become an issue, you can configure the standby server to offload some of the work from the other nodes. In that case, you would need to purchase an additional server to sit idle to maintain the N+1 formula.

This approach is usually applied to load balancing, but I believe it should be applied to SQL Server clustering as well. If you have only a two-node configuration, it can be hard to justify the cost of letting that hardware sit. As you increase the number of nodes, the potential protection provided by a node that sits fallow can be significant. Having a spare node can still be a hard sell to management, but I'll discuss some techniques to rationalize the extra hardware in Chapter 12.

Active/Active/Active/ ...

SQL Server 2005 Enterprise Edition supports the same number of nodes as the Windows Server version being used, which means you could have an eight-node active/active/active/active/active/active/active/active configuration. I've configured four-node clusters, as shown in Figure 7-4, for production use, and I've configured an eight-node cluster in a test environment. Having four active nodes is complicated enough; a cluster of eight active nodes in a production environment is enough to make your head explode (well, mine at least).

Keep in mind that you must configure each active node so that in the event of a failure, all nodes can run on a single server without clobbering each other. In an eight-node active environment, that means a lot of configuration and a lot of testing. I'm interested to see one of these in production (as of this writing, I haven't).

If you have more than three physical nodes, I strongly advocate using the N+1 principle. One server should always be sitting fallow, waiting to help out in the event of a hardware failure. That node should always be physically as "beefy" as the strongest node in your cluster. Trust me, when the hardware failure occurs, you'll be happy you configured it that way. An active/active configuration on a two-node cluster requires more care in configuration, but it's an acceptable situation. If you have the funds for a cluster of three or more nodes, there really is no excuse for not having a passive node for failure scenarios.

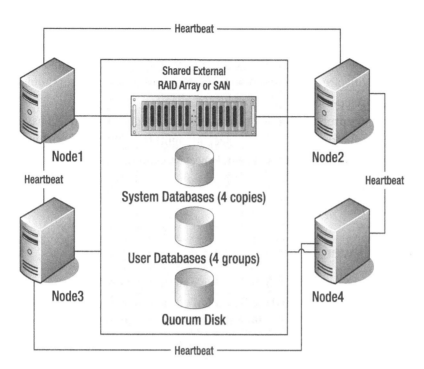

Figure 7-4. *A four-node cluster*

Multiple Instances

While a standalone installation supports 50 instances, a clustered environment can only support 24 instances. Why 24? It has to do with the assignment of drive letters, such as A, B, C, D, E, F, G, and so on. While there are 26 letters in the alphabet, only 24 of those letters are available for assignment to hard drives. Since the discrete point of disk failure is now a mount point, it's limited to the number of available drive letters.

In any event, I dislike the use of multiple instances on a single node. It requires more configuration and more to manage. At the moment, however, server consolidation is popular, so running multiple instances on a single node might be a scenario you need. Keep in mind that under a cluster environment, an instance is also considered a virtual server, so you must have a separate IP address for each instance. You also need to take a great deal of time reviewing your configuration. You don't want to be in the position where clustering is ineffective because you didn't partition your resources properly, allowing for all of them to be run on a single node. Management will not react favorably.

Failover in a Cluster

Hopefully, the process of failover will never occur. You could have a controlled failover if you're installing new software or patches, but in a perfect world, a true failure should never happen. This isn't a perfect world, though.

If you've done things properly and no hardware failure ever occurs, you will have recouped no benefit (other than the ability to sleep at night) from the significant amount of time you spent planning for the failure event. However, dealing with a failover without planning accordingly (both in the failover configuration and in how to react) is sometimes more chaotic than losing a server altogether.

Planning for Failover

Windows clustering isn't a simplistic tool to just move all running services from one server to another. It provides a detailed configuration of each cluster resource, and you may configure each of those resources differently. Usually I encounter cluster environments in which all the defaults are used, but that is often not in the client's best interest.

As important as it is to properly configure the cluster resources, it's also important to prepare yourself for the event of a failover. What actions do you need to take, if any? Will the applications work as expected? Logical failover planning is just as important.

Physical Failover

After installing SQL Server on a cluster, check to be sure that you haven't created any unexpected resource dependencies. Every resource can have a dependency, and many have dependencies immediately after the install. For example, SQL Agent is dependent on the SQL Server instance running, as shown in Figure 7-5. If the instance fails, SQL Agent won't be able to access the MSDB database, so naturally it will fail as well.

SQL Server 2005 is much better about putting only minimal logical dependencies in place. The instance depends on both the clustered disk resource and a network name. The network name depends on having an IP address. Every dependency probably needs to be in place, but it's still a good idea to check them over.

You may want to create your own dependencies as well. If your application depends on full-text search capabilities, you may want to configure resources to have some sort of dependency on the full-text search service or on the drive that holds the full-text catalog.

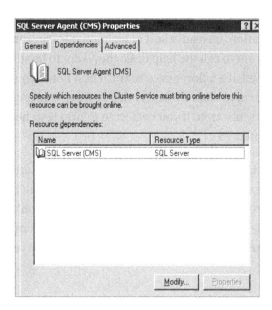

Figure 7-5. *SQL Agent cannot run if SQL Server has failed; thus, SQL Agent will fail as well.*

⬛**Tip** One of my many mantras that I share when teaching SQL Server to fledgling DBAs is, "Know thy application." It's one thing to support the back-end database, but you can't properly support that database without knowing how it's used. I have one client who runs an application that uses the full-text search functionality for one of its primary functions. If full-text search isn't running, the application is useless. I would never have known that if I hadn't taken the time to try to understand how the application uses the database. It only takes a few hours of observing the application in use.

Logical Failover

As important as it is to plan for physical failover, you also need to spend time considering what actions you need to take in the event of a *logical* failover. Maybe you're one of the lucky ones, and you won't need to do anything. Users who experience a brief outage will go back into the application out of habit. You won't need to perform any additional work or create any custom applications. Clustering will do everything for you.

Most of us are not so lucky. A failover event usually causes a great deal of activity that has nothing to do with clustering or SQL Server. For example, you might need to follow one of these plans of action:

- *Notify the help desk*: For many users, an error equals a call to the helpdesk. Many users don't try to restart the application; instead, a sort of technopanic consumes them. It's actually good that they want to call the help desk; they want to be sure they didn't do something wrong. Well, if a failover occurs, you'd best notify your help desk to expect calls and tell them to reassure callers that nothing is wrong with the system and they can simply restart it. If you neglect to inform your help desk, you could be making some enemies.

- *Restart custom applications or services*: Not everything can be automated. Certain applications that run in the cluster environment (or interact with it) may halt if they experience a failure. I once dealt with a middle-tier application that would simply hang in memory if it lost the connection to the database. Simply restarting the application wouldn't work; the only way to clear it out of memory was to reboot the server.

If you have manual tasks that should occur after every failover, document them. Store them on a separate server—not in the clustered environment—and even write them down on paper. Make sure everyone knows where those failover instructions are located. Don't be surprised if you discover during your first production failover that you need to take manual steps. Remember, disaster recovery planning is iterative, and you learn every time something goes wrong.

Server Resource Planning

When clustering goes wrong, it's often when you have an active/active configuration without enough system resources to handle a failover. Each node can handle its own application or the other node's application, but not both at the same time.

While resources such as CPU and I/O may just result in extreme performance degradation, a memory constraint can result in a *failed failover*. In this case, there isn't enough memory to fail one SQL node over to the secondary node, so the entire process fails. It can also result in what I like to call *clustering schizophrenia*, where both nodes begin failing almost repeatedly, neither knowing which role it should be playing. This is a rare situation, but it's a joy to watch and a nightmare to resolve.

In any active/active/active/ . . . configuration, the sum of the maximum memory on all nodes should not exceed the maximum memory for any single node. And all of those individual servers should be exactly the same, right?

SQL Clustering and AWE Memory

One great new feature of SQL Server 2005 is how clustering uses memory when Address Windowing Extensions (AWE) is enabled. As I mentioned in the previous section, if memory resources are misconfigured in a way that prevents both instances from running on a single box, clustering will tend to, well, freak out.

When AWE memory is enabled (usually only done when more than 4GB of memory is installed), SQL Server interacts with the operating system to dynamically reconfigure the memory of the running instances so that they run together. There might be an extreme performance hit, but at least the failover will work.

Failback in a Cluster

Just as important as preparing for failover, you should invest time in planning the process to use in restoring the failed node. Restoring a failed node to its former position in the cluster is referred to as failback. Will things fail back automatically, or will you have to move them back over to the other node manually? As Figure 7-6 shows, if you choose to fail back automatically, you can configure how long the repaired node will need to be up before the cluster services decides it is restored. You can also set the failback process for a specific resource, or you can group resources together and have them behave as one.

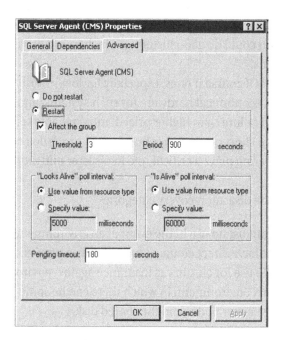

Figure 7-6. *Here SQL Agent is set to restart automatically in a failback situation.*

Personally, I prefer to control failback manually. As long as I have the resources to run both applications on a single node with minimal performance impact, I like to control exactly what happens when. I've encountered scenarios in which the replacement server is installed and ready to receive cluster resources, but it hasn't been completely rebuilt. The server team still needs to install some applications, service packs, or hotfixes, causing reboots, which in turn cause more failover events. Of course, such a server shouldn't be joined to the cluster until it is fully prepped, but you'll find (hopefully not the hard way!) that people do sometimes place a node into a cluster before that node has been fully prepped for its task. And that's when automatic failback can lead to trouble.

Note I despise all automatic operations that I didn't designate to be automatic in the first place. Yes, it's personal bias, and perhaps without grounds, but not being in control of things that I should be always worries me.

Clustering and Disaster Categories

SQL Server clustering is fairly limited in what type of disaster it protects against. Essentially, it's only useful if there is a problem with one of the physical servers. You could still lose the shared storage and lose everything. The individual servers must be in the same location, because they're directly attached to the storage, so there's no help as far as environmental issues are concerned. If you have a robust external storage system such as a SAN (more on SANs in Chapter 10), you could do geo-clustering, which would protect you in environmental disaster situations.

So does clustering have any value? Of course it does, especially for low-priority systems. Businesses often prefer to select economical hardware for such systems, and economical hardware is more prone to failure than higher priced, more reliable server platforms. All it takes is for one cable to short out, a power fluctuation, or a failed cooling fan to damage a single node. Clustering plays a critical role in disaster mitigation, but just one role.

Here's how clustering fits in with the disaster recovery categories:

- *Environmental*: Clustering is of almost no use in the event of an environmental failure, because the servers must have direct contact (and thus close proximity) to the shared disk. The only possible use for clusters as insurance against environmental disaster would be in a SAN environment, in which there can be some physical separation between the cluster nodes and the shared disk.

- *Hardware*: A hardware disaster is really the only scenario in which clustering has any appreciable impact. If any physical node in the cluster fails, the only data lost will be the current transaction.

- *Media*: Clustering provides no protection from media disasters, because all SQL Server data is kept on a shared device. If that device fails, all data is lost. If the media for the individual server (holding the operating system) is damaged, the ability to fail over to another node will protect you to a point. If the media storing the quorum is damaged, the clustering will fail altogether.

- *Process*: There are some scenarios in which clustering can protect against process errors. If the error is a long-running, incorrect transaction (such as issuing a `DELETE` without a `WHERE` clause), initiating a manual failover will cause the incorrect transaction to roll back. Of course, hard-booting a server would accomplish the same thing, but in a cluster environment, the users would have only a brief hiccup in availability.

- *User*: As with process errors, if you can catch the user error in time (which implies you know what was done when, which is rare), you could use a manual failover to roll back the mistake while maintaining availability.

Caveats and Recommendations

There was a day when I was very high on clustering SQL Server. If budget allows, I still think clustering is a technology to be considered as a piece of the entire disaster recovery puzzle. However, with today's hardware, there just isn't the same driving need for clustering as there has been in years past.

As with all technologies, you can follow some general guidelines to keep yourself in a safe harbor, so to speak. Consider the following guidelines when implementing clustering in a SQL Server environment:

- *Never consider SQL Server clustering as the primary means of disaster mitigation*: Clustering can play an important role, but its applications are specific to high-availability issues rather than disaster mitigation.

- *Make sure you understand failover scenarios*: Be clear on what actions the cluster will take in the event of a failover. If you don't, you could be in for a surprise.

- *Perform all service maintenance with the cluster utilities*: Controlling a service directly, either from the command line or from the Services Control Panel applet, could be interpreted as a failure event, causing all services to fail to a standby node.

- *Have replacement hardware on hand*: Hardware fails. Death, taxes, and hardware failure are life's only truths. Yes, there is the occasional exception, but you should always focus on extremes when planning disaster recovery. Having a spare hard drive or power supply can save you a world of time, even if you have the Diamond-Studded Platinum level of support from the hardware vendor.

Summary

While useful and efficient for dealing with specific hardware issues and software upgrades, clustering leaves a lot to be desired when it comes to disaster recovery. It doesn't mitigate much in the way of risk, and it's only truly effective in response to a hardware or software problem on one of the nodes. The benefit of easing the upgrade process is solely in the realm of high availability, so that doesn't help us much either.

So why even use clustering? Well, it's ubiquitous, and several applications and resources can take advantage of it. After all, clustering isn't a function of SQL Server but, rather, a feature provided by Windows. Clustering offers some (limited) level of risk mitigation, so why not take advantage of it? Clustering isn't difficult to install, nor is it difficult to apply service packs. In many ways, running a clustered environment with SQL Server 2005 is no different than having a single server.

Similar to clustering, though much more complex and native to SQL, database mirroring is a more robust feature in SQL Server 2005 that mitigates a number of risks. Mirroring is the topic of Chapter 8.

CHAPTER 8

■■■

Database Mirroring

If there's a crown jewel in the SQL Server feature set, database mirroring could arguably be that jewel. An interesting combination between log shipping and clustering, database mirroring has the potential to eliminate the impact of environmental, hardware, and media disasters for companies that normally couldn't afford a hot remote standby system.

To Microsoft's credit, it knew upon the initial release of SQL Server 2005 that database mirroring wasn't quite ready for prime time. I'd been testing it throughout the beta and Community Technology Preview (CTP) programs, and I personally found it to be quite stable. Initially, SQL Server 2005 had no GUI for configuring a mirroring session, and manual configuration was a bit difficult, if for no other reason than the number of steps required. Still, Microsoft released SQL Server 2005 with database mirroring disabled. It provided a documented trace flag to enable mirroring if desired, but the company admitted to not having enough customer feedback to support it for production use. The feature wasn't fully supported until Microsoft released SP1. I appreciate that Microsoft didn't release a feature it wasn't sure was stable.

While database mirroring might be called the crown jewel of the SQL Server 2005 platform, that doesn't mean it's a jewel without flaws. Like any technology, it has its quirks, unexpected behavior, and oddities. In this chapter, I'll take a look at the architecture of database mirroring, show you how to configure it, compare the different features it provides (contrary to popular belief, database mirroring is *not* "all about availability"), and explain how it is best used.

Mirroring Architecture

From a purely conceptual level, the basic architecture of database mirroring is quite simple. In fact, it looks somewhat familiar because it's really a functional combination of clustering and log shipping. Like clustering, database mirroring *can* provide seamless failover (you must configure it to do so). Like log shipping, it maintains two separate copies of the database. Like clustering but unlike log shipping, database mirroring *can* (again, there's a catch) have no more data loss than a single incomplete transaction. And like log shipping but unlike clustering, there is technically no limit to the distance between the two copies of the database. Theoretically, you could have a database in Chicago that maintains a mirror of itself in Shanghai. Does it sound too good to be true?

Once you take a closer look at the architecture, you'll see that the plumbing behind the conceptual architecture unveils a wealth of moving cogs. It isn't as simple as being managed by a specific service (clustering) or as basic as automating standard activities such as backing up and restoring transaction logs. Database mirroring is deceptively complex and has a number of dependencies that you must consider when implementing it.

The Basics

Taking a cursory look at database mirroring, as shown in Figure 8-1, you'll see that the architecture looks a lot like log shipping. It consists of a primary database (the principal) that forwards database transaction activity to a standby database (the mirror). An optional component (the witness) monitors the activity between the principal and the mirror.

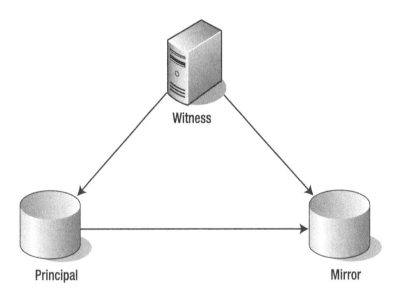

Figure 8-1. *Simplified view of a mirroring configuration*

Note that I specifically said that the principal database forwards "transaction activity"—not the transaction logs themselves.

So far, things seem simple enough. Let's start out by examining these three components.

Principal

The starting point for all mirroring operations is the principal database. It's always a user database, and it always must be in Full Recovery mode (i.e., all transactions must be logged). System databases cannot be mirrored. (Do you feel a potential problem coming on?) The principal database is considered to be the primary, functional database; client applications normally connect to the principal, not to the mirror.

The principal database is always available to users—with one specific exception, which I'll cover shortly. Figure 8-2 shows how the principal database appears in the SSMS GUI.

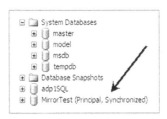

Figure 8-2. *MirrorTest, which is playing the principal role in the mirroring configuration, is labeled as "Principal, Synchronized," indicating that the mirror and the principal have exactly the same data.*

The principal is the point at which all data entry occurs. Even if a database is configured for mirroring but the rest of the mirroring infrastructure is missing, damaged, or disabled, users will still be able to get to the principal to enter data. If the components other than the principal are down or disabled, the SSMS GUI will refer to the principal as disconnected, as you can see in Figure 8-3.

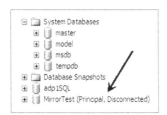

Figure 8-3. *The principal database as it appears in SSMS when the other components of the mirroring solution are unavailable*

If other components are causing the mirroring to fail, appropriate messages will appear in the SQL Server error log, as shown in Figure 8-4. Luckily, these types of messages won't fill the log on the principal node; other components of the mirroring solution will alert the principal that they've recovered on their own.

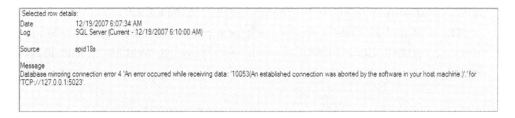

Selected row details:
Date   12/19/2007 6:07:34 AM
Log   SQL Server (Current - 12/19/2007 6:10:00 AM)

Source   spid18s

Message
Database mirroring connection error 4 'An error occurred while receiving data: '10053(An established connection was aborted by the software in your host machine.)'.' for 'TCP://127.0.0.1:5023'.

Figure 8-4. *This error that refers to a failure of the mirroring process appears on the principal. Because the error is logged, it can also be triggered as an alert.*

Even though the mirroring session is stopped, you may still access the properties of the database-mirroring configuration through the SSMS GUI on the principal to make modifications. If the principal were to fail (or if you were to attempt to make changes to mirroring on the mirror node while it's in a failed state), *the database mirroring options won't be available through SSMS.* You can still use T-SQL to make some changes, though.

Mirror

The database on the receiving end of a mirroring session is called the mirror database. You can create it by restoring a backup of the principal database and leaving that restored version in an unrecovered state (just like with log shipping). The mirror continually receives transaction data (*not* transaction log backups) and restores it as quickly as it can or as quickly as it is told to do.

In normal operation, a database that is acting as a mirror should appear as it does in Figure 8-5.

System Databases
  master
  model
  msdb
  tempdb
Database Snapshots
MirrorTest (Mirror, Synchronized / Restoring...)

Figure 8-5. *When all is well with database mirroring, the mirror database should appear as synchronized and restoring.*

If, for some reason, the mirror is still in a state of "synchronizing," that means it's not identical to the principal and is in the process of receiving new data. This can happen when database mirroring is first established, or if mirroring is set to run in an asynchronous mode and the mirror database is in the process of catching up.

In the event that a principal database fails but the mirror remains available and database mirroring is *not* configured for automatic failover, the mirror database will show as disconnected, as you can see in Figure 8-6.

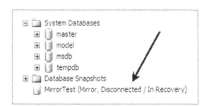

Figure 8-6. *Remember, the mirror database should always be either restoring or in recovery—never simply online. Once the mirrored database is online, it's the new principal!*

If you attempt to access the database mirroring properties in SSMS for the witness database while the principal was down or unavailable, you will receive the error shown in Figure 8-7.

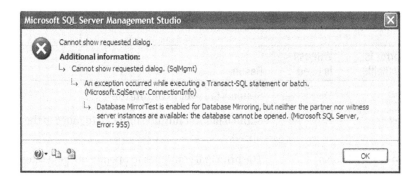

Figure 8-7. *Usually, you only see this error when automatic failover is deliberately not being used.*

While you can configure a standby database used in log shipping as readable, the mirror database is inaccessible. You cannot read it, back it up, and so on. You can use the mirror database for reporting purposes by means of database snapshots, but that method of viewing the mirror database is limited. I'll cover that method in more detail in the next chapter.

Witness

While the principal and the mirror are both databases, the witness is not—it's a separate SQL Server instance. The witness is an optional component of a mirroring environment, but it's required if you automate failover. People often ask, "Do I need to have a third server for every mirroring session?" No. One instance can act as the witness to any number of mirroring sessions. SQL Server Express can act as a witness, so really the witness can be any server available.

The role of the witness is to do nothing but help decide if a failover needs to occur. It continually talks to both the principal and the mirror, and if either is unavailable, it facilitates automatic failover. The witness doesn't decide that a failover is necessary, however. The witness and the mirror both have to agree that the principal is unavailable before an automated failover occurs. For example, it's possible that the witness can't contact the principal, but the mirror can. In such a case, the mirror would not agree, and failover would not occur.

This method of determining failover is vastly superior to that of database clustering, which relies primarily on a heartbeat network connection. Database mirroring essentially uses the heartbeat as well, but when three nodes are involved (the principal, the mirror, and the witness), *two* nodes usually must agree that a failover should occur. Table 8-1 illustrates the possible failure situations and how they interact with database mirroring. As you can see, if automatic failover is important, a witness is not only required, but it's critical that it remain running.

Table 8-1. *Failover Matrix*

Principal Is Available	Mirror Is Available	Witness Is Used	Result
No	Yes	Yes	Systems fail over to the mirror.
No	Yes	No	Manual failover must be initiated to move to the mirror.
Yes	No	No	The principal continues to operate but generates an error that it cannot connect to the mirror.
No	Yes	No	Manual failover must be initiated to move to the mirror.
Yes	Yes	Yes, but down	No failover occurs. An error is noted, and until the witness is restored or replaced, all failover is manual.

Understanding the Details

OK, you have a principal database, a mirror database, and an optional witness. What are the other components to database mirroring that make it so complex? So far, you know where the original data resides (in the principal), where the standby data resides (in the mirror), and the component that facilitates failover (the witness). Now it's time to explore how these pieces connect and how they communicate. This is where things get complex.

Connections

Communications for database mirroring occur over TCP/IP connections. A port number is an important facet of such connections—you likely know that. However, with database mirroring, you need to be concerned about an additional facet: the endpoint.

Ports

Database mirroring connects by means of TCP ports bound to a specific IP address. These ports are not reserved or defined in the way that SQL Server has a reserved port (1433, which incidentally isn't used by default in SQL Server 2005), but you must define and hard-code them explicitly. You cannot have dynamic ports when it comes to database mirroring.

You should know what ports to use before you even begin setting up database mirroring. Yes, you could use whatever points you want at the time of installation, but your network administrators may be more than a bit unhappy with you. As you'll see in Chapter 10, ensuring that there is connectivity from one server to another over a specific TCP port is no trivial task. Simply picking a port number without first discussing your specific needs with your networking staff is not only unwise, it's also rather rude.

Tip For a list of reserved port numbers, go to www.iana.org/assignments/port-numbers. This is an old list, and a number of the reserved ports no longer have a corresponding application. Still, only use ports that are listed as "unassigned."

Endpoints

When configuring database mirroring within the GUI, you can simply put in the TCP port number to use. However, SQL Server 2005 implements a distinct object to open that port for use: an endpoint. As you can see in Figure 8-8, there are endpoints for every connection to the database, whether it's a straight query, an HTTP request, and so on. All connections are implemented as endpoints.

Figure 8-8. *Database endpoints as seen at the instance level*

The T-SQL command for creating an endpoint isn't trivial either.

```
CREATE ENDPOINT [Mirroring]
    AUTHORIZATION [SPYGLASSTAB\jluetke]
    STATE=STARTED
    AS TCP (LISTENER_PORT = 5022, LISTENER_IP = ALL)
    FOR DATA_MIRRORING (ROLE = PARTNER, AUTHENTICATION = WINDOWS NEGOTIATE
, ENCRYPTION = REQUIRED ALGORITHM RC4)
```

Not only do you have to specify the protocol, the port number, and the IP address, but you also must define who has authorization to use the endpoint that you're creating, how it authenticates requests, and whether or not encryption is required.

TAKING THE FEAR OUT OF ENCRYPTION

The first time I heard that SQL Server would include native support for encrypting communication and actual stored data, I have to admit I panicked. The first thing that came to mind was the WITH ENCRYP-TION clause that you can use when creating a stored procedure. That particular encryption algorithm is more than weak, and as far as I know it's homegrown. My imagination quickly constructed images of encryption algorithms being created by means of a secret decoder ring that was obtained by collecting 20 UPC symbols off of some sugary breakfast cereal. My fears turned out to be nothing but paranoia.

SQL Server 2005 uses industry-standard algorithms for encryption. These same algorithms are applied to both encrypting communication between servers and encrypting data stored within a table. Some of the standard algorithms currently supported are Data Encryption Standard (DES), Triple DES, RC2, RC4, and 128-bit to 256-bit Advanced Encryption Standard (AES) as well as X509(1) certificates (up to 2,048-bit encryption). However, just because these algorithms are industry-standard doesn't mean they're unbreakable. With enough computing resources and enough time, a hacker can break nearly any encryption scheme.

Communication

While database mirroring revolves around duplicating database transactions from one database to another, it does so differently than log shipping. Log shipping ultimately relies on a file transfer of a transaction log backup. The transfer of that file is not guaranteed. If it fails for some reason, you must restart it manually (or use some sort of scripting retry process). There is no automated method for ensuring the file is copied successfully.

Database mirroring, on the other hand, uses a queuing technology to guarantee the transfer of information. *Message queuing*, as it's usually referred to, is only concerned with the transfer of a piece of information from point A to point B. Figure 8-9 shows the basics of message queuing.

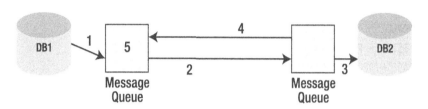

Figure 8-9. *The basic steps involved in message queueing*

Figure 8-9 illustrates the following steps:

1. A database, or some other application, writes a piece of information to its local message queue.

2. The first message queue contacts the remote queue, signaling an attempt to send a message. It then copies the information.

3. At any time, the second database or application may retrieve the information, which is now stored in the remote queue.

4. Once the data is received, the remote queue signals the local queue to confirm receipt.

5. After receiving a confirmation receipt, the local queue removes the original information from the queue. It will only remove it from the local queue if it's sure the remote queue has received it; otherwise, it will continue to retry the original send.

Message queuing is only concerned with guaranteeing queue-to-queue communication. What happens outside of the queues (in Figure 8-9, DB1 and DB2) is irrelevant. Queuing is effective when working with data connections that may disconnect periodically, or when asynchronous communication is desired. Establishing some sort of direct connection from one database to another tends to result in trouble and frustration once a network issue occurs (I'll discuss hardware implications in greater detail in Chapter 10).

Queuing is implemented in many different ways. The idea and technology has been around for quite some time. We have Microsoft Message Queuing (MSMQ) and IBM Web-Sphere MQ, not to mention a plethora of handwritten queuing techniques. Database mirroring uses a new queuing technology native to SQL Server 2005 only: Service Broker.

It's actually more accurate to say that a database mirroring session is a Service Broker application—just a very specialized version of one. An awful lot of creation and configuration goes on behind the scenes. Technically, after creating endpoints that are marked FOR DATABASE_MIRRORING, you only need to set the partner level—that is, what role the database plays in mirroring.

```
CREATE ENDPOINT Endpoint_Mirroring
    STATE=STARTED
    AS TCP (LISTENER_PORT=7022)
    FOR DATABASE_MIRRORING (ROLE=WITNESS)
GO
ALTER DATABASE MirrorTest
SET PARTNER = 'TCP://SPYGLASSTAB:7023'

ALTER DATABASE AdventureWorks
  SET WITNESS = 'TCP://SPYGLASSTAB:7042'
```

Once you've activated all endpoints FOR DATABASE_MIRRORING and you've set the databases with partner or witness roles, the Service Broker part of things is set.

A Service Broker application is extremely complex to configure simply by virtue of the number of steps involved. Luckily for us, the steps to configure Service Broker are performed automatically when you configure database mirroring. With the release-to-manufacturing (RTM) version of SQL Server 2005 and all of the betas and CTPs, you had to manually configure the Service Broker aspect for a database mirroring session. Be thankful things have changed since then.

Client Connections with the SQL Native Access Client

Although database mirroring has value regardless of how you connect to the server (there's always the possibility of a manual or automated client-side failover process), the only way to achieve truly seamless failover from a client perspective is to use SNAC. SNAC is technically just the SQL Server 2005 OLE DB driver, but it requires installation on all client machines for database mirroring automated failover to work as advertised.

When a client using SNAC connects to a principal database participating in a mirror operation, it immediately receives information about the location of both the mirror and the server. Should the principal fail, the SNAC-enabled client will automatically redirect further database requests to the mirror (which should now be the principal). You don't need to rename any servers, change any database connections, or modify any DNS entries.

As Figure 8-10 illustrates, the client immediately learns the following facts:

- Server A and Server B are in a mirroring session.

- Server A is the principal.

- Server B is the mirror.

- Server C is playing the role of a witness.

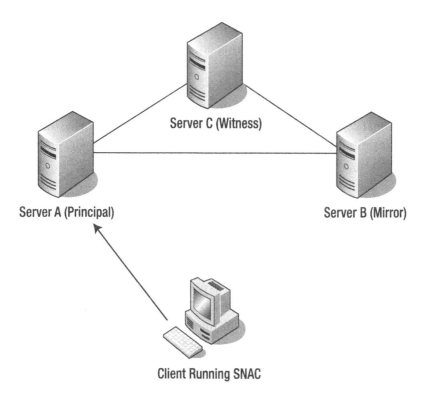

Figure 8-10. *Client connection to the principal and the relationships between the principal, the mirror, and the witness*

This transfer happens each time the client connects initially. If the configuration changes and you have a new server as the witness—say, Server D—the client will learn of it.

The connection string for the 2005 OLE DB driver—I'm sorry, SNAC (I love saying that for some reason)—includes a spot to designate the location of the mirror database.

```
Data Source=Mirror1;Failover Partner=Mirror2;
Initial Catalog=MirrorTest;Integrated Security=True;
```

The `Failover Partner` is a fallback in the event that the client doesn't have or somehow loses the name of the other failover partners. SNAC automatically collects that information when it connects to the principal, so when would you ever need this setting in the SNAC connection string? Actually, you'll need that hard-coded failover partner more often than you think.

Mirroring Levels

Mirroring runs in three distinct modes, each with a specific role. I'm going to say that again: *mirroring runs in three distinct modes, each with a specific role.* If you want to use database mirroring effectively, you must first burn that fact into your brain. Contrary to what you may hear, database mirroring doesn't necessarily have to do with high availability.

Only one of the three mirroring modes provides a truly robust means of automated failover. The other two mirroring modes focus on providing a standby of sorts; one is concerned with performance, the other with data protection. While often labeled differently in the interface, the three mirroring modes are generally referred to as High Performance, High Protection, and High Availability.

Mirroring Mode: High Performance

When you select High Performance, SQL Server configures the connection such that all communication will be asynchronous. The goal of the High Performance mode is to keep the principal database performing as efficiently as possible. Records inserted into the principal are sent to the mirror, but not necessarily on a real-time basis. By using asynchronous communication, the principal and the mirror only need to do their best to keep up. This may seem like a significant deterrent to using High Performance, but database mirroring is designed to minimize the likelihood of the two nodes being out of sync, even in this scenario.

The largest risk of data loss occurs when the two nodes sync up initially and transfer new data from the transaction log of the primary database to the mirror database after it has been restored without recovery. At that point, failure of the principal would guarantee data loss if the mirror were brought online. Once the two nodes are synchronized, database mirroring no longer uses the active transaction log at all when sending new information over the wire; it comes directly from the in-memory log cache directly to the service broker automation. Barring any huge data changes within a short period of time, it's unlikely that the asynchronous connection will ever be out of sync for long. In the event of a failure, there is *no* witness defined to facilitate automated failover.

Failover

During a failure situation, mirroring simply stops, and the mirror database is left in an unrestored state. You must manually intervene and tell the mirror database that it should now assume the role of the primary database. Remember, there is no witness available to facilitate failover.

Depending on the Service Pack level SQL Server is using, you probably won't be able to access the graphical tools to perform the failover in the High Performance configuration. From the command line, you'll actually have to break the mirroring session completely:

```
ALTER DATABASE MirrorTest SET PARTNER OFF:
```

This command literally breaks the partnering session. Remember that this mirror database has been sitting in an unrestored state the entire time, so you'll need to bring it online:

```
RESTORE DATABASE MirrorTest WITH RECOVERY
```

Once the mirror database is online, there's no going back without re-creating a new mirroring session.

Failback

It's in the failback process that you feel the sting of having no mirror. The only way you can bring the database back online is to break the mirroring relationship completely. Of course, that means you must rebuild the mirroring relationship. Thanks to the help of the GUI, rebuilding database mirroring is relatively painless, as you'll learn in the upcoming "Configuring Mirroring" section.

As long as your clients are running SNAC, they *should* revert to the new primary database when it comes back online—that is, if it has the same name. You may have to stop a client application and restart it, or point it to a new server name if a new server name was required in the repair of the primary failure. Other than that, the clients should have no problems (or at least they won't complain as they might with log shipping).

Mirroring Mode: High Protection

In High Protection mode, all changes are synchronous, but no mirror is available to provide automated failover. In the event that the principal fails, *no automatic failover occurs.* That's right, no automatic failover. It's already slowed down by being synchronous, plus you have no automated failover, so what's the benefit?

When the mirror fails, the DBA has to make the decision to abandon mirroring altogether to make the principal a standalone server. Actually, you need to make this decision in conjunction with the business owners of the application (more on that in Chapters 11 and 12). In some cases, it's wiser to stop entering data than to continue without a mirror.

Failover

You must manually intervene during a failover in High Protection mode. The process is exactly the same as in High Performance mode. You must first break the mirroring session with `ALTER DATABASE SET PARTNER OFF` and then bring the database online with `RESTORE DATABASE <<databasename>> WITH RECOVERY`. This effectively brings the mirror online, but the mirroring configuration is gone.

A failover event also means that you now have a stand-alone server handling what should be mission-critical data (if it isn't mission-critical, you should use another mirroring mode). The real question that you and the business unit must answer is, "Do we want to have this server operational?" In many ways, High Protection mode feels like high-powered log shipping—that is, its role in life is merely to be a standby database, used only as a last resort.

There is one key difference between High Protection mode and log shipping or some other means of having a standby system: synchronous data transfer. Log shipping moves data from point A to point B relatively slowly. With data mirroring in High Protection mode, all data transfer is synchronous. Any data modified at point A must first be modified at point B. Some systems are more concerned about data loss than High Availability—that's where High Protection data mirroring comes in.

Failback

Since you have to destroy the database mirroring session completely if you want to bring the mirror online, failback lets you reestablish the mirror session from the start. As with High Performance mode, failback should have little or no impact on your clients, as long as the name of the principal server has not changed.

Note The database mirroring TCP ports are stored in the `sys.database_mirroring_endpoints` table. They are disabled in the mirroring setup interface. When re-creating or reconfiguring the sessions in both High Performance and High Protection modes, if you need to use different TCP ports, you'll need to remove these entries from the `endpoints` table.

SYNCHRONOUS VS. ASYNCHRONOUS MIRRORING

Both High Protection and High Availability modes use synchronous communication, while High Performance mode communicates asynchronously. Knowing how the principal and the mirror communicate is critical. Why, you may ask? Well, for starters, one method might have your users chasing you through the cubicles with pitchforks and torches, while the other might have your boss calling security to walk you out of the building.

Synchronous communication in mirroring is essentially a two-phase commit. The principal doesn't commit its data until it receives confirmation from the mirror that the data in question was committed successfully on the mirrored database. I've said this before, and I hope that it's clear conceptually. It is in the practice of synchronous, two-phase commit communication where potential problems can occur.

Let's say a user is entering data in his application, which is connected to the principal. Every time the user hits Save, he must wait until both the principal *and* the mirror complete saving the data. If the network must undertake a long physical distance or a complicated journey to get the data from the principal to the mirror, that poor user will sit and wait and wait and wait and . . . well, you get the idea.

If mirroring is run with asynchronous communication, as it is in High Performance mode, there is always the chance that the principal and the mirror will be out of sync due to network holdups, deliberately pausing mirroring operations, or large amounts of data changes in a short period of time. If the principal fails at any point while the two nodes are in a synchronizing state, there is a chance that the mirror node will not represent all of the data that was present on the principal. Bosses and executives generally don't like it when data is lost. Granted, High Performance mode does its best to stay in sync, and in most normal operations it is in sync, but remember, what can go wrong probably will go wrong. Always assume the worst when designing for disaster recovery.

Mirroring Mode: High Availability

Finally, the *pièce de résistance* of mirroring modes: High Availability. This mode includes a principal, a mirror, and a witness. When the server is in High Availability mode, communication is synchronous. Not only is failover automatic, but both failover and failback can be done literally at will. While High Availability mode does require a witness, there should be no reason why an organization can't run in High Availability if it want to. The witness could be an older server running SQL Server Express Edition, so no additional SQL Server licensing fees would be required.

However, remember that High Availability mode communicates synchronously— that is, it runs in two-phase commit mode. That means slow insert, update, or delete operations. High-volume data-entry systems may experience pauses while users are entering data. It's best not to use High Availability mode with applications that have data-bound controls, in which updates are automatically transmitted for every field that is updated on a form. It's best to use High Availability mode when data is captured from the form and then inserted or updated in one action. Granted, users will still see a delay after hitting Save, but at least they won't feel the delay throughout the entire data-entry process.

Failover

In the event that a principal fails in High Availability mode, mirroring will automatically transfer users to the mirror node, as long as they're using SNAC. At most, users will have a single transaction fail; when they retry the same transaction, it will succeed.

Failover in High Availability mode is a thing of beauty. It's faster than a SQL clustering failover because it only has to fail over to a single database, it requires no client redirection, and, in many cases, no one but the DBA knows a failover even occurred. You can also initiate failover manually if server patches require a reboot of the principal node.

Failback

In the event of a failover, failback is simply a case of the mirror and witness nodes both agreeing that the principal is unavailable for any of the following reasons:

- A network error of some kind

- DBA error on the principal node (been there, done that)

- Principal server failure

- Failure of the SQL Server instance

It would be possible for a clever programmer to actually check to see if any of these types of errors have occurred and to retry the transaction against the mirror. There should be no risk of updating the mirror while the principal is still running. While in mirror mode, only the principal can update the database.

Failback is another story. Yes, it should be seamless to users when it happens, and quite easy once the principal is restored. *That is, if you remember not to back up the transaction log, truncate it, or switch to Simple Recovery mode while the mirroring configuration is in a failover state.* Remembering to leave the transaction log alone during a failover state is all you need to do during a failover situation. Once you restore the principal, you can usually just fail back immediately to the principal. Sometimes the principal may be so badly damaged that you have to eliminate and reconfigure mirroring from scratch, but High Availability mode is designed to minimize those situations.

ORPHANED USERS: AN OLD FRIEND

Anyone who has backed up and restored a database to a new server has probably run into the problem of orphaned users. Regardless of what mode you're in, you'll experience the same issue in all database mirror failover situations. If you haven't dealt with the issue of orphaned users, here's a quick recap.

SQL Server has both logins and users. Logins are used to identify (authenticate) you to the SQL Server instance. Users are defined at the database level and are linked by means of a Security Identifier (SID) that's recorded when the login is created. If Windows Authentication is used, this SID is the actual SID that's used on the operating system. If SQL Authentication is used, the SID is generated randomly, based in part on the internal ID of the SQL Server instance.

If you move a database from one server to another, all of the users will appear to have "disappeared" from the GUI. If you try to add a user, you'll get a message saying that user already exists. If you drop and re-add the user, you'll lose all of the object-level permissions. If you use Windows Authentication and the server is in the same domain, you can simply re-add the Windows user or group as a login. The user will reappear with all of his object-level permissions intact, because the SID generated when the Windows user or group was added as a login is exactly the same as it was on the previous server.

If you happen to use SQL Authentication, you aren't so lucky. When you add in a new login, the SID that's generated will be relatively random and *won't match* the SID that's recorded with the user. Now all of those users and logins are out of sync. There are a number of ways around this (just search for "orphaned users" in BOL). The one I prefer is the old standby; the stored procedure sp_change_users_login. You can use this to sync up the SIDs so that the SID for the database user is the same as the SID for the login.

If, during the course of a mirroring session, logins are added, you'll need to add them to the mirror node in the event of a failure. The master database cannot be mirrored, so make sure you record any additional logins that have been added since the mirroring session started.

Configuring Mirroring

For the purposes of this chapter, I'm keeping things as simple as possible. Let's say you have three instances—DBMIRROR1, DBMIRROR2, and DBMIRROR3—and you want to configure mirroring for one of the databases. You choose to use the High Availability mode, because it's the most popular choice. The first step is to create a fresh (yes, fresh—not one from last night) backup of the database that you want to protect—in this case, MirrorTest. The reason you need a new, clean backup is that you must have all of the committed transactions as part of the backup, including the database and the active transaction log. If a log backup occurs before you back up the database, you'll receive an error later when you try to enable mirroring.

Tip Creating a full backup resets your LSN chain as it relates to differential backups, but there's a way around that. Do you remember the `WITH COPY_ONLY` clause back in Chapter 2? Now is the perfect example of when you should use it.

Next, copy the backup to the instance you want to use for the mirror database (in this case, it's on the same PC) and restore it. Read that last sentence carefully, because it's important. *You're restoring the database, but you're not recovering the database.* You need to leave the mirror database in a state where it can continue to receive new records, as shown in Figure 8-11.

Figure 8-11. *Before configuring any level of database mirroring, you must prepare a suitable mirror database and leave it in a state ready for additional transaction logs.*

I recommend that you use `WITH COPY_ONLY` to make a full backup to a device, as well as a log backup. Restore both the full backup and the log backup (which is essentially a tail-log backup), but don't recover the database. Now you're all set to begin configuring database mirroring.

There are numerous ways to bring up the GUI for configuring mirroring. Figure 8-12 demonstrates how to go through the Tasks menu item.

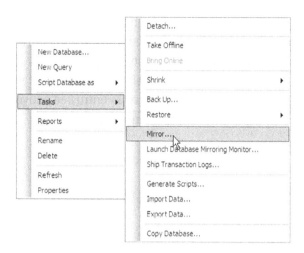

Figure 8-12. *When using the Tasks menu to access mirroring, be sure to right-click on the database you'd like mirrored.*

Figure 8-13 demonstrates how to bring up the GUI by going to the properties for the database. I generally hate including screenshots that simply show how to launch something, but oddly enough, a number of clients have had difficulty setting up mirroring intuitively.

Figure 8-13. *Every database has a Mirroring option on the Properties screen.*

■**Caution** The GUI has changed a bit from service pack to service pack—nothing major, just subtle changes. These screenshots are all based on SP2; future service packs may change the look a bit, but the process remains the same.

The first step in configuring database mirroring is to launch the Configure Security wizard, as shown in Figure 8-14. Personally, whenever presented with a wizard, I'm a bit concerned that I need to have all of my ducks in a row before beginning it. (If you've ever installed the original release of Reporting Services, you know what I mean.) However, there's no need for concern here, unless you intend to mirror across untrusted Active Directory domains. For simplicity and your sanity, I won't attempt that in this walk-through (say, "Thank you, James").

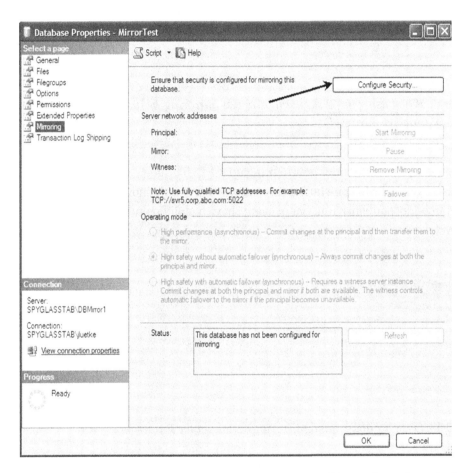

Figure 8-14. *The key to configuring database mirroring is this Configure Security button, which automates the creation of TCP endpoints.*

Oddly enough, the Configure Security wizard gathers a significant amount of information, some of it seemingly irrelevant to security. This wizard is actually configuring endpoints, which need to be secured. I guess the Create Endpoint wizard would be a bit of an esoteric wizard name for the average DBA.

As you can see in Figure 8-15, the wizard first determines whether or not a witness instance is required. Even if you intend to run in High Protection mode (no witness), say yes to this and, if nothing else, reference the local instance. Why? You can always remove the witness later, and this way you can see what's involved in configuring a witness.

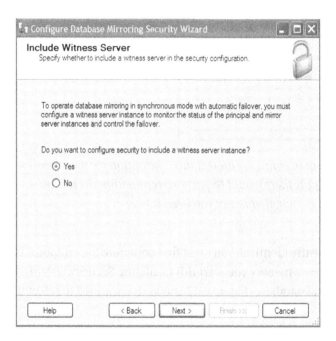

Figure 8-15. *Remember, the witness can be a SQL Express instance, so theoretically, running on any other server in your environment (the workload on the witness) isn't excessive unless it's monitoring a large number of mirroring sessions.*

You have the option of configuring some or all of the required endpoints, as shown in Figure 8-16. Since you're configuring this for the first time, both the principal and the mirror instances are required (and thus grayed out). Again, the witness is optional, but go ahead and include it.

Figure 8-16. *If you had chosen not to configure an instance, the option for the witness server instance would be grayed out, plus there would be fewer screens within the wizard. I recommend configuring a witness whether or not you need it.*

The next three steps are nearly identical. You must first configure the endpoint for the principal instance. Note that wherever you start this Configure Security wizard, it will assume that this is the principal database. Figure 8-17 shows that the area to select the instance is grayed out.

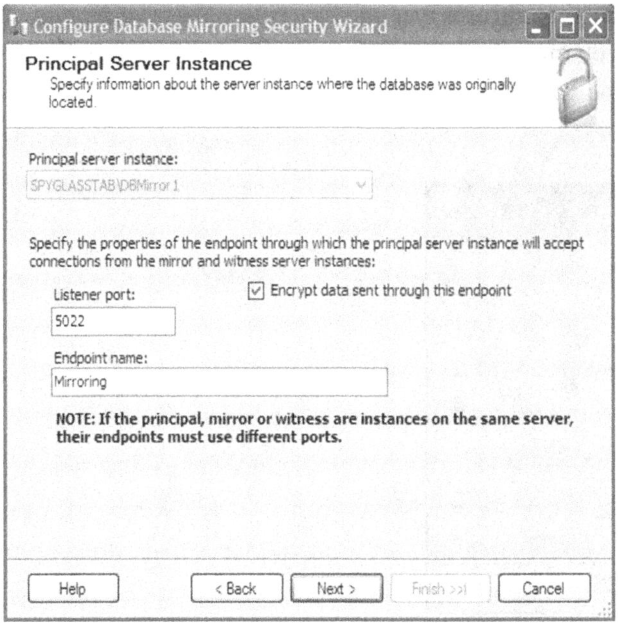

Figure 8-17. *You first create an endpoint for the principal instance, then create the same types of endpoints for the witness and mirror instances. In this example, they're all on the same server, so the computer is the same.*

The interesting thing with mirroring endpoints is that each instance has only one port dedicated specifically to mirroring traffic. If you create another mirroring session on the SPYGLASSTAB\DBMIRROR1 instance, the entry for port and encryption will be grayed out as well. Yet database mirroring is done at the database level, not the instance level. Anybody feel the potential for a bottleneck?

Incidentally, the wizard creates an endpoint with the following settings:

```
CREATE ENDPOINT [Mirroring]
AUTHORIZATION [SPYGLASSTAB\jluetke]
STATE=STARTED
AS TCP (LISTENER_PORT = 5022, LISTENER_IP = ALL)
FOR DATA_MIRRORING (ROLE = PARTNER, AUTHENTICATION = WINDOWS NEGOTIATE
, ENCRYPTION = REQUIRED ALGORITHM RC4)
```

The key phrase in this code is FOR DATA_MIRRORING. As far as SQL Server is concerned, this isn't an ordinary TCP endpoint that you're configuring. It's specifically designated for all database mirroring activity in and out of this instance. After using the GUI to create the endpoint, you may want to re-create it with either a stronger or weaker algorithm than RC4. Encryption has an obvious impact on how secure the communications are, but also on speed: a stronger algorithm means slower communication. Consider this food for thought—now back to configuring mirroring.

Next, you need to configure the mirror server instance—namely, the endpoint it's to use for mirroring. To do this, you must first connect to that instance to create the database mirroring endpoint, as shown in Figure 8-18.

Figure 8-18. *You're configuring this on the same computer, so the mirror will simply be another instance on this computer.*

After establishing the connection to the instance holding the mirror database, you can now create a database mirroring endpoint, as shown in Figure 8-19.

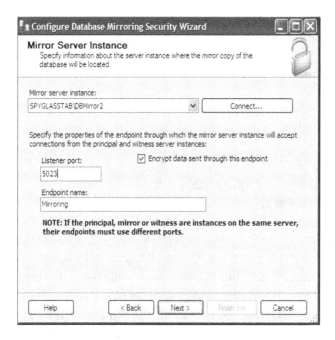

Figure 8-19. *After connecting to the mirror instance (in this case,* Spyglasstab\DBMirror2)*, you can create a database mirroring endpoint.*

Even though you've chosen a different port number (out of necessity), I highly recommend using the same port number on all instances involved in mirroring. It makes troubleshooting and monitoring for your network administrators much easier (and yes, you'll need to work with them to successfully configure a database mirroring configuration—more on that in Chapter 10).

Finally, you need to configure a database mirroring endpoint for the witness instance, as shown in Figure 8-20. Again, you're forced to use a different port, because this instance is on the same computer.

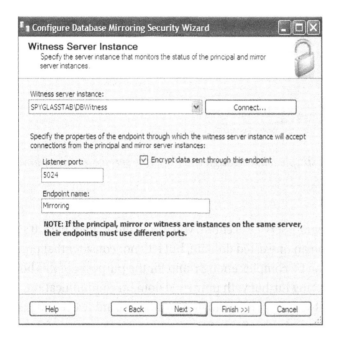

Figure 8-20. *After connecting to the instance that will act as the witness, you can again select the database mirroring endpoint for that instance. Since this is the witness, this is really the only configuration necessary for mirroring.*

The endpoint you create for the witness instance will be used for all database mirroring communication.

Next, you need to indicate how all three instances—the principal, the mirror, and the witness—will communicate with each other, as shown in Figure 8-21. If you leave each of these blank, the first assumption SQL Server will make is that they all use the same service account.

Figure 8-21. *All instances in this simple walkthrough use the same service account, so you can leave them blank.*

If each instance uses a separate service account, you would enter them here. It's possible that each instance runs on an untrusted domain, but let's not consider that possibility here. Database mirroring can be complex enough, and for the purposes of this book, I don't want to complicate mirroring further with untrusted domain communication.

Figure 8-22 shows the final screen of the Configure Security wizard (we're still just configuring security). The result of the Configure Security wizard is the successful completion of three actions: creating a mirroring endpoint on the principal instance, the mirror instance, and the witness instance.

Figure 8-22. *If you have a green light on all three nodes, you're ready to continue configuring mirroring.*

After completing the Configure Security wizard and successfully creating mirroring endpoints, you're prompted to start the mirroring session, as shown in Figure 8-23. However, do not start mirroring at this time.

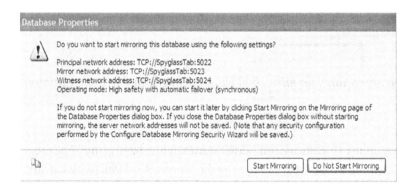

Figure 8-23. *Note that the Do Not Start Mirroring button is highlighted, meaning it's the default selection. Never start mirroring immediately; instead, first review the configuration and select what type of mirroring you'd like.*

If you were to start mirroring immediately after completing the Configure Security wizard, it would automatically start in High Availability mode (High Safety mode with automatic failover)—that is, if it could start at all. If you look closely, the names of the servers are not fully qualified domain names (FQDNs), so it's likely that mirroring would fail, as shown in Figure 8-24.

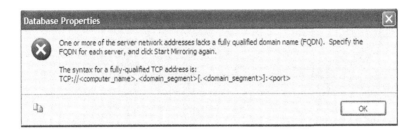

Figure 8-24. *You'd receive this error if you simply used the computer name as the location of the principal, the mirror, and the witness instance.*

You were warned about this earlier, as you can see in Figure 8-25. This leaves me, the author, in a quandary. If I were to complete this walkthrough, I'd have to give the FQDN of my server. The paranoid DBA in me doesn't want to do that.

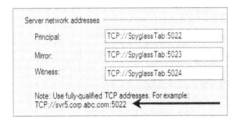

Figure 8-25. *FQDNs are required for mirroring. Thus, starting with the configuration shown here would fail.*

I could just put in my IP address, but I don't want anyone having my IP address either. Instead, I'm going to use what's known as the *loopback address*, which every server translates to 127.0.0.1. This sidesteps the need for an FQDN for each instance. Once I make that change, I can turn on mirroring, as shown in Figure 8-26.

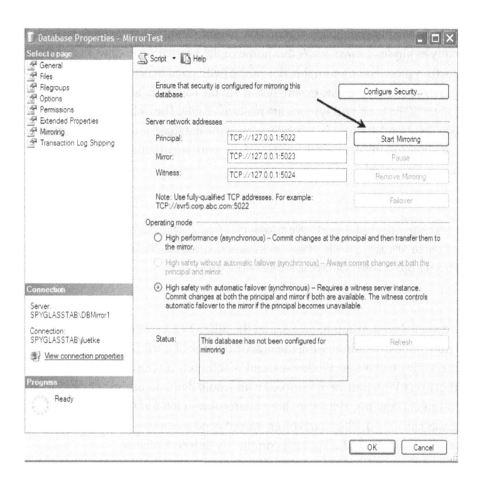

Figure 8-26. *Using the loopback address, you can now start mirroring.*

The database mirroring session is now running in High Availability mode, so failover will be automatic, and all communication is synchronous. However, once you've configured mirroring, you can easily change the mirroring mode. Next I'll explain why you'd want to use one mode over another.

Guidelines for Selecting a Database Mirroring Mode

Although I've discussed how database mirroring works and how to configure it, I still haven't addressed what I think is the most important question of all: what do you do with database mirroring? Database mirroring is certainly not a cure-all for disaster mitigation, nor is it a High Availability solution. Then again, I believe there's no such thing as a technical cure-all. Mirroring is extremely useful, but make sure you consider the possible ramifications of any given use.

When discussing availability, you need to be clear about whether you're referring to availability as physical, *measurable* downtime or the perception of downtime. Often, too much focus is placed on measurable downtime (with good reason—it's easily quantifiable) at the expense of the user experience. If I'm the user of an application, it doesn't matter to me if the back-end systems are really available. The only thing that matters to me is whether I can continue to work. So what if the database is technically "up"? If I can't continue filling out my data-entry form (or if my work is lost), the system is unavailable as far as I'm concerned.

░**Note** User experience is also quantifiable in terms of uptime. It's often overlooked and downplayed because it can be difficult to quantify. It takes time, cooperation, and coordination with end users, and potentially some type of client-side coding, to capture timing data.

It's extremely important to be clear on the difference between physical and perceived downtime when discussing the practical usage of mirroring or any other high-availability technique. While the trend is definitely on the decline, it seemed for a while that every IT department I worked with would demand uptime charts for their mission-critical systems. However, those charts always left out the basis on which the uptime was calculated. The charts often looked good when presented to management, but the user base would often paint a completely different picture.

░**Note** Many people believe they can use statistics to prove whatever point they want to make. While there is a certain amount of truth to that, a real statistical analysis always includes the methodology used to collect the data and what that data represents. Upper management generally prefers a concise, graphical representation of information, but you should always be prepared to present the methodology you use in your analysis, as well as what each term represents.

Some also believe that *user* downtime cannot be measured with any assurance of accuracy. I disagree. A simple way to get accurate, quantifiable data is to shadow a user and use a stopwatch. Don't have a stopwatch? Many cell phones provide some sort of stopwatch functionality, as do many modern watches. Ideally, the application would have some sort of stopwatch functionality that you could enable with a certain startup flag.

If you believe user perception is worthy of consideration when selecting a database-mirroring mode (and I think user perception should be considered), you should consider the following situations:

- *Low user downtime*: If the user experience is one of the major business drivers that you must consider, then running database mirroring in High Availability or High Protection mode (both use synchronous communication) will definitely have an impact on that user experience. Depending on the network factors and the location of the mirror database, the impact on users could be significant. Even what seems like a minor network delay of 50-100 milliseconds (yes, milliseconds) could result in a visible delay for users. If you want to minimize the impact on users, High Performance mode (which is asynchronous) might be a better choice.

- *Low system downtime*: If user experience isn't a factor, you should always run database mirroring in High Availability mode. When database mirroring has a witness instance and is running in synchronous mode, failover is extremely fast, no matter what the distance. If the users are using SNAC, the failover will be nearly seamless.

- *Uptime first, data second*: If you're concerned with uptime at the expense of data loss, then High Performance mode is the most likely choice. While failover requires manual intervention, it's extremely fast. Also, it uses asynchronous communication, so there will be no direct impact on the user experience.

- *Data first, uptime second*: Sometimes the most important factor in a data system is the protection of that data. Any lost data could mean a loss not only in revenue but also in terms of customers (and thus, future revenue). Imagine an online retailer: would it be better to lose 20 minutes' worth of data or have 20 minutes of downtime? I would choose the downtime. Losing 20 minutes' worth of potential orders plus all of those customers would have a huge impact on bottom line. (Would you use a retailer who charged you yet sent nothing and had no record of your data?) High Protection mode is the best choice in this scenario. Failover requires manual intervention, and all communication is synchronous. The chances of accidental entry of data are almost nil.

Disaster Categories

So how effective is database mirroring when it comes to dealing with disaster scenarios? How well does it protect your data? It turns out that database mirroring can literally protect you in every scenario (with some exceptions):

- *Environmental*: As long as the mirror database exists at a separate physical location, database mirroring can be the perfect protection against any sort of environmental disaster. In particular, if you can run the mirror database in High Availability mode, everything will be protected.

- *Hardware*: Even if you mirror from one server in your data center to another in the same physical location, database mirroring can be the perfect protection against hardware failure.

- *Media*: Database mirroring involves a complete copy of the database, which you can maintain in parallel with the production server. If you lose an entire disk array, no problem—the entire database exists at the mirror location, wherever that may be.

- *Process*: There is the possibility of protecting against process errors if the mirror database is running in High Availability mode. In that mode, you can pause mirroring while performing the process. If the process succeeds, you can resume mirroring; if the process fails, you can break mirroring and fail over. It isn't the perfect process, but it could work.

- *User*: As with process disasters, you might be able to pause mirroring if you can catch the user disaster in time. That's a pretty big "if," though.

Caveats and Recommendations

While database mirroring sounds like a panacea to all disaster scenarios, no technology or solution is without its own issues. Don't forget these tips:

- *Don't forget SNAC*: To take full advantage of database mirroring, make sure that all clients have SNAC installed.

- *Choose the appropriate mirroring model*: Be aware of all of the needs involved when choosing a mirror. Optimizing for immediate failover may not be the best for the application involved. Will all the data be protected? Will the users notice a performance impact while mirroring is enabled?

- *Understand your failover and failback scenarios*: Even though failover and failback in database mirroring are significantly less painful than in log shipping, some situations may require you to break the mirror and re-create it.

Summary

Is database mirroring too good to be true? I don't believe so. When it comes to mitigating disaster situations, there really isn't a better solution. Not only can it provide a high level of disaster mitigation, but it can also ensure transactional consistency. Some of my colleagues recommend replication as a superior means of disaster mitigation, but I see replication fitting a different business role—one of secondary usage in disaster recovery. I'm placing my money on database mirroring as the best solution for mitigating database disasters. In the next chapter, I'll talk about database snapshots—how to create them, restore them, and manage them.

CHAPTER 9

■■■

Database Snapshots

One of the most useful and potentially problematic features of SQL Server is the database snapshot. It provides two basic pieces of functionality: 1) a point-in-time view of a database (a data time machine, if you will) and 2) the ability to restore the production database to that point in time extremely quickly. However, a database snapshot is not part of, nor should it ever be a part of, a backup/recovery process. It needs a live database in order to function. It can play an important role in a disaster recovery plan, though.

In this chapter, I'll examine the architecture of database snapshots, their practical usage, and how they play into a disaster recovery plan. There are many creative uses for database snapshots other than disaster recovery scenarios. I'll mention some of these uses briefly, because they can conflict with disaster recovery using database snapshots.

Understanding the Architecture

For practical purposes, a database snapshot behaves just as a read-only database; its implementation, however, is quite different. A database snapshot is simply a file or collection of files associated with a specific database. When a data page in the source database changes, the original data page is first copied to snapshot file before updating the source database. This process is called *copy-on-write*. Figure 9-1 illustrates the copy-on-write process, which happens only once per data page; after a data page in the source database has been modified and copied to the snapshot file, it will never be copied again. The snapshot is intended to represent the database at a particular point in time, so it only needs the original copy of the data page, not subsequent changes.

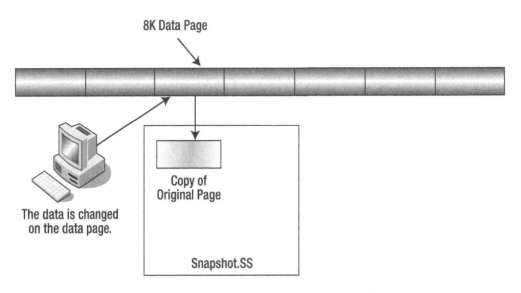

Figure 9-1. *SQL Server's copy-on-write process for generating snapshots*

The snapshot doesn't care what type of data is on the page; it could be table data, index data, or information catalog data—even GAM, SGAM, or Index Allocation Map (IAM) pages. There's no evaluation of the information being copied, so the process is extremely fast.

Theoretically, the snapshot file(s) could grow to be as large as the source database (if every data page were modified). However, the snapshot file uses no preallocated space in the way a normal database file would. It's a *sparse file*, a feature of NTFS where only nonzero information is stored on disk. Normally, when a file is written to disk and it contains "blank" information, that empty space is "zeroed out," meaning it is filled by setting all of the bits to 0. Sparse files do not do that. So if data pages written to the snapshot file contain empty initialized space, that empty space will not be stored within the snapshot file.

Keep in mind that *any* change to a data page results in the entire page being written to the sparse file. If the page is fairly full, the size advantage of using sparse files will be for naught. For an OLTP database, the chance of the snapshot growing to a significant size is high.

It's also possible to have multiple snapshots of the same database. You might want to do this for a number of reasons (which I'll discuss later), but the net effect is that changed data pages need to be written to multiple locations simultaneously. Of course, this increases disk usage and I/O, particularly with an active OLTP database.

As previously mentioned, for practical purposes, a database snapshot is a read-only database. You can run SELECT queries against it, extract data from it via SSIS, and so on, but you can't back it up, change any properties for the database, or perform any other operation you could normally perform on a database.

When you query against a snapshot, SQL Server checks an in-memory map of what pages the snapshot has. If it doesn't find the requested page, it redirects the request to the main database. Figure 9-2 illustrates the process.

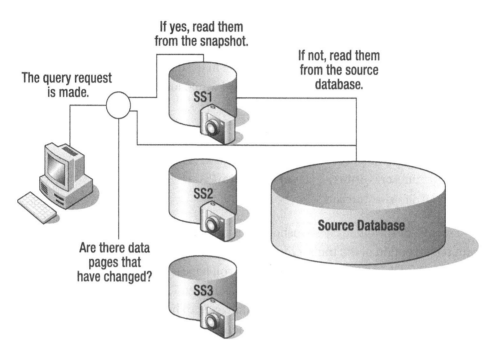

Figure 9-2. *Processing a query involving a snapshot*

The process is completely seamless to the end user. The snapshot will return data just as if it were any other database.

A snapshot file is maintained for each `.mdf` or `.ndf` file in the source database. If the need arises to return the source database to the way it looked at that point in time, you can simply restore the snapshot. All modified data pages will be replaced, and the transaction log will be reset—it is equivalent to a point-in-time restore using the transaction log, although no full database backup, differential backup, or transaction logs are required. It's extremely fast, although any data inserted, updated, or deleted since the snapshot was created will be immediately lost.

Creating Database Snapshots

Since they behave as read-only databases, it's no surprise that you create snapshots using the `CREATE DATABASE` command:

```
CREATE DATABASE AdventureWorks_SS ON
(NAME=AdventureWorks, FILENAME='D:\data\AW.ss')
AS SNAPSHOT OF AdventureWorks
```

As opposed to a normal CREATE DATABASE statement, the NAME option here refers to the logical name of the source file, not the logical name to be assigned to the snapshot. Note that I'm already using a naming convention of *DBName_SS* for the snapshot.

You must create a snapshot file for each file in the database. So if you have three files in the AdventureWorks database, the command would look like this:

```
CREATE DATABASE AdventureWorks_SS ON
(Name=AdventureWorks_Data1, Filename='D:\data\AW1.ss'),
(Name=AdventureWorks_Data2, Filename='D:\data\AW2.ss'),
(Name=AdventureWorks_Data3, Filename='D:\data\AW3.ss')
AS SNAPSHOT OF AdventureWorks
```

Essentially, the database snapshot needs to look physically like its source database (with the exception of the transaction log). There needs to be a snapshot file that corresponds with each individual database file. If you have a large database with dozens of files, creating a database snapshot is no trivial matter. The easiest way to deal with creating a database snapshot of a multifile database is to begin by creating a script to re-create the database. Figure 9-3 shows the menu involved in generating such a script.

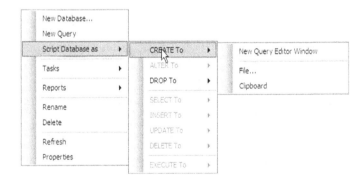

Figure 9-3. *Simply right-click on the database to bring up the scripting option.*

Once you have a script to re-create your database, simply remove all of the elements from the script that are unnecessary to specify when creating a snapshot. For example, you won't need to specify any initial file size. Leave only the CREATE DATABASE statement and the original file names. For the physical file names, simply rename them to use a .ss extension.

Note When the `CREATE DATABASE...AS SNAPSHOT OF` command is issued, the source database is "captured" at that particular point in time, but uncommitted transactions are not included.

Once you've created a database as a snapshot, you cannot drop, detach, or restore the source database (or specific files within the database), but you can back it up normally. You also cannot back up, detach, or otherwise move the snapshot files.

You remove snapshots by using the `DROP DATABASE` command:

```
DROP DATABASE AdventureWorks_SS
```

Take care in removing snapshots, particularly if your naming convention doesn't include some indication that what you are removing is in fact a snapshot. The risk is that you will write a `DROP DATABASE` command and then unthinkingly follow that command with the name of a database, and not of a snapshot. You won't be able to drop the source database of a snapshot, but it is possible to type in the wrong database name. Since T-SQL commands execute without a confirmation prompt, you could be initiating a disaster scenario! That would qualify as a process error.

Restoring Database Snapshots

I generally prefer the phrases "reverting to a snapshot" or "snapping back," but technically, you're restoring the database from the snapshot files. The command to restore a database snapshot is probably *too* simple:

```
RESTORE DATABASE AdventureWorks FROM DATABASE_SNAPSHOT=AdventureWorks_SS
```

The great thing about restoring is that it returns the database to that point in time immediately. The troublesome thing about restoring is that it returns the database to that point in time immediately. There's no "snapping back."

As with the `DROP` command, if you don't use a naming convention that identifies the snapshot as a snapshot, it is possible to accidentally restore the wrong database, particularly if you're writing the T-SQL statement on the fly. Just as I would write the word `WHERE` before constructing a `DELETE` or `UPDATE` statement, I recommend writing the `RESTORE` statement with `FROM DATABASE_SNAPSHOT` first.

A number of requirements must be met before you can restore a snapshot:

- *There can be no other snapshots of the source database*: You must delete all other snapshots before reverting. Needless to say, be very certain you know which snapshot you need if you maintain more than one on any given database.

- *All full-text catalogs must be dropped*: Since full-text catalogs are still stored outside of the database itself, reverting to a snapshot would invalidate any catalogs; full-text search would be unaware of the change in the database.

- *All filegroups in the source database must be read/write and uncompressed*: Snapshots and compression don't mix, and it's necessary to write to filegroups in order to restore them to their previous state.

- *All filegroups that were online when the snapshot was created must be online when the snapshot is applied*: This is because those filegroups must be written to in order to restore them to their original state (i.e., to their state when the snapshot was taken).

Reverting to a snapshot also breaks the transaction log chain. It rebuilds it during the revert action, but be sure to back up the existing transaction log before applying the snapshot; you may need it if a more drastic restore operation is required.

Note It is extremely important to back up the tail of the transaction log before applying a snapshot. Without that tail-log, you will lose data if you need to restore the database using a full backup that precedes the snapshot. With normal restore operations, SQL Server 2005 prompts you to back up the tail-log first—it doesn't do so with snapshots. This is critical, because the instant the snapshot is applied, the transaction log is reset, and those "tail" transactions are inaccessible.

Keep these restrictions in mind as we continue. If you haven't already guessed it, they have a profound impact on the practical usage of database snapshots.

Managing Database Snapshots

The use of database snapshots can be quite appealing; however, they carry a heavy management burden. Even though you can create them only using a T-SQL script, they appear in SSMS under a special Database Snapshots folder, as shown in Figure 9-4.

Figure 9-4. *All database snapshots, regardless of what database they point to, appear together in the same Database Snapshots folder in SSMS.*

Another potentially confusing aspect to the presentation of database snapshots in SSMS is that once opened, they look exactly like any other database. Even viewing the properties of a database snapshot gives the impression that you're looking at an actual database. Figure 9-5 shows the problem.

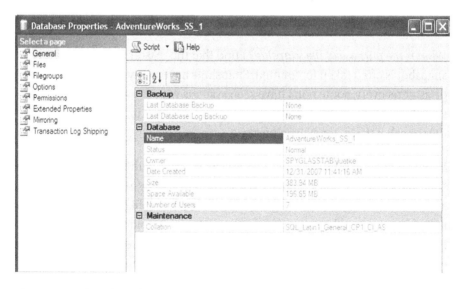

Figure 9-5. *Other than the Name property that I've chosen (*AdventureWorks_SS_1*), nothing indicates that this screen shows the properties of the database snapshot.*

If left unmanaged and only used marginally, database snapshots do little more than consume disk space and clutter the Management Studio landscape. There are no automated methods supplied for managing the database snapshots—no automatic naming convention or linking a database snapshot to its home database. Developing an effective management routine for database snapshots should be a requirement before even considering their use.

Applying a Naming Convention

I have seen, firsthand, extremely poor naming conventions for database snapshots. Even the barely adequate naming schemes (as shown in Figure 9-4) leave questions about the role of each individual database snapshot.

An appropriate naming convention should be able to answer the following questions for any given snapshot:

- *What database does the snapshot point to?* All database snapshots appear in the same place in SSMS. Unless you're in luck and have only a single production database on your SQL Server instance, including the name of the source database is critical.

- *When was the snapshot created?* Knowing the creation date of a database snapshot is not an item of convenience for the DBA. A snapshot is a point-in-time view of an entire database, so the creation date drives exactly what will be contained within the snapshot.

- *What is the purpose of the snapshot?* I find that the reason for using a database snapshot is often taken for granted. Snapshots have many uses—some related to disaster recovery, some not. I have seen systems with literally hundreds of active snapshots, all named in a way that makes it an exercise in frustration to try to find the snapshot to use for a given purpose.

- *When will the snapshot "expire"?* I have seen systems with hundreds of database snapshots. Why? Because snapshots don't "expire." They aren't self-maintaining, and you can't set a "lifetime" when you create them. Unlike with a database backup file, you cannot set them to expire after a certain date or a specific number of days. Having some sort of marker in the name that indicates the expiration date is necessary in order to control snapshot "expiration" programmatically.

I recommend that you apply these four guideline questions when naming a database snapshot. As a result, a practical name might be:

```
AdventureWorks_010120080900_YearStartProcessing_10
```

This name is in the following format:

```
[Database]_[CreationDate]_[Reason]_[Days to Live]
```

When I see a snapshot named in this way, I know exactly what database it points to, the data that it holds and why it holds it, and when it would be safe to remove it from the SQL Server instance. It is true that the name is rather verbose, but there's a benefit from that verbosity.

Depending on your environment, you may choose to use a naming convention that does not explicitly differentiate a snapshot from a normal database. Why might you do that? A snapshot is sort of a "database view." In many systems, views are named in a manner that the consumer of that information does not realize it is not a physical table, either for pragmatic or security purposes. Database snapshots could be used in a similar fashion. Using the example in the previous paragraph, perhaps simply *Year2008Start* would be sufficient, and preferable, if the snapshot is to be exposed to users for writing ad hoc queries or reports.

As with any naming convention, the key to success is to simply pick a naming convention and stick to it. Having multiple naming conventions for different uses can quickly lead to confusion.

Linking a Snapshot to Its Database

If you have the unlucky and unhappy reality of having existing database snapshots that are poorly named, use this handy query that returns each database name and all of its associated snapshots:

```
USE master
SELECT s1.[name] 'SourceDB', s2.[name] 'Snapshot'
FROM sys.databases s1
INNER JOIN sys.databases s2
ON s1.database_id=s2.source_database_id
```

■**Caution** Be careful when executing the query that returns each database name and associated snapshots. The SourceDB column exists in sys.databases but not in sys.sysdatabases. Be sure to specify the correct source table in your FROM clause.

Figure 9-6 shows some example results from the preceding query. You can see how snapshot names are correlated with their respective database sources.

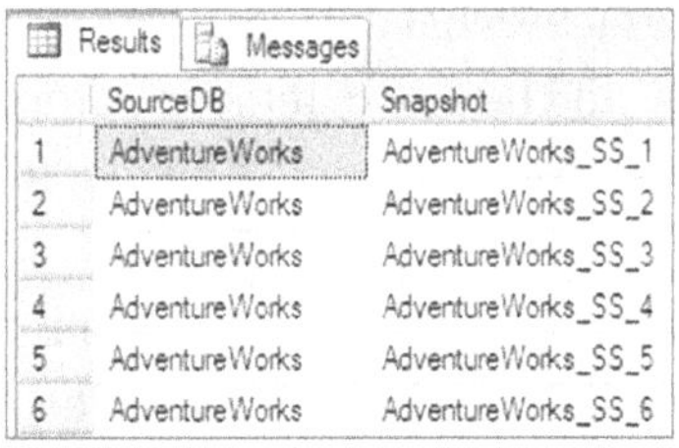

	SourceDB	Snapshot
1	AdventureWorks	AdventureWorks_SS_1
2	AdventureWorks	AdventureWorks_SS_2
3	AdventureWorks	AdventureWorks_SS_3
4	AdventureWorks	AdventureWorks_SS_4
5	AdventureWorks	AdventureWorks_SS_5
6	AdventureWorks	AdventureWorks_SS_6

Figure 9-6. *Query results correlating snapshots to their source databases*

You could include the Creation_Date field from sys.databases when listing snapshots. However, the purpose of a given snapshot can only be derived automatically when you follow a solid naming convention.

Using Database Snapshots to Address Process and User Error

Snapshots can be used for many purposes. For disaster recovery, though, the utility of snapshots lies primarily in their ability to help you deal with process and user errors.

Dealing with Process Errors

With respect to disaster recovery, database snapshots are probably best used to deal with process errors. These errors occur during either an automatic or manual process, such as planned maintenance or database updates. Take a snapshot of the database before the process (and use a descriptive name for the snapshot, such as AdventureWorks_BeforePriceUpdate_SS). If there's any sort of problem with the maintenance or update, simply apply the snapshot. Once you're satisfied that everything is working properly, delete the snapshot. Everyone at one time or another has done DELETE FROM TABLE and then gone, "Whoops, I forgot the WHERE clause." With database snapshots, there should be no excuse for data loss due to errors like that.

Dealing with User Errors

The most difficult situation to deal with is a simple keying error. Maybe an order-entry clerk typed in the wrong quantity or removed an entire account. Discovering those issues and correcting them is a DBA's worst nightmare.

There are two ways you can use snapshots to deal with this type of situation. You can 1) create a periodic series of snapshots to restore from, or 2) use a snapshot to try to identify what exactly has changed with the production database. Both methods have major benefits and major shortcomings.

In the first scenario, you could create an automated job to generate snapshots on an hourly basis. The snapshots should be named so that the time of day is easily recognizable—something like `AdventureWorks_SS_0700`. If you have a serious user error, simply apply the appropriate snapshot. The upside of this technique is that there is almost no downtime for your database; the downside is that there will be data loss. If availability is your primary concern, this technique works nicely.

The second scenario works essentially the same way in that you create periodic snapshots, but probably less frequently (maybe once or twice a day). When a user error occurs, you can query the snapshot to see what the database looked like before the mistake was made and generate a script to either replace the lost data or remove improper information. The key benefit to this approach is that data loss is unlikely; the drawback is that it could take quite some time to diagnose the situation, especially if you don't have access to an automated database-compare tool.

Deciding which approach to use comes down to knowing what is most important for your system: uptime or zero data loss. Be sure that the business owners of the system understand the benefits and drawbacks of each approach.

Understanding Other Uses for Database Snapshots

Snapshots are far more than just a disaster recovery tool. In fact, disaster recovery is probably the least of their many uses. The following sections briefly introduce you to some of the other benefits that can be had from using snapshots.

Point-in-Time Reporting

In environments where data changes frequently, it can be useful to create a snapshot to keep a history of the state of a database. You could create a snapshot each month and use that to compare sales data from month to month. Of course, you could achieve the same thing by using Reporting Services and using historical reports.

Creating a Reporting Interface to a Mirrored Database

One way to leverage the standby end of a database mirror configuration is to create a snapshot of that database. Users can then at least have a read-only view of the data. This technique can come in handy when multiple developers or users need a temporary snapshot of the database, either for reporting or testing purposes.

Leveraging Snapshots in Development

One area I see database snapshots being used extensively (perhaps excessively) is within development environments. Since SQL Server 2005 expands on the level of development that you can do with the database, having a technique to test a database change and quickly revert back is ideal. Enter database snapshots.

Say you create a new set of stored procedures, but before putting them on the server, you make a database snapshot. After applying them, you notice that you did more harm than good with your changes. You apply the snapshot—rinse and repeat. This can apply to raw development, unit testing, and quality assurance—you name it.

This poses a potential problem. If the developers have the rights to create snapshots, uncoordinated "snapping back" could be surprising to other developers. If you're in charge of creating snapshots, that may create an undue and sporadic workload. These are not technology problems, though; these are process issues that you need to address before using the technology.

Be Careful When Restoring

Looking through this list of potential uses, there are a number of situations where you could use snapshots in non–disaster recovery situations. Take care in mixing snapshot functionality within the same database if you ever anticipate "snapping back." Remember that list of requirements for restoring a snapshot? You must remove all existing snapshots. If you have to revert back, and other snapshots exist for something like point-in-time reporting, those latter snapshots will be completely gone. Restoring to a snapshot will result in data loss not only to the database itself, but also to all other snapshots created on the same source database.

Database Snapshots and Disaster Scenarios

So how do database snapshots fit in with the disaster categories? You've already seen that they fit well with process and user errors. Here's how they work with five disaster categories:

- *Environmental*: Since database snapshots require an active database in order to be used, they are of absolutely no help in the event of a tornado, fire, flood, or power outage. One of the requirements of the source database is that it cannot be restored. The only way snapshots can be included in an off-site backup is if you take a cold backup of all the database files.

- *Hardware*: As with environmental errors, snapshots have nearly no application when it comes to hardware errors. In a situation where the disk array survives and the server can be prepared, the standard recovery process of bringing a database back online should return the database to the point of the failure.

- *Media*: Snapshots have absolutely no use in the event of media failures. You can't back up a snapshot, and you can't restore a database that has snapshots attached to it, so if you lose the disk array that the database uses, the snapshots will be completely invalid.

- *Process*: Database snapshots shine with process errors. Any automated or manual process should be preceded by the creation of a snapshot. Used properly, snapshots should nearly eliminate the likelihood of a process error.

- *User*: I've already discussed two techniques for dealing with user errors. Snapshots have limitations, but they do provide a level of recovery that was previously unavailable in SQL Server. Restoring a snapshot can be extremely quick, which is critical for 24/7 systems.

Caveats and Recommendations

Follow these recommendations and best practices when using database snapshots, whether for recovery or for other purposes:

- *Follow proper naming conventions*: As you've already seen, naming snapshots properly is critical to using them effectively. Poorly named snapshots are of little use to anyone. It should go without saying at this point, but whatever naming convention you choose (e.g., DBNAME_DATETIME_SS), you should be consistent with its usage.

- *Manage the number of snapshots*: Snapshots have no automated expiration, so if left unchecked, they will continue to grow as necessary. If you have one or two snapshots, this probably won't be an issue. However, keep in mind that a database snapshot could theoretically grow as large as its source database, so maintaining a number of snapshots could consume disk space quickly. This is most likely to occur when using snapshots in a development or quality assurance environment.

- *Consider the impact on performance*: Obviously, adding a database snapshot creates additional resource demands on the server. Changes to the source database result in additional I/O. Queries against the database snapshot require additional processing time to determine whether the snapshot or the source database should be accessed. With a single snapshot, the impact should be negligible; the increase in resources would probably be measurable, but it's unlikely it would be perceivable. But change from one snapshot to ten, and you have a different story. If you have a large number of snapshots defined on an OLTP database, you may have a perceivable performance impact. It is unlikely that using database snapshots will bring the server to its knees, but a decrease in performance is something to keep in mind when using them.

- *Be wary of using snapshots as a single approach to dealing with user error*: Snapshots can be effective for mitigating user error, but they have serious limitations. There is no way to guarantee or specifically determine the amount of data loss when reverting to a snapshot. Be careful not to place total dependence on snapshots for dealing with user error. Also, make sure that the business owner of the system is aware of the consequences of using them.

- *Beware of granting access to the CREATE DATABASE command*: Anyone with the right to create a database can create a snapshot. If you have a development environment in which developers need to be able to create their own databases, they will also be able to create their own snapshots. As mentioned before, this can be extremely useful in a development/test/QA environment, but left unmanaged, it could completely consume disk space. If your environment dictates that developers create their own databases, make sure that you take the necessary steps to verify that you are managing your system resources effectively.

Summary

Database snapshots add yet another technique to your toolbox for dealing with disaster recovery. Snapshots represent an intriguing technology initially intended for high-availability databases, but as you've seen, you can use them in a number of creative ways. They aren't without their own set of issues, so you should always use them with caution. In Chapter 12, I'll show you how database snapshots fit in with all of the other disaster recovery options available within SQL Server 2005.

CHAPTER 10

■ ■ ■

Hardware Considerations

Following is a comment I hear from DBAs on a daily basis:

> *The server administrators must ensure everything gets written to tape; that isn't our*
> *responsibility.*

This is never said with disdain or defensively. The DBAs who say it really believe it isn't their responsibility. In many organizations, this is true by policy. Each department has specific responsibilities, and "crossing silos," so to speak, is not only discouraged but also forbidden. There is logic to this: you want staff members to confine their duties to a specific scope to avoid utter chaos. So when I say what I'm about to, I don't want you to think that I'm implying that you're slacking off or not doing what you believe is in the best interest of your company. Saying that hardware "isn't my responsibility" is a common viewpoint in the DBA world. However, the fact that it is a commonly held belief does not make it correct.

I believe that all DBAs are responsible for the hardware supporting their platform.

I fundamentally disagree with the notion that responsibility ends with one's particular job function or area of expertise. This line of thinking will ultimately end in, well, disaster. Is this a controversial claim? Absolutely. I have yet to be convinced otherwise, though. If you disagree, I'd love to have a good argument over a cup of coffee (in the morning) or a beer (any other time).

I am not saying DBAs have the responsibility to know absolutely everything there is to know about servers, tape devices, storage arrays, and network configurations. There are varying degrees of responsibility. What I am asserting is that if there is a technology that integrates somehow with SQL Server, DBAs have the responsibility to know enough to be able to discuss possible issues and solutions with a specialist in that technology.

When it comes to disaster recovery, what are the critical hardware factors involved? Well, simply put, hardware breaks eventually. Software only breaks if there is a flaw in the code; the passage of time alone does not cause software to degenerate. Not so with hardware.

Beyond out and out failure, hardware can present challenges by virtue of its very design. Bulk data storage, whether on hard drives or backup tapes, is based on magnetic media. A really strong magnetic field could cause data corruption. Network communication relies on a complex series of name-to-address resolution operations, routing from switch to switch to firewalls, which are thankfully becoming increasingly more prevalent. Server virtualization, while software-based, is being driven by the infrastructure community, not DBAs. What impact does that have?

In addition to all of the expensive solutions promising continual data protection and such, there is the ubiquitous question of power (the kind that comes from outlets in the walls, not political). Lack of sufficient power, power fluctuation, and loss of power all create a headache for the DBA.

If all of this weren't bad enough, there's the issue of heat. Without a proper HVAC system in place, the best-designed disaster recovery solution will fail simply due to heat wreaking havoc on the internal hardware.

I've glibly mentioned a large number of subjects that will appear in this chapter. I in no way expect to fully explain each of them. Those of you who are familiar with some of these subjects may object to some of my explanations ("Hey, that isn't exactly how it works"). I expect that. My goal with this chapter is to merely provide information for less-experienced DBAs to help them become conversant on the topics in this chapter when dealing with the appropriate experts in their organizations. What I present in this chapter is very much my interpretation, my viewpoint, and my recommendations (if you've read this far into the book, you already know that).

So what makes hardware issues so important that they warrant their own chapter in a book about SQL Server disaster recovery? For me, the answer is simple: hardware issues tend to be random in nature, while software issues tend to have detectable patterns. This isn't always the case, but I think everyone out there would say that hardware issues can be very difficult to troubleshoot. To exclude some sort of discussion of hardware in a book regarding disaster recovery would be almost negligent.

For each topic, I will present the technical details I believe to be crucial to becoming conversant on the topic, and I'll list issues related to disaster recovery that I've experienced.

Online Disk Storage

If there is any single type of hardware that a DBA *must* understand, it is hard disk storage. This *is* your data, your database, your SQL Server instance, and your operating system. No hard disk storage, no job.

> **Note** Many DBAs have a strong understanding of disk storage, configuration, and optimization when it comes to databases and potential issues involved. No DBA knows everything (myself included), and some may know nothing about disk storage (I hope I'm wrong about that). Even if you feel you fully understand the topic, don't disregard this section. Even if you learn one new tidbit, it's worth it.

One of the more frustrating aspects of storage technology is the overlap in terminology. It is easy to sound like a Luddite just by using the right term in the wrong way. When mistakes like that happen, you often won't even be given the respect to have your misunderstanding corrected by your hardware counterparts.

From a hardware perspective, the basics of storage I/O are relatively complex, even when a single internal disk drive is involved. I'll skip what happens when the write or read request goes through SQL Server to the OS and jump right down to the hardware.

Block Size vs. Stripe Size

It's common to confuse the terms *block size* and *stripe size*. Be clear and always use the proper term:

- *Block size*: Refers to how the disk storage physically stores information, and more specifically to the smallest number of bytes read or written at one time. When a disk partition (a drive letter) is formatted, it is created with a certain block size (see Figure 10-1). The default block size is 512 bytes. Considering that SQL Server writes data in 8K blocks, 16 reads or writes are required to transfer data for one SQL Server block. It is possible to change that block size, but only when creating the partition.

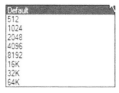

Figure 10-1. *Disk-partition block sizes*

- *Stripe size*: Applies specifically to certain methods of disk configuration where a parity stripe is written to provide redundancy (I'll cover these types of configurations shortly). Many hardware controllers are hard-coded to a specific stripe size, giving the impression that the block size configured for the disk itself isn't relevant.

AN ARRAY VS. A PARTITION

Surprisingly (at least to me), the difference between a partition and an array is often misunderstood by those who don't deal with storage as a regular job function. The result of that misunderstanding is often "getting what you asked for" rather than "getting what you need."

An array is a physical portion of a disk array that has been configured to use a certain number of disks with whatever level of fault tolerance is required. The storage administrator (who could be the same person as the server administrator, if you are using local drives) chooses which disks will participate in the array and then sets a specific level for protection and redundancy.

At the operating-system level, the server administrator configures one or more partitions on the newly constructed array. Each of these partitions is configured to use a specific file system, such as FAT, NTFS, or FAT32. After the file system is specified, the drive is created, formatted, and made available for use. Drive letters—C:, D:, and so forth—correspond to partitions.

As the DBA, you should be clear about what you're asking for when it comes to disk space. If you aren't careful, you could end up with one huge drive array with multiple partitions. If that happens, and if I/O is your concern (and if it isn't, you shouldn't be a DBA), your options for maximizing I/O performance just got a lot smaller.

When discussing disk performance, people often use block size and stripe size synonymously, when in fact the two are quite distinct. Be sure that you know the difference (which means being able to describe the difference) when discussing disk configuration with your hardware colleagues.

From a disaster recovery standpoint, I want to minimize the number of times that a drive is actively writing. If my disk is formatted in something other than 8K blocks, I'll face additional discrete writing operations at the low level of the disk. This increases my chances (however slim they may already be) of having a checksum or torn-page error. Even though SQL Server 2005 supports page-level recovery, I'd rather not recover an individual page if I can avoid it.

Locally Attached Storage

Any storage device that is directly attached to the database server is considered local storage. This includes drives within the server itself, or a disk drive attached to the server by means of an internal controller. For simple space management, disk drives are often placed in an externally powered disk cabinet attached directly to a server, as shown in Figure 10-2.

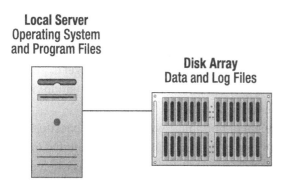

Local Server
Operating System
and Program Files

Disk Array
Data and Log Files

Figure 10-2. *In this typical deployment of locally attached storage, no other server may access the external disk array.*

For smaller implementations, the disk arrays are physically stored within the database server. There's absolutely nothing wrong with this, although it does place a lower limit on scalability (there is a limited amount of space for additional drives in an internal drive bay). Either way, when it comes to locally attached storage, you have two internal disk connectivity specifications to choose from: Advanced Technology Attachment (ATA) (or Serial Advanced Technology Attachment, known as SATA) and Small Computer System Interface (SCSI).). There are also two external connectivity specifications: USB (2.0) and FireWire.

ATA vs. SCSI

Personal computers generally have ATA or SATA drives. In short, ATA is an interface type for communicating with storage devices such as hard disks, CD-ROMs, DVD drives, and so on. ATA and SATA devices are relatively inexpensive and have become competitive with SCSI devices in terms of performance.

SCSI is usually associated with server configurations. Originally, it significantly outperformed ATA and provided options for RAID configurations that ATA-type drives couldn't offer. These days, SATA drives rival SCSI drives as far as performance. The one downside is that SATA controllers are generally limited in the number of drives they can support.

■**Note** SCSI, contrary to popular belief, has nothing to do with RAID specifically, nor does SATA. RAID is implemented either as a feature of the operating system or the disk controller itself. Plenty of SATA controllers out there don't support hardware-level RAID. The same can be said—but far less often—of SCSI controllers. ATA and SCSI are simply specifications for how to communicate with devices—nothing else. In common conversation, we sometimes talk of SCSI and RAID as being almost synonymous, but that isn't the case.

USB/FireWire

Not every company can afford expensive external storage devices. With the advent of USB 2.0 and FireWire, throughput to an external storage device is no longer extremely slow: it's just slow when compared to a local hard drive. There may be situations in which using a USB-based hard disk is an acceptable approach.

In Chapter 2, I brought up the concept of portability with respect to backups. By "portability," I mean the ability to easily make use of a backup in the event that original hardware on which that backup was made is not available. What happens when either you don't have the tape-drive capacity or a tape drive is temporarily damaged? How can you ensure the data is portable? Well, it certainly isn't a fast, sexy technique, but simply purchasing a number of large, portable USB drives for use as backup devices could work in a pinch. Would I advocate this as a long-term approach? Never. However, given the choice of no portability or low-tech USB hard drives, I'd take the latter.

Avoid early iterations of USB, though. I would only consider USB 2.0 or FireWire for locally attached storage. The original specifications for USB 1.0 or 1.1 are just too slow to use effectively for read/write data access.

■**Tip** Don't be quick to rule out simplistic approaches to solving any problem. Often, the most basic approach is the most effective. Resist the urge to have the "cool" technology. Having a cool technology solution to a problem isn't impressive to executive management, who only cares that a solution works and has the lowest cost possible.

RAID Configurations

Back in the day, RAID was a server-only feature, and an optional one at that. These days, no one would even dream of putting a server into production with a single hard disk. RAID configurations are now becoming commonplace even in desktop PCs.

You have a variety of RAID configurations to choose from, each with its own benefits and drawbacks. Some RAID specifications have essentially disappeared (RAID 2, 3, and 4), while new specifications have appeared as RAID itself has matured and evolved.

RAID 0

RAID 0 refers to simply taking a group of disks and striping data across them. This can be the fastest disk implementation possible, depending on the how well the I/O controller driving them behaves. The minimum is two physical drives (see Figure 10-3); the more drives you add to the RAID 0 array, the faster the disks will behave. This implementation is all about performance. While RAID 0 can be blazingly fast, if a single drive in the array fails, all data will be lost. In disaster recovery, RAID 0 is the "RAID that shall not be named" of disk configurations. Avoid it.

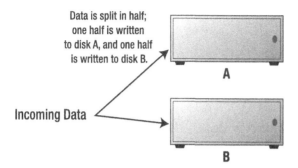

Figure 10-3. *RAID 0 at work. This setup offers no protection and no redundancy—just speed.*

RAID 0 is rarely used in business environments, but when I do see it, I always ask as many people as possible, "So, it's no big deal if you lose all of the data on your S: drive, huh?" This usually causes panic and lots of screaming, often accompanied by an angry mob carrying torches and pitchforks and storming the IT offices.

Personally, I use RAID 0, deliberately and with excellent results, in my personal gaming PC, which is built for speed—no data protection required. Try this at home only if you understand the implications (one dead drive means one dead PC).

RAID 1

Usually referred to simply as *mirroring*, RAID 1 is designed to protect a single drive against failure. Two drives are configured to appear as one array. All data written to the primary drive is also written to the mirror drive, as shown in Figure 10-4. If the primary drive should fail at any point, the secondary drive will take over and become the primary. Depending on the type of RAID controller involved, failover could be nearly transparent, require a reboot with no reconfiguration, or require a reboot with administrator intervention. RAID 1 always consists of two distinct drives—no more, no less. Because there is only a single drive, there is a ceiling to the speed capabilities of this RAID level. However, speed is not important—data protection is.

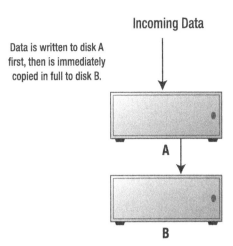

Incoming Data

Data is written to disk A first, then is immediately copied in full to disk B.

A

B

Figure 10-4. *RAID 1 offers pretty solid protection against data loss, but is not so fast or efficient when it comes to maximizing space usage.*

RAID 5

When dealing with RAID 0, there is clearly no protection against drive failure. If any drive in the stripe set fails, the entire array will be lost. The focus with RAID 0 is one of performance only. While RAID 1 does provide protection against drive failure, it does nothing to optimize performance, because throughput is still limited to what one drive can handle. RAID 1 is focused on data protection, not performance.

RAID 5 has long been the choice for the best mix between data protection and performance. Data is striped across all disks, as it is with RAID. In addition, one parity stripe is maintained as protection against loss of a drive. With that one parity stripe, a RAID 5 array can lose a single disk and continue to function. The remaining disks use their parity information to infer what the missing data is (see Figure 10-5).

Of course, if there is a disk failure, the culprit should be replaced as quickly as possible. Most controllers supporting RAID 5 will rebuild the array on the fly. While the RAID 5 array is down a disk or in its parity-rebuilding phase, loss of an additional disk would mean a loss of the entire array.

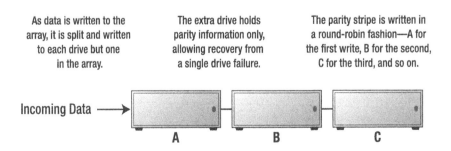

As data is written to the array, it is split and written to each drive but one in the array.

The extra drive holds parity information only, allowing recovery from a single drive failure.

The parity stripe is written in a round-robin fashion—A for the first write, B for the second, C for the third, and so on.

Incoming Data →   A   B   C

Figure 10-5. *RAID 5 allows for the loss of one drive while keeping the data array operational.*

RAID 6

Generally used only with SATA drives (where the number of devices is limited), RAID 6 is for those who are ultraparanoid about data loss. RAID 6 involves not one but *two* parity stripes. That means it would take three discrete disk failures before any data would be lost (see Figure 10-6).

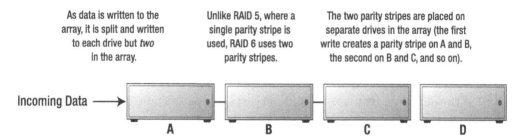

Figure 10-6. *With RAID 6, two drives can be lost, and the array remains available.*

The drawback with RAID 6 is that essentially two entire disks are wasted on storing parity information. If you had four 1TB drives arranged in a RAID 6 array, you would be left with only 2TB of usable storage.

MEAN TIME TO FAILURE

Disk drives include a specification, usually entitled "mean time to failure" (MTTF), which lists the amount of time that a drive should function before it fails. The key word here is *failure.* A disk drive has mechanical parts, and it will fail eventually. A drive won't necessarily fail when it has passed its MTTF rating (I've got a 20MB disk drive that is a decade old that still runs), but assuming that the drive will run through the life cycle of the server is a dangerous game to play. Having some sort of parity or mirror drive should be a given.

I recall a hardware colleague who once said to me, "Losing one drive, yeah, that could happen, but the odds of losing two or more are astronomical." For the longest time, I repeated that mantra, focusing on cost and potential array performance rather than protecting data. I personally learned my lesson when my own server lost not one, not two, not three, but four of its six drives within a week. Apparently, a bad batch of drives had hit the market, and my server was lucky enough to house them. These were quality, expensive drives as well, with a respectable MTTF rating.

RAID 0+1 and RAID 1+0

RAID 0+1 and RAID 1+0 both represent ways of combining striping (RAID 0) with mirroring (RAID 1) to gain performance while still maintaining solid protection against drive failure. Sometimes the plus sign (+) is omitted. In particular, RAID 1+0 is often referred to as RAID 10. However, one thing to watch out for is that some vendors use the term *RAID 10* to refer to what is really RAID 0+1.

Yes, there is a difference between RAID 0+1 and RAID 1+0. System administrators and vendors are sometimes confused about the difference. I once ran into a RAID controller that supposedly supported RAID 10, but upon implementation, I discovered that the controller really implemented RAID 0+1. That difference had a negative consequence, which I hope to clarify shortly.

The difference between 0+1 and 1+0 isn't simply academic. There is a major difference in terms of performance and data protection. Don't let anyone simply shrug their shoulders at you and insist that the two approaches are basically the same. Be sure you know which type you're implementing. RAID 0+1 is a mirror of stripes; RAID 1+0 is a stripe of mirrors.

■**Caution** Some RAID controller hardware vendors claim to support RAID 10, while in practice, they really implement 0+1. Don't rely solely on published specs or documentation; verify that when vendors say RAID 10, they *mean* RAID 10.

RAID 0+1 tends to perform slightly better than RAID 10. This performance increase is due to focusing on striping before mirroring, as shown in Figure 10-7.

Data is written to a stripe, then the entire stripe is mirrored.   **RAID 0+1**

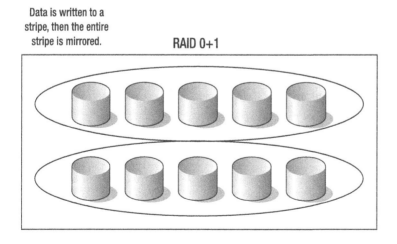

Figure 10-7. *RAID 0+1 writes a stripe first, then mirrors the stripe.*

If a drive is lost with a RAID 0+1 stripe set, it must be replaced by the entire mirrored stripe set—a process that may not be instantaneous or straightforward (depending on how RAID 0+1 is implemented by your vendor).

RAID 10 is better suited for disaster recovery, because it focuses on mirroring each drive first, then striping them all for performance (see Figure 10-8).

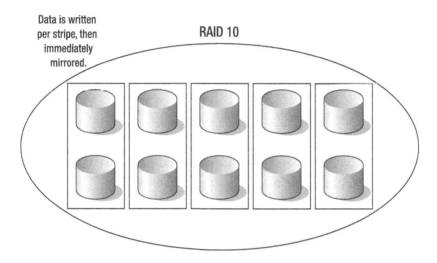

Figure 10-8. *RAID 10 immediately mirrors each write to a drive.*

If an individual drive is lost in a RAID 10 array, the mirror of that drive will come online immediately. In fact, it's possible to lose multiple drives and have the array still function as long as you don't lose both a drive and that same drive's mirror.

RAID 5+1

RAID 5+1 is a single-parity array in which each drive is mirrored. You need a minimum of six drives for this configuration, as shown in Figure 10-9.

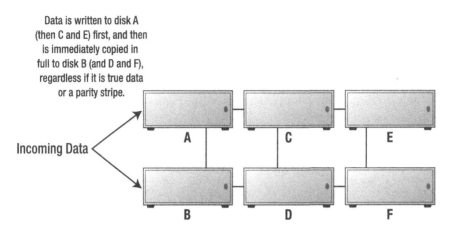

Data is written to disk A (then C and E) first, and then is immediately copied in full to disk B (and D and F), regardless if it is true data or a parity stripe.

Incoming Data

A   C   E

B   D   F

Figure 10-9. *RAID 5+1 provides excellent protection from drive failure.*

With RAID 5+1, it is possible to lose an entire stripe and still keep the array functional. The disks can be replaced and the parity stripe rebuilt online.

Vendor-Specific RAID

Once we cross over into the world of SAN hardware, there are a number of variations on the concept of RAID. Most SAN vendors have their own specifications that exceed or extend the data-protection capabilities of the standard RAID configurations. These nonstandard configurations usually maximize performance as well, without sacrificing data-protection capabilities.

Remote Storage

As long as storage is attached directly to a server, even via an external SCSI cabinet or a portable USB hard drive, there is a certain level of control that a DBA maintains. Once remote storage is used, control over I/O specifics can become difficult for a DBA. There are two basic types of remote storage: network-attached storage (NAS) and a storage area network (SAN).

NAS

The most basic of remote storage, NAS is nothing more than a set of disks with a basic operating system to make them appear on the network as if they were drives being shared from a full-blown server. NAS is certainly cost-effective; however, NAS devices are generally not designed for robust data protection. Generally, NAS devices are used for file server storage, not any sort of transactional database system.

I would personally only involve a NAS device in a backup process, probably just to store backup files. If they are on the same network backbone as your database server, they will hopefully have a reliable network connection. I would never use a NAS device to actually house active database files. Perhaps it is paranoia on my part, but I've run into one too many SQL Server databases that failed due to a network hiccup between them and the NAS devices.

SAN

In almost every large organization, all critical data is stored on a SAN device. Even mid-sized and smaller businesses are able to afford entry- and mid-level SAN hardware. You may wonder, what is a SAN device anyway? A SAN is a centrally administered storage server shared across a network of one or more application or database servers, as illustrated in Figure 10-10.

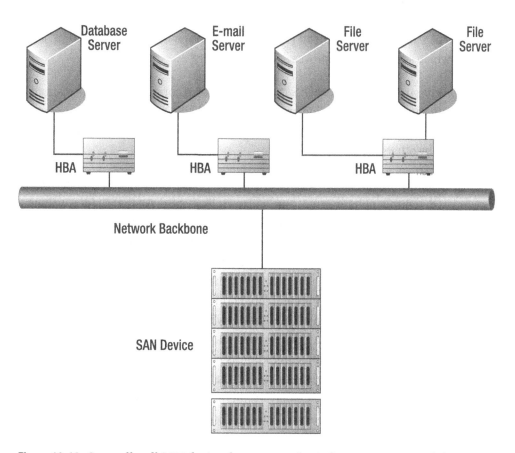

Figure 10-10. *Generally, all SAN devices have a complex infrastructure around them.*

A SAN is a complete storage system with highly tuned disk processing and high levels of memory cache. Designed to serve a large number of requests and multiple servers, SANs are sophisticated and complicated hardware devices. A SAN generally includes

- *The SAN itself*: Comprised of a huge number of drives, its own internal operating system, CPUs, and large amounts of RAM, the SAN can present multiple RAID arrays via separate I/O paths and logical unit numbers (LUNs).

- *Host bus adapters (HBAs)*: HBAs are special controller cards installed on servers to enable connectivity to the SAN itself. The type of adapter depends on the connectivity protocol used. Some connection protocols don't require a special piece of hardware but, rather, a software driver to enable communication over an existing network.

- *Some sort of HBA switch*: This is where the *network* in *storage area network* becomes apparent. NAS devices are simply plugged into existing network switches; SANs usually have their own network and thus require their own switching device. The switch coupled with an HBA creates a storage-only communication network, which significantly improves a SAN's reliability.

- *A communication protocol*: SANs have their own connectivity protocols, and these can vary widely depending on the vendor of the SAN and the requirements of your own infrastructure. The most popular are Fibre Channel and iSCSI, but there are many others.

Depending on the significance of your hardware investment, a SAN might be peppered with redundant hardware. There will most likely be disks that sit idle, waiting to be hot-swapped into a RAID array; redundant power supplies and HBA switches; and so on. Even entry- and mid-level SANs can have significant redundant systems in place.

SAN hardware generally requires a dedicated individual to act as a storage administrator. If you don't have such an individual in your organization, then you'll find it difficult to ensure that the SAN is configured optimally for your SQL Server storage.

The problem you're most likely to run into with a SAN configuration is having all of the data placed on a single array, without you knowing for certain what type of array it is. From a performance standpoint, combining as many disks as possible into a single array is generally best. From a recovery standpoint, that may not be the case. No matter how much hardware redundancy there may be, there's always some single point of failure. Ideally, you want to physically separate transaction logs, data files, backup files, and perhaps specific filegroups onto different data arrays. Don't be intimidated by the complexity of a SAN, and argue your point when it comes to disaster recovery.

SAN-A-PHOBIA

It's common for DBAs making the transition from locally attached storage to a SAN environment to be skeptical about the I/O configuration for the various data files/filegroups for their database. Their skepticism and paranoia is, at times, valid. Some SANs are installed and configured by an outside vendor with little or no knowledge to transfer to in-house staff (this is more common with small- to mid-sized companies where IT budgets are tight). While the DBA requests separate I/O for certain files or filegroups, the ultimate configuration may be one, single, huge disk array. To make things worse, there may be only one path into the SAN, shared by everyone.

Tape Storage

Backups must be portable. Traditionally, portability is a side effect of magnetic tape storage. I always advocate that backups should ultimately end up on tape storage. Ideally, I'd like to see multiple copies of backups retained: perhaps one on disk and one on tape.

Tape drives have multiple storage formats. At the time of this writing, the more popular are

- *Digital Linear Tape (DLT)*: These drives come in a number of varieties, with storage capacity going up to 800GB and support for native hardware data compression (probably about a 1.5 to 1 ratio).

- *Linear Tape-Open (LTO)*: Also available in a number of flavors (currently LTO-1 to LTO-4, with LTO-5 and LTO-6 on the way), LTO is (at least as I've seen) growing into the de facto tape storage format for Windows-based servers. Currently, the LTO format supports up to 800GB in uncompressed storage (with built-in hardware compression available). LTO-5 and LTO-6 are slated to support 1.6TB and 3.2TB, respectively.

Tape drives may also be configured into tape libraries, groups of drives acting as one to increase capacity, or tape autoloader mechanisms, which robotically replace tapes as they fill (again, to increase capacity).

One of the greatest challenges with tape storage is in the practical aspect of cataloging and storing tapes. In most organizations, tape storage is either maintained centrally, using backup software to assist in maintaining a record of what backups are on what tape, or by a third-party that houses the tapes in an off-site storage location. Sometimes cataloging and storing tape drives is done extremely efficiently. Sometimes it is not. As a DBA, you must have a handle on how this is done, so you can effectively request the correct backup tape and receive it in a timely manner in a disaster scenario.

Archival Storage

In talking with colleagues, I often argue about the difference between true data archiving and data partitioning. I see archiving as the removal of data from an active system, more or less "boxing" the information for long-term storage (think of a warehouse full of file cabinets with handwritten records). Data partitioning, in my opinion, is the moving aside of *soon to be archived* data.

The idea behind partitioning is to separate seldom-used data from more active records (usually for performance purposes) while ensuring that the data is still accessible with no administrative intervention. Such data is not archived in the sense that I prefer; such data is not completely removed from the system.

I seem to be losing the argument that archiving and partitioning are separate and distinct functions of data. The popular view today of data archival essentially matches my own view of partitioning. "Archived" data isn't really archived at all. Rather, it is moved to a separate device while still retaining uninterrupted user access. C'est la vie.

■**Note** One belief I do stand by is that archiving in any form is not the equivalent of backing up your data, and thus is not sufficient for disaster recovery purposes.

Tape

A tape library might be used as a method of true archiving. However, it is extremely important to resist the urge to kill two birds with one stone and use the same "archival" tapes as your backup source. The business need for data archiving is different than one for disaster recovery. You may find that the archival process does not include all data required to restore a system to a functioning state; instead, archiving might only retain records that have business significance. Never rely on an archival process for backups.

Low-Cost SAN or NAS

"Archival" hardware devices are becoming common now, with basic NAS or SAN devices used to house data that may still be accessed (unlike the tape scenario) on demand. If your organization decides to use this type of data-life-cycling approach to archiving and wants to include portions of your database, stamp your feet and shout up at the sky, "THIS ISN'T THE SAME AS DISASTER RECOVERY!" That is, if your organization wants to use these devices as part of your disaster recovery approach.

Continuous Data Protection

When approaching disaster recovery, our ultimate goal is no data loss, ever. There is a trend in the market right now to offer either software- or hardware-based continuous data protection (CDP). Data is continually being transferred to either another device (high-speed disk to low-speed disk, or low-speed disk to tape). While I have high hopes for these approaches, numerous aspects to their implementation make me worry. Also, be aware that CDP is quickly becoming a buzzronym, so use the acronym with care.

CDP systems usually involve a combination of software and hardware to achieve a continual transfer of live data to a secondary, sometimes remote, system. If the active system fails, the CDP-based system will come online in a matter of minutes (sometimes seconds).

Some CDP systems are hardware-based geolocated SANs, where data is transferred bit by bit to a remote location. These geolocated SANs are generally composed of expensive hardware—a luxury that many of us cannot afford. For those who can afford geolocated SANs, they should not serve as a replacement for a disaster recovery plan. What if the network link hiccups and corrupts data? What if the secondary data center is completely destroyed?

CDP is a great augmentation toward a disaster recovery plan, but it is not sufficient on its own. Backup/restore planning is still necessary, as is preparing for user or process disasters, and so on.

Virtualization

A popular practice these days is to consolidate multiple servers onto a more powerful server using some sort of virtualization software. Virtualization refers to the creation of separate virtual hardware environments, as shown in Figure 10-11.

Not too long ago, I would have cringed at the thought of virtualizing any database server, even in a test environment. At the time, I believed I was correct in my squeamishness with virtual hardware. Times change quickly, though, especially in the world of technology, and the virtualization software available today is quite sophisticated.

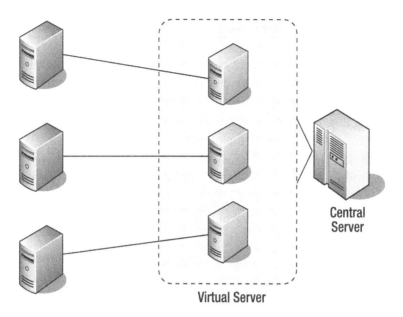

Figure 10-11. *Virtualization places all of your software eggs in one hardware basket.*

Virtualization software has become quite complex, allowing the administrator to designate specific hardware on the host system for each individual virtual system. From a disaster recovery standpoint, virtualization still places a heavy responsibility on the host system. However, if you were to take the individual budgets for several smaller servers and combine them, the result could be a much more robust, stable, high-end host platform. Yes, if you lose the host, you'll lose everything, but if you invest in higher-end hardware for the host, there will be a lower probability of hardware failure in the first place. Even if there is a hardware failure, your increased investment probably includes a significant improvement in hardware support as well. I'm still not sold on the virtualization approach, but I believe it at least deserves the merit of evaluation rather than the convenience of abject dismissal.

Network Issues

One of the most misunderstood of all hardware problems, network issues are often the most difficult to troubleshoot, much less resolve. Networking has always been considered a complex, almost mysterious subject. I recall early in my career doing support for Windows 3.1 and Windows 3.11. The latter included peer-to-peer networking, which we all feared troubleshooting. Of course, the main problem was that we just didn't fully understand how things worked. The following sections detail some critical networking topics on which you need to have some basic understanding in order to work effectively with your network administrators.

Latency vs. Bandwidth

When people start talking about network issues, the first thing that comes to mind is bandwidth:

> Business analyst: *Our application runs fine if you run it with the database server on a local network. When a customer connects from a remote network, the performance is impacted to the point of making the application unusable.*

> Manager: *Looks like we need more bandwidth.*

I don't know how many times I've listened to a conversation like this, mentally banging my head against an imaginary wall. Without performing other tests on the network (and testing for bandwidth issues is quite difficult), declaring "we need more bandwidth" is a hasty and probably incorrect solution. Latency is more likely to be the cause of the performance problem.

I generally explain bandwidth and latency with the analogy of a freeway. I often drive to the airport in Chicago, which means I travel on Interstate 90 (I-90), which is a toll road. It is also a road that is in a constant state of repair (there's a joke that Chicago has two seasons: winter and construction). As you get close to Chicago, I-90 becomes four or five lanes and has a speed limit of 65 mph. Of course, you won't necessarily move at 65 mph.

The slowdown is not due to a lack of lanes. Instead, it is due to all the cars stopping to pay tolls or slowing down while moving through construction zones. The size of I-90 could increase to ten lanes, and I'd still have to slow down when nearing Chicago. Networks are a lot like the stretch of I-90 with which I've become so familiar, as you can see in Figure 10-12.

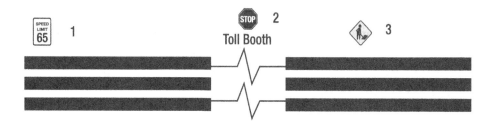

Figure 10-12. *Networks, bandwidth, and latency are easily understood if you think of them as highways, lanes, and tollbooths and construction.*

The following aspects of networking are well illustrated by the highway analogy:

- *Networks have a speed limit*: Essentially, networks function at the speed of light, because they're simply passing electrons over a wire or fiber-optic cable. Similarly, I-90 has a general speed limit of 65 mph. It's not the Autobahn, but the interstate still offers a decent speed limit.

- *Network transmissions need to stop periodically*: Routers, firewalls, and switches need to interrogate network packets being sent, briefly stopping them before forwarding them on. Similarly, I have to stop at tollbooths on the interstate (it seems like every five miles).

- *Poor-quality cabling or malfunctioning devices can cause network packets to be resent*: Similarly, road construction slows down my approach to the airport.

Why does separating bandwidth from latency matter to disaster recovery? Any process, backup, or mitigation technique can be affected by network difficulties. Database mirroring in particular is susceptible to latency issues. If network packets are taking 200 to 300 milliseconds to get from point A to point Q on a network, and database mirroring is set to synchronous mode, users will see a definite lag when typing in data. More often than not, latency is the cause of network problems rather than a lack of bandwidth (unless you're connecting systems using a dial-up connection).

Name Resolution

The current Windows standard (Windows 2000 and later) for name resolution is DNS. However, a number of features still require the older Windows Internet Name Service (WINS) resolution. WINS and DNS are very different.

WINS maps a NetBIOS computer name to a specific IP address, recording it in a Jet database (yes, that would be a Microsoft Access-type .mdb file). NetBIOS names typically do not have an Internet-style name at the end. For example, you would have a name like JAMESLAPTOP rather than JAMESLAPTOP.Somedomain.com. If support for NetBIOS names is required, a WINS server must be running on the network. If it isn't, connecting to a machine by its NetBIOS name may not work.

DNS maps a fully qualified domain name (e.g., JAMESLAPTOP.Somedomain.com) to an IP address and stores that information. This is a far more robust name-to-IP address-mapping technique than WINS. If you're lucky, your network will have no need for WINS or NETBIOS naming.

Why is name resolution important to disaster recovery? I don't think I can count the number of times I've been informed that my database server was down when really it was a problem with name resolution (either WINS or DNS was unavailable for some reason). When someone tells you your server is down, check for yourself rather than taking it on faith.

Routing and Firewalls

Ah, routing. I can't name how many times I've run into an issue that ended in someone mumbling, "Oh, there just isn't a physical path defined." If that doesn't mean anything to you, read closely.

Routers and switches are network devices that basically have information on where the next step in the network communication path is. Going over the Internet, you may hit dozens of routers or switches. No router or switch has a complete path defined between every network node; it generally has information about where to forward the request (something like a default gateway).

When you add a new server on an internal network, it may be necessary to update your internal routers. Furthermore, switches that send requests to that server should remain on the internal network, or those requests should be forwarded to a special zone that exists between the internal network and the outside world. If you don't do these things, then requests to the new server may be sent off into oblivion. With the latest switch and router hardware, the sort of reconfiguration I've just described is less of a problem than it was formerly, but a lot of older network devices are still in use. Don't forget about establishing a physical network location if you happen to have some of these older devices.

Why is all this important to disaster recovery? What happens when you replace a downed server? Will it have the same IP address? Perhaps not. It may be necessary to manually update your internal networking devices so they route information to the replacement server.

Authentication

The current Windows standard for authentication is Kerberos, which itself is not a Windows standard. Kerberos is an industry-defined authentication method. The authentication method used previously by Windows was NT LAN Manager (NTLM). This is essentially the same authentication method that was used when DOS PCs were networked.

Kerberos hands out a "ticket" when a user authenticates, and this ticket only contains the information that the user is who he says he is. NTLM, on the other hand, provides a token that has not only the authentication of the user, but also a list of the resources to which the user has access. (Anyone remember being told to log off and back on to the network after a permission change?)

Problems arise when both authentication schemes are active on the network. SQL Server tries to authenticate first with Kerberos and then move on to NTLM if Kerberos fails. At times, it seems like the order gets reversed. Have you ever seen errors like these?

```
"Could not create SSPI context."
"No server principal name found."
```

There are literally dozens of variations, and the most common resolution is to ensure that a Service Principal Name (SPN) gets created in Active Directory. If you see these errors, just check the Microsoft Knowledge Base; you'll get a hit right away with directions on troubleshooting the issue.

Power

Often an overlooked hardware gremlin, power issues can present themselves in a variety of seemingly unrelated events. Random reboots, network hiccups, and even corrupt backups can be the result of an inconsistent power supply. Some power problems can be handled by simply installing redundant power supplies. Sometimes there's nothing you can do to protect against power issues.

Power Surges/Lapses

I recently encountered a mission-critical server that was disabled by a lightning strike. It had surge protection and a basic Uninterruptible Power Supply (UPS). Apparently, neither was sufficient. Considering the massive amount of power a lightning strike can generate, it's hard to conceive of any sort of protection being sufficient in the event of a direct strike.

Just as devastating as a direct lightning strike is a massive power failure. On August 14, 2003, someone working at a major power plant made a slight mistake while configuring something. The result was the now infamous Northeast Blackout of 2003 in which the upper East Coast of the United States and eastern Canada lost power. For databases housed in data centers with their own backup power supplies, this incident may not have caused a massive panic attack for the DBAs. In smaller organizations without a dedicated backup power generator, let's just say that sedatives were probably needed for those DBAs.

UPS

A UPS is actually very poorly named. The goal of a UPS is not to act as a backup power generator for prolonged activity without main power. Instead, its goal is to supply enough power to a server long enough to shut it down in a safe and controlled manner. Many UPS vendors supply software utilities that automate this process. If power is in question, the answer "we have a UPS on the server" is not an appropriate response to the question "are we prepared if we lose power to the SQL Server?"

Heat

Temperature is secondary to, but tightly coupled with, hardware. Because all computing components essentially channel and use electrical power, they generate heat. How much heat is generated depends on how many devices are involved and what methods are used to control temperature.

Most devices (such as computers, laptops, servers, and network devices) employ at least a single fan to control heat. Many use multiple fans and heat sinks as well as redundant cooling methods in the event of a single failure. Data centers and dedicated server rooms also have fairly sophisticated methods of controlling the environment, including moisture and temperature.

As a recently rehabilitated computer gamer (OK, I have my relapses), getting a PC to perform optimally usually means ensuring that heat is kept to a minimum. Some gamers go so far as to employ Freon-based cooling systems to ensure that their over-clocked CPU and graphic cards won't crash while playing the hottest new game on the market. I doubt that any single database server would generate the same sort of heat that a top-of-the-line gaming PC would, so elaborate internal cooling systems would probably be wasted on a SQL Server machine. Still, heat issues can impact any electronic system, so we should remain diligent and account for temperature control in our disaster recovery discussion.

Internal System Heat

If you've ever had a PC or server simply lock up with no response from the operating system, you've most likely overheated the system. Internal cooling for a computer—whether a PC or a server—is a critical function.

CPUs generate an incredible amount of heat. They have heat sinks physically attached to them to keep them at a reasonable temperature. Fans are used to blow hot air out of the casing in an attempt to maintain temperature. Usually server hardware devices have a number of redundant cooling fans. However, fans are mechanical devices and will fail. If a computer reaches an internal temperature that is dangerous for the CPU, the hardware will halt operation by design. Some systems have hardware-based heat sensors that will shut down a server if it even comes close to overheating.

Ensuring that a server has sufficient cooling is nothing to take for granted. Even with the appropriate amount of cooling fans, a system can still overheat. The outward-facing fan assemblies will also slowly collect dust and can become clogged. I've even seen some servers physically positioned so their cooling fans are pushed against a wall; as a result, there is no place to blow out the hot air generated within.

External Heat Issues (HVAC)

We all appreciate effective air conditioning in hot summer months. However, the HVAC technician is one of the most underappreciated players in the IT world. Without a properly environment-controlled data center, there can be no such thing as high availability, and disaster recovery becomes a constant concern.

Any room that houses server equipment will be hot. Very hot. Why? All of the server devices use internal cooling methods to blow the hot air away from the CPU. All of that hot air has to go somewhere; thus, the temperature of the room will rise. If left uncontrolled, servers will overheat and lock up randomly or reboot.

There was a time when server rooms and data centers didn't exist. People only used server closets. The smaller the physical space that a server occupies, the faster it will overheat the environment and cause havoc. Today, building codes (at least in the United States) define what qualifies as a true data center. There are specific rules about controlling humidity, minimizing the risk of internal flooding, and maintaining a consistent temperature. If you walk into a real data center today, you may want to even put on a sweatshirt.

Even if you have only a handful of servers to manage, being able to maintain the temperature is crucial to a successful disaster recovery plan.

Hardware and Disaster Categories

Do hardware considerations have an impact on how we look at disaster categories? Absolutely. The following list shows how the specific hardware issues apply to each category:

- *Environmental*: Much of what I've mentioned involves controlling the environment. Power and heat issues affect every device in your data center.

- *Hardware*: This chapter is all about hardware. The question is: do you understand your hardware components enough to help ensure that your SQL Server data is insulated from hardware-related issues? This chapter offers a basic overview; there's always more to learn.

- *Media*: Understanding different RAID levels is critical to ensuring that your data is protected in the manner it requires.

- *Process*: Hardware environments present their own types of process errors. You, as the DBA of a critical system, should be notified if there are changes to the hardware environment. For example, you need to know if someone is upgrading a DNS server, potentially making your SQL Server unavailable to users.

- *User*: Hardware specialists (just like DBAs) can make mistakes. Don't be surprised if you're faced with a hardware-related user error (e.g., if someone accidentally shuts down the wrong server in the data center).

Caveats and Recommendations

If I could give only one recommendation, it would simply be, "know thy hardware." The less you understand about your hardware environment, the more you're at the mercy (or will) of the hardware experts around you. Perhaps I'm a bit on the paranoid side, but I would rather have a basic understanding of as many technologies as possible than rely on faith that others will do what is necessary to protect and preserve the data for which I'm responsible.

In addition to "know thy hardware," I do actually have a few other thoughts to leave you with:

- *Be conversant*: I'm not advocating that you become an expert on hardware, a SAN specialist, or anything like that. The key is to be able to converse with those who are. The more you know the more effective you can be when it comes to developing and implementing a sound disaster recovery plan.

- *Don't confuse bandwidth with latency*: The majority of network problems that I've faced have actually been due to latency issues rather than bandwidth. Truly understanding the difference is necessary when interacting with the network specialist to see what types of tests are being performed.

- *Don't confuse backing up your data with archiving your data*: If your organization implements some sort of data-archival plan, you must remain adamant that archiving is not sufficient for a backup/recovery plan, and it should not be mixed with an existing plan. The two serve different business needs.

- *Don't confuse redundancy with backup*: Having redundant hardware devices is not the same thing has having backup devices. Even if you have a redundant power supply in your server, losing a power supply *will* place you at risk. You should also attempt to obtain a backup power supply to replace the failed redundant power supply to ensure availability.

- *No one knows everything*: This chapter provided a brief overview of some of the hardware issues you may face as a DBA. You can't be expected to know everything, and you can't expect others to know DBA-specific items as they relate to hardware. Keep the dialog going with your hardware staff, and both of you should benefit. Never stop talking.

Summary

In this chapter, I covered numerous issues related to hardware, specifically discussing how they might affect SQL Server. As a DBA, you must have at least a conceptual understanding of a wide range of topics in order to interact successfully with the rest of the business. As I said in the opening, I consider it to be bordering on irresponsibility to play the ostrich with your head in the sand. The less you know about the big picture, the less effective you'll be at your specialized position.

CHAPTER 11

■ ■ ■

Disaster Recovery Planning

Now that I've covered all of the technical variables involved in disaster recovery planning, it's time to take that information and combine it in the most effective manner. Up through SQL Server 2000, this meant making a solid backup plan, documenting it, and testing it. You could also use clustering to mitigate certain scenarios, such as hardware/ application failures or operating system errors.

As you've seen, SQL Server 2005 introduces a number of new technologies that you can apply to disaster recovery. Not only do you have new options, but you can also combine those options in interesting ways that will fundamentally change the way you think about disaster recovery. You'll still always need to back up databases, but now you can mix that with clustering, database mirroring, or using database snapshots for user or process disasters. A creative combination can result in an extremely well-protected database.

Unfortunately, all of these additional technologies go for naught without actual disaster recovery planning—that is, documenting, testing, and practicing. Disaster recovery planning should be considered an ongoing process, constantly reevaluated and adjusted to meet new requirements. It's not a static project to be completed. Instead, it's a DBA's ongoing job responsibility.

In this chapter, I'll discuss the individual steps in the process of disaster recovery planning, and I'll show you examples of actual disaster scenarios.

Putting It All Together

Dealing with technology is easy. Planning is not.

Planning for anything in the IS/IT world is deceptively complex, no matter what the topic. Deciding not to invest time in planning can result in some extremely surprising results. On the other hand, if you go to the other extreme and spend too much time planning, you waste time and resources needed to carry out the actual work. Focusing on the wrong subjects during the planning phase can lead to mass confusion when it comes to actual implementation. Throw in the chaos that can surround planning meetings (much more on this in Chapter 12), and the prospect of disaster recovery planning is enough to keep you up at night.

To try to help you sleep better, I'm going to propose an approach to disaster recovery planning that you can apply to other situations as well. The approach I take is based on the experiences I've had, both positive and negative.

Guiding Principles

The first step is to establish some principles that everyone involved in planning for disaster recovery can and should follow. Establishing common ground with others on your team will take you a long way toward having a successful disaster recovery plan. Here are the main principles I (try) to follow:

- *Do not confuse plan with task*: I'm guilty of doing this on a regular basis. In most scenarios involving disaster recovery planning, I'm involved more with helping the planning portion and less with carrying out the plans. When I'm in a position where I need to both establish and document the plan, I may come up with great ideas and simple procedures but then neglect to actually put them in place. Planning should be abstract. Tasks are real. A plan implies a task list. By focusing on the planning side, ignoring the concrete tasks involved is easy to do.

- *Plan for the big picture, but act on the wallet-sized photo*: When working on a disaster recovery plan, keep your big-picture goals in mind: reducing data loss and maintaining system availability. However, you need to discuss the simplest of steps toward achieving those big-picture goals.

- *Document while doing*: Yes, we all hate documentation, but it must be done. If you're the sole DBA, a disaster can always occur. If there are multiple DBAs where you work, they'll need to be familiar with what's being done. I'm horrible with documentation myself. I find that the best way to ensure documentation is to continually write things down and never wait until after the fact to create the documentation.

- *Assume nothing*: I'll avoid any cliché comments about this. The bottom line is that a disaster recovery plan should include the most obvious of information. You never know what information will be obvious to whom when the plan is needed.

Note Don't be shy about stating the most obvious principles. They may seem intuitive to you, but the same concept may mean something completely different to someone else. Just like everything else with disaster recovery, expect the worst.

Risk, Response, and Mitigation

As mentioned in Chapter 1, disaster recovery planning is a combination of preparing a response in the event of a disaster *and* reducing the likelihood that a given disaster will occur. Therefore, you must create a plan that identifies potential events, the *risk* of those events (the probability of occurrence and potential impact), the response plan, and what you'll do to mitigate those risks.

Identifying Risk

It's often difficult to know where to start. All too often, people rush in and throw any solution in place before taking a moment to consider the situation. Risk identification should be a formal, documented part of a disaster recovery plan.

Note that I'm calling this *risk identification* and not *risk management*. I'm not advocating a long, drawn-out process or an exhaustive analysis of financial risk. There is a place for that sort of thing, and it certainly has value, but when creating a disaster recovery plan, you need to keep things simple and iterative in order to get the process moving. If you hire a risk-management firm to help you analyze your company *before* you move on to establishing response and mitigation plans, it could be six months before anything is actually done. And in the technology world, your environment may have already changed.

■**Tip** Don't waste time analyzing and documenting obvious risks that have been addressed already. Known issues and deficiencies have the highest risk rating possible. If you know you aren't currently backing up your system and you know you really should be, it's comical to think that you should take the time to identify the impact of not having a backup—just do something. That doesn't mean you shouldn't include it in the documentation of your overall plan, but don't bother analyzing what you already know.

I've defined risk as a combination of likelihood of occurrence vs. the impact of occurrence. It sounds like I might have a mathematical formula in mind; I do. Don't worry, though; you won't need a degree in statistical analysis or actuarial science. I have very simple formulas in mind. I do think it's important to quantify things somehow, and not just because I'm a database geek and like to quantify things. Without quantification, setting a priority list is simply a judgment call. If left this way, you open the door for political squabbling as to who is in the best position to make the judgment call (I'll discuss this more in Chapter 12).

I use one of two formulas (more like one formula with different numerical definitions). The first assigns a ranking to both probability and impact and multiplies the two:

```
PROBABILITY * IMPACT = RISK
```

The result is the numerical, overall risk of the disaster, which you can use to rank your activities. Pretty simple, isn't it? Well, it has a few drawbacks. First, if you select a wide range of numbers to represent probability, it will take more time and thought to choose the appropriate risk level. I never use a scale of more than 1–10 for either, and usually I try to keep it to 1–5, with the highest number being the greatest probability or impact. Trust me, if you move to a scale greater than 10, you'll spend far too much time on risk identification.

The other drawback to the arbitrary weighting technique is that if you use a narrow scale, as I've advocated, you'll have numerous ties, which again will require you to make a judgment call. If you do have numerous high-level ties, this tells you two things: 1) you have a lot of work to do, and 2) you aren't working iteratively. Work on things in smaller groups and get started.

The second formula that I'll accept (but personally dislike) involves "real" numbers. Probability is represented as a percentage, and impact is represented as a dollar amount:

```
PROBABILITY (.01-1) * IMPACT ($0.00) = RISK ($0.00)
```

The reason that I say I'll accept it rather than like it is that often in order to justify spending time on planning and putting any response or mitigation plans in place, you have to attempt to cost-justify the activities to upper management. It's a reality that I sometimes face, and you may too. I personally think it's a bit silly: you cannot cost-justify disaster plans. Companies don't cost-justify things such as liability or workers' compensation insurance—those are costs of doing business. In fact, what you really want is for all of the money spent on disaster recovery to be wasted, because that means you'll never have a disaster scenario in the first place. (Don't get your hopes up—you will.) Try "selling" disaster recovery up the corporate ladder with that line of thinking and see how high you climb. They'll probably take away your ladder; you'll be lucky if you're left with a footstool.

The end documentation, whatever the method, should be simple. Remember, you don't want to get bogged down in this step, but you don't want to ignore it either. Tables 11-1 and 11-2 show two real examples of what I've presented as documentation (and later worked from with my clients).

Table 11-1. *Assessing Risk with Rankings*

Disaster	Type	Probability (1–5)	Impact (1–5)	Risk	Response?	Mitigation?
Tornado	Environmental	2	5	10	Yes	No
Disk failure	Media	3	4	12	Yes	Yes

Table 11-2. *Assessing Risk with Percentages and Dollar Amounts*

Disaster	Type	Probability (%)	Impact ($)	Risk	Response?	Mitigation?
Tornado	Environmental	.05%	$10,000,000	$500,000	Yes	No
Disk failure	Media	.10%	$10,000,000	$1,000,000	Yes	Yes

When beginning disaster recovery planning, simply create a spreadsheet with one of these ranking techniques and start filling things in as you and the client think of them. You can go back to the spreadsheet after a failure occurs and you find something you've missed.

Note Don't doubt the positive power of mistakes. While stressful at the time, every failure that occurs is an opportunity to learn more about your environment. Trust me, you'll make mistakes. There will be factors you won't have considered. That's OK. Just learn from them, and don't make the same mistakes again. Treat every problem as a learning experience, and document what went wrong and how things will be changed. Your management should be impressed when you share that sort of thing.

In the Response and Mitigation columns, as shown in Tables 11-1 and 11-2, you can either put simple Yes/No responses as to whether a mitigation or response plan is in place, or you can link to whatever response or mitigation plan is used. Response and mitigation have a many-to-many relationship with disasters.

Once you have some sort of ranking, start coming up with response and mitigation strategies. I highly recommend using a simple technique like this for risk identification. The more complicated you are, the harder it will be to move on to the next step (which is actually doing something about the risk).

Developing a Response Plan

The first step after identifying and ranking some risks (remember, don't try to do everything at once) is to come up with a response—that is, what actions you should take if the disaster occurs. Unlike mitigation planning in which you try to prevent the disaster or the impact of the disaster in the first place, response planning is *not* optional. Never rely on simply trying to avoid the issue; come up with a plan of action when the issue occurs. Even though you've assigned probability to each disaster, always assume even the least likely disasters will occur eventually.

It's possible that you have multiple response plans for a single disaster, or multiple disasters covered by a single response plan. A backup/recovery plan obviously can act as a valid response to a wide range of disasters. Something as catastrophic as a tornado should obviously have more than one response plan tied to it. Of course, you'll need to do backup and recovery, but you'll also need plans in place to acquire a new facility, obtain a new server, and so on. Let's look at some mitigation plans and techniques.

Defining Mitigation Plans

While a response plan is required for every disaster, a mitigation plan is optional. However, you're better off if you can prevent a disaster or minimize the impact then have to react to it. Think of mitigation planning as proactive disaster recovery. However, you cannot skip response planning and rely on mitigation plans. (Well, you could, but I certainly wouldn't approve, and you're just asking for trouble.)

Since we're focusing on SQL Server disaster recovery, you essentially have a single response plan for any disaster situation: a backup/recovery plan. With mitigation plans, however, you can have a wide variety of plans given the type of disaster. Clustering is good for addressing hardware disasters. Log shipping and database mirroring are prime candidates for dealing with environmental, hardware, and media disasters. A database snapshot is an excellent tool for dealing with process errors and can prove useful for some user-based errors. However, no specific technology provides mitigation for all disaster categories, much less for all specific disasters you could imagine.

This is where SQL Server really shines, in my opinion. Forget the performance improvements, CLR integration, native web services—all the sexy features. The product pays for itself by providing intuitive methods for creating multiple mitigation plans that reinforce each other.

Complementary Technologies

SQL Server 2005 should truly change the way we think about disaster recovery plans. New technologies provide for creative approaches to mitigation and can be combined in interesting ways to protect against multiple disaster categories. The traditional method of disaster mitigation involved either failover clustering or having some sort of remote standby database used either log shipping or replication. (For the record, I don't endorse replication to create a standby database.)

We need to move away from the belief that a single technique will suffice. If we have the opportunity to put more than one mitigation process in place, why not use all our options? After all, we expect hardware installations to have redundant systems, such as multiple power supplies and RAID protection for disk arrays. I've combined some examples of mitigation techniques for your consideration. This is far from an exhaustive list; the intent here is to spark your imagination and expose you to new ways of viewing disaster recovery planning.

Clustering and Log Shipping

You already know that clustering provides no protection against environmental disaster—only protection for the physical server nodes that provide access to the data. What about the data itself? Log shipping is an excellent, inexpensive way of establishing some sort of protection against environmental disasters. To make sure that data is stored in a second location, augment clustering by implementing log shipping.

Clustering and Database Snapshots

Database snapshots can be useful in an environment where user disaster is probable. You've already seen how you can use database snapshots in multiple ways to respond to some sort of user mistake. By simply combining a database snapshot with a hardware-protection technique such as clustering, you can account for a wide variety of disaster situations.

Note that you must store the database snapshots on a clustered resource. Storing them on a local cluster node will invalidate the snapshots in the event of a failover. Database snapshots as implemented by the initial release of SQL Server 2005 have a number of limitations, but as long as you store them on a clustered disk resource, clustering won't increase those limitations.

Clustering and Database Mirroring

Whenever I'm presenting at a conference or teaching, people often ask if they can combine clustering and database mirroring. The hardware protection of a cluster and the real-time duplication of data off-site is an attractive combination. Cluster failover is quick, as is database mirroring. You also avoid the complicated failover and failback procedures required by log shipping.

However, the combination of clustering and mirroring comes with some complications. Controlling which feature is first to fail over can be difficult. Ideally, if you have a hardware issue, you'll want clustering to fail over to a secondary physical node rather than have database mirroring fail over to a remote location. As SQL Server 2005 stands at this writing, it's difficult to establish this level of control. Yes, you can combine clustering and database mirroring, but would I necessarily recommend it? No. There are too many variables for my tastes. If you do decide to use this combination, be aware of timing issues.

Database Mirroring and Log Shipping

I've mentioned the combination of database mirroring and log shipping during lectures, and the response I see on the faces of my audience is generally one of, "Did I hear that right? Is he drunk?" Yes, this seems redundant and includes additional configuration with little to gain from it. It is redundant: that's the point. You always consider redundancy when implementing hardware. Why not expect the same thing from software?

Both database mirroring and log shipping are designed to protect primarily against environmental disasters. Mirroring provides for fast and simple failover to a remote mirrored database. Log shipping allows for a remote standby database, but failover is a complicated process. Each has its benefits, and each has its drawbacks. By combining the two, you get the fast failover capabilities of database mirroring and the ability to have data stored at multiple locations (mirroring only permits one mirror database).

Basic Documentation for Disaster Recovery

Having a disaster recovery plan is important to even the smallest organization. However, an undocumented disaster recovery plan is next to useless. In addition to the specific steps to be taken in the event of a failure (from a technology point of view), a disaster recovery plan must include basic, logistical information.

There are also some caveats when it comes to documentation. Some of these will seem obvious to the point of being silly, but I can tell you from experience that they happen:

- *Don't rely on electronic documentation only*: You should always have a hard copy of the plan available. What happens if you lose power to your facility? A hard copy of the plan can be invaluable. Also, be sure to update it on a regularly scheduled basis.

- *Don't store the documentation on the server that you're protecting*: Relying on an electronic copy is dangerous enough. If you store it on the very server you're trying to protect, you might as well not bother with it.

- *Establish an owner of the plan*: Guess what? That probably means you. This is a critical component, as you'll see in Chapter 12. A single person must ultimately be responsible for maintaining the plan. That doesn't mean the owner does all of the work or is the only one writing the plan, but the owner is necessary so that someone is accountable.

- *Establish an authoritative, master copy*: For most of you reading this, you'll have a relatively large environment with multiple people working on or with the plan. That means multiple copies of that plan. How likely is it that all the copies will be in sync? Be explicit, and identify which copy is to be considered the authoritative version of the document.

- *Make sure that everyone knows about the plan*: I've run into situations in which the company had a disaster recovery plan but only two people knew about it. I've also run into situations in which I heard the phrase, "I know it's around here somewhere" used frequently. Be sure everyone knows there's a plan and how to access the plan.

The following list describes some of the key elements that your disaster recovery plan should contain:

- *Risk matrix*: Disaster recovery planning is an ongoing process, so you must have a risk matrix that shows exactly what disasters you've considered and those that have recovery and mitigation plans.

- *Mitigation plan*: Yes, you should document the actual steps of a mitigation plan. However, you also need to include information about where that mitigation plan is applicable.

- *Backup/recovery plan (response)*: Since we're specifically talking about SQL Server disaster recovery, a response plan equates to a backup/recovery plan. You must include the actual backup/recovery scheme, plus details on how it should be used given any specific disaster (as listed in the risk matrix). The inclusion of examples can be incredibly useful.

- *Contact*: Commonly missed, a simple contact list of relevant individuals can make the difference between total stoppage of work and a speedy return to normal operations. Don't forget to include the main DBA, a manager, a business manager, hardware vendor support, and other key figures.

- *Licensing and installing media*: This is perhaps one of the most commonly missed components in a full disaster recovery plan. Often the existence of media to reinstall SQL Server, as well as the license key required, is taken for granted. Also, don't forget to keep the current service pack installation and any hotfix installation files currently in use (I'd burn those to a CD as well).

- *External support*: If you maintain any support from a third-party vendor, make sure you have the support agreement available. Incidentally, you should include the hardware or software support agreement as part of the documentation of the disaster recovery plan. You never know when you'll need to remind a vendor that it has a responsibility to actually help you.

Testing

In case you didn't already notice, *test* is a four-letter word, and other four-letter words often accompany it. It's a rare individual who cannot only tolerate testing but actually enjoy it. Most people in the IT industry despise testing. No one can deny how important it is, though.

Some lucky organizations have extremely capable staff in every technology area, and their ability to adapt and work without documentation is astounding. These organizations usually skip testing and planning, yet somehow manage to respond to any scenario thrown at them.

However, even these organizations have the need for documentation and testing. The fates have a wicked curveball. As capable as any IT group may be, it's better to be prepared than to rely solely on individual skills. Reacting to a disaster on the fly also takes more time without a specific, tested plan. A lot of organizations believe they're one of these lucky, highly effective groups, but chances are, they aren't. While I have actually seen extremely capable groups in action, they're extremely rare.

Without exception, testing disaster plans should never be optional. Periodic disaster drills should be run at least once a year and should include as many factors as possible. Testing isn't just a training exercise; it helps to uncover flaws in implementation or planning itself.

You should even go so far as to test something like the capabilities of external support if you have it. If the vendor guarantees a four-hour response time to replace hardware, see if it can hold up to that claim.

Real-World Scenarios

All of the following scenarios are based in part on actual events that I've either observed or participated in. No scenario is based on a single event or organization; rather, they're aggregations of my more interesting experiences throughout the years. Are some of them extreme? Yes. Does that mean they're deliberately exaggerated? No. I have many stories that are just too unbelievably bizarre to put into print; no one would believe me.

Panic-Induced Disaster (User/Process Disaster)

Panic-induced disaster is a common scenario—by far, the most common that I encounter. It's actually a post-disaster disaster. At some point, someone decides that they need to restore a database (or restore a system or replace hardware), and they act quickly—too quickly, in fact.

When presenting or training on the topic of disaster recovery, I stress not being afraid to take action. It's easy to fall into the trap of analysis paralysis and waste precious time debating the best action to take.

The quickest way to learn is to make a mistake. The quickest way to make a mistake is to act based on panic. Ergo, in this particular scenario, we learned a lot.

The Scenario

I had assisted a company in setting up an effective backup scheme for its production database. The platform was SQL Server 2000, and the backup/restore plan specified that we needed to restore the database quickly. Users only accessed the main application during business hours (7 a.m. to 6 p.m.), but web-service-based processing and replication occurred on nearly a 24x7 basis. Due to budget constraints, no third-party tools were available to speed the backup process, so we were left with SQL Server native backup techniques. The databases weren't exceptionally large (around 30GB), so we opted for as simple a plan as possible while achieving our base goal. After discussing the business impact and the technical requirements, we chose the following backup scheme:

- Full backup nightly

- Differential backups every hour (with only the most current being kept on disk)

- Log backups every 30 minutes

This gave us a simple scheme for the staff to follow, plus our restore scenario would be a maximum of four restores: one full, one differential, one log backup, and one tail-log backup. After testing for timing, management deemed that the plan met all business requirements. We documented the plan fully and meticulously with each step, with the understanding that server support staff may be the ones executing the restore plan.

(If you happen to notice potential issues already, good for you!)

The Result

I was teaching a SQL Server 2005 class in a city far from my home base when around 8 p.m. I got a call on my cell from a member of the server staff. While replacing a server, the primary application database "wouldn't come up." Of course, the staff member didn't remember seeing any specific error message or database state. He informed me that they'd begun the restore procedure and asked if I could check in later that night and apply the additional backups.

"No problem," I responded.

I was wrong—it turned out to be a problem.

What Went Wrong

The first thing I discovered was lost data. I forgot to include a crucial piece of information in the documentation I put together: the tail-log backup. That was the first mistake. Since the on-staff DBAs and I always backed up the tail of the log out of habit, I just missed that step in the documentation. Obviously, though, anyone other than the on-staff DBAs and myself would not have been aware of the tail-log. The full backup was in the process of restoring, so we lost 17 minutes' worth of data. Or course, it may not have been possible to back up the tail-log, but I verified later that it wasn't even attempted.

The second mistake was simply not following the directions. We'd written everything out in T-SQL statements, and the restore process was started by means of Enterprise Manager. The default restore option was to recover the database at the end of a restore.

That meant that when the full restore finished, the database was live and no further files could be restored. In the documentation, we had listed RESTORE DATABASE...WITH NO RECOVERY. If that command had been executed, I would have been able to finish the process. Instead, I was stuck with a database that was available, but missing about 18 hours' worth of critical data. I had to start over.

The third mistake was making undocumented changes to the backup scheme. This was a subtle issue. I finally finished restoring the full backup, then turned to apply the differential backup. Much to my surprise, I received an error saying that the differential backup was not associated with the full backup. I ended up having to restore each individual transaction log backup, which took me until almost 6 a.m. to complete. Since processing and replication weren't occurring, a bottleneck occurred once users came into the office. It took until at least 3 p.m. before the application started responding in the usual fashion. I later found out that a developer had taken a full backup to refresh the test system just after 7 p.m. the night before. From that point on, every differential backup was associated with the developer's backup. Oh, and the developer deleted the full backup once it was restored onto the test system to conserve disk space, so I wouldn't have been able to use it even if I'd known about it.

How SQL Server 2005 Would Have Helped

My client had been running SQL Server 2000. Had the company been running SQL Server 2005 or higher, the following features would have helped significantly:

- *Tail-log*: If the tail-log had been available for backup, SQL Server 2005 would have given the server staff a warning to back up the tail-log before proceeding. Even if they weren't sure what to do there, it would have prompted a phone call to me much earlier. I've run into this mistake in SQL Server 2000 systems regularly, and the simple inclusion of a warning message can make all the difference in saving as much data as possible.

- *Defaults*: Knowing what the defaults are for any given operation is critical. With a restore process, the default action is to recover the database—that is, roll forward the committed transactions and roll back the uncommitted ones. From that point on, no further restore operations are possible. How could SQL Server 2005 have helped with this? There are more functions in SQL Server 2005 that leverage the ability to continually restore backup files. Log shipping and database mirroring are the first that come to mind. Had SQL Server 2005 been implemented, the critical nature of the WITH RECOVERY default would have been more apparent and would have probably been stressed in the documentation.

- WITH COPY_ONLY: In SQL Server 2000, anytime a full backup is taken in the middle of a standard backup scheme, all following differential backups are then associated with that full backup. There is no way around this. In SQL Server 2005, you can add the WITH COPY_ONLY clause to a full backup command; this instructs the database engine not to consider this a full backup in terms of differential backup association. If the company had been running SQL Server 2005, the developer could have used this clause, which would have saved significant time in the restore process, since the differential backup could have been applied.

The Overheated Data Center (Environmental/Hardware Disaster)

Overheating is a common scenario in small- to mid-sized companies that have rapidly evolving IT needs. They never have the time to spec out a proper data center with appropriate HVAC capacities. Usually, there's very little leverage of existing hardware resources, leading quickly to rapid server proliferation.

For my fellow gaming geeks in the audience, you know that the price you pay for extreme performance is extreme heat. Gaming PCs have high-performance fans, heat sinks on the CPU(s), heat sinks and fans on the graphics cards, and, for the true gamers out there, some sort of custom water-cooled system. Heat is the source of all evil when it comes to gaming. The same is true of server stability.

The Scenario

The client had rapidly growing IT needs. This was during the dot-com boom, so of course technology was being pitched as the savior for every possible business problem. Like every other company trying to keep up with the Joneses, my client was investing large amounts of money in software and hardware.

Unfortunately, the company neglected (and no one had advised it) to invest money in data-center needs, such as more power, environmental protection, and most importantly, proper temperature control. The server room was about 12 square meters, with racks so close together you literally had to squeeze your body in between them. The average temperature in the room well exceeded 90 degrees. The only means of cooling the room was to open a small window. (It would be very difficult for a person to squeeze through it, much less pass any equipment other than network cables through it.) There was an ongoing battle between the IT manager and an informed-yet-rogue consultant about whether the window should be open or shut. The IT manager usually won the ongoing battle, insisting the window should be shut.

The Result

As you might expect, the servers would randomly reboot throughout the day. Some would exhibit periodic hardware problems that would resolve themselves if the server was powered down for five minutes. All of this was due to heat.

The hardware vendor was blamed for the "bad hardware," and significant time was wasted with fruitless arguments between the network manager and the hardware vendor. The randomness of the reboots and the hardware issues also wasted significant consultant time attempting to troubleshoot or some how proactively alleviate issues (usually by scheduled reboots). Instead, the consultants should have been working toward implementing the systems for which they were hired as specialists.

The constant reboots and downtime caused obvious frustration with the user base, which included the CEO. While the end users complained to their hearts' content and received essentially no response, one complaint from the CEO caused entire software packages to be thrown out. Millions of dollars worth of hardware and software investments were discarded. However, the hardware itself was never shut down and removed, so the heat issues continued.

In the end, the company (like many companies from 1995 to 2000) lost a lot of money, and the CEO was resistant to any IT investments from that point on. It took more than five years to recover and return to a conservative but consistent IT budget.

What Went Wrong

Multiple issues were at work here, and interestingly enough, none of them were technical. If there was any single root cause of the company's financial problems, it was simply being a victim of the Before Dot-Com-Bust (BDCB) era. From the mid 1990s to about the spring of 2000, business and technology were more or less analogous to prospectors flocking to California and Alaska during the great gold rush. If you happened to hit the technology mother lode, you'd be rich beyond your wildest dreams. And it was a rush to be the first one to get there.

Obscene amounts of money were poured into technology. Most IT/IS departments even within a mid-sized company had a blank check. It was almost like playing the technology lottery: keep buying things, and the company might just get rich. Entire companies were formed and backed by venture capitalists based on an idea that involved technology (usually some sort of web site, hence the dot-com boom and bust). Having a sound business plan was almost a waste of time.

It really isn't surprising that this overheating situation occurred. The same sort of thing probably happened to lots of companies during that time frame. There were very specific problems at work here that still happen in the present day:

- *Dependence on a single physical location*: If you choose to have all of your information in the same place, you're taunting the fates to strike you down with some sort of environmental disaster. While centralizing systems can make things more efficient and cost-effective, it only takes one leaky pipe to destroy everything.

- *Lack of training*: If you ask someone to do a job he isn't trained for, it's a certainty that mistakes will be made. In this particular example, the IT staff did not realize that heat has a drastic effect on the stability of any server.

- *Inappropriate server environment*: This was not a data center, nor did it resemble any version of one apart from containing servers and networking equipment. This was essentially a storage closet. There was no HVAC control, no moisture control, and clearly no protection from external elements. This is an obvious case of an inappropriate environment. However, identifying a flawed environment is not always so obvious.

- *No disaster recovery planning*: If the organization in this example had performed any sort of disaster recovery planning, the impact of heat or the impromptu server room might have been reviewed and considered for both response and mitigation. Simply planning for disaster recovery can result in positive changes in any environment, regardless if any disaster occurs.

How SQL Server 2005 Would Have Helped

In this particular case, the version of SQL Server in use really didn't matter. Environmental disasters are, by their very nature, technology-agnostic. It doesn't matter what type of software or hardware you're using.

However, training could have helped in this or a similar situation. No one understood the impact of temperature when it came to server hardware. If an actual SQL Server DBA had been part of the staff, and technologies such as clustering, database mirroring, or log shipping had been implemented, the DBA would have more or less been obligated to investigate why the servers were rebooting on a regular basis. Eventually, someone would have discovered the cause (or convinced management of the cause).

■ **Note** DBAs naturally become the glue that holds the IT staff together. To be successful as a DBA, you need to know a little bit about development, hardware, operating systems, networking, and so on. You're likely to interact with all these groups, no matter how separate your IT department is. Whenever there's an issue with the system from the business users' perspective, you usually hear, "There's a problem with the database." Sound familiar? The DBA is often the logical point of contact for business users when interacting with IT.

Must. Have. More. Power. (Environmental/Hardware Disaster)

Whenever I bring up the topic of power when talking about disaster recovery, people's thoughts immediately jump to redundant power supplies or ensuring all servers are connected to an Uninterruptible Power Supply (UPS). However, the issue of power can be involved in a significant number of disaster scenarios, some of them extremely subtle.

The Scenario

This manufacturing company was growing quickly during the economy boom of the mid to late 1990s. The company directive was to "keep up with the Joneses" from a technology standpoint. A well-constructed server room complied with most of today's data-center standards. It was temperature and moisture controlled, physically secured, and so on. Like most companies during that time period, this company had significant server proliferation. Each month, it would add two or three new servers. Each new server was implemented with care, and the integrity of the server room was always taken into consideration. All in all, this was a quality IT organization and an impressive server environment. Barring a physical disaster, it seemed as if no environmental disaster could occur.

The power supplied to the entire facility assumed a certain level of growth, mostly from the manufacturing floor. For that purpose, the power was more than sufficient. However, no one took into account the power needs of the server room, which was quickly becoming a full-fledged data center.

After about four years of continued server additions (and the network infrastructure required to support it), servers started rebooting randomly. It was infrequent at first, but grew to the point where each server rebooted at least twice a day, for no apparent reason. This organization had affiliates in Europe and China, so these reboots affected not only local productivity, but also the productivity of the international offices. The impact was costing the company a significant amount of money.

The Result

Needless to say, executive management was growing less and less patient with the IT department. No one was able to identify an exact cause. Significant time was invested in troubleshooting the issue. Initially, SQL Server or Exchange problems were thought to be the cause, and outside consultants were brought in to assist. Then the operating system was blamed. More consultants. Then the hardware. More consultants. More hardware. More money. The executives grew more and more upset.

Finally, an internal employee, who once worked as an electrician, came up with a crazy idea: maybe there wasn't enough power coming in to the server room itself. Sure enough, the staff performed a few tests and discovered that there indeed wasn't enough power to run all of the IT hardware they'd been accumulating over the previous five years. Electricians were brought in, and the problem was resolved, but not before costing the company millions of dollars, as well as damaging the perception of IT in the eyes of the executives.

What Went Wrong

This is one scenario where literally nothing was done incorrectly. The company had a great server environment and a quality staff. It was just an extremely difficult issue to troubleshoot. If anything was done wrong, it was relying too much on consulting companies to assist with the problem. Granted, this occurred during a time when companies put a lot of faith in consulting companies to act as "experts" for the changing technologies. The company sunk a lot of money into external help troubleshooting the issue. To be fair, it was almost impossible to troubleshoot. It took someone's hunch to find the problem.

The one item the IT staff truly lacked was an appropriate mitigation procedure. Downtime occurred every time a server rebooted. While each individual instance of downtime was relatively small, there were so many reboots that a significant cost was incurred from lost productivity. Having some sort of standby situation might have helped. At the time, though, the only affordable high-availability solution for them was clustering. Although they did have SQL Server and Exchange on a cluster, that didn't help with this particular issue.

The one true lesson to take from this example is that things go wrong. Even the strongest IT department can be presented with a disaster they haven't anticipated. This further demonstrates that disaster recovery planning should be an ongoing process.

How SQL Server 2005 Would Have Helped

The company lost money in the effort to troubleshoot the issue. More importantly, though, money, respect, and credibility were lost because of lost productivity caused by the continual reboots. Overseas affiliates began to question whether the organization was capable of maintaining such a complicated IT infrastructure.

If SQL Server 2005 were available, database mirroring would have provided for a remote failover site, reducing the perception of downtime. It wouldn't have eliminated the consulting costs of troubleshooting the rebooting issue, but it would have reduced the perception of the severity of the issue and allowed for continued productivity. Sometimes damage to an IT department's reputation can ultimately be more costly than downtime or external consulting costs.

"I Don't Think My Data Is in Kansas Anymore" (Environmental Disaster)

While an environmental disaster can be as subtle as temperature control or access to sufficient power, most people think of an environmental disaster as something catastrophic— usually a natural disaster. Every place on the planet is susceptible to some sort of natural disaster. Where I live, the most common natural disaster is a tornado.

If you've never lived in a location that has a weather system prone to tornados, you may not know that when tornados form, they form quickly. There is very little warning (although techniques identifying the proper conditions for a tornado have improved dramatically). You usually don't have time to react or try to secure anything. Basically, you have time to seek shelter, and that's it.

The Scenario

A city in the Midwest not far from where I live was essentially obliterated by a tornado. The base of the tornado was almost half a mile wide, and it was so strong that it completely destroyed every building in its path. One of those buildings was a mid-sized manufacturing plant.

The machinery on the manufacturing floor was connected to a database that contained every conceivable piece of data related to the company's day-to-day operations. It even contained accounting-related data. This system was critical to the plant's ability to do business, so the IT staff were careful and backed up everything nightly and placed the tapes in a fireproof safe.

The Result

The safe was housed at the plant. It was great that the staff had the foresight to place the backup tapes in something durable and fireproof. However, the problem was that after the tornado struck and completely destroyed the plant, no one could find the safe. It probably ended up in a nearby forest, at the bottom of a lake, or perhaps embedded into the concrete foundation of a house 40 miles away.

The company did receive government-aid money and was able to reconstruct the building and purchase new equipment, but its data system was gone. The information stored on that system was gone. The plant managed to stay in business, but what was once a mid-sized company became a small business, rebuilding from the ground up. It was able to establish a new customer base, but it will probably be a decade before the company returns to the size it once was.

What Went Wrong

Having a durable, fireproof safe to store backup tapes was an excellent idea. Even though this was an extreme environmental disaster, the safe may have protected the company's data. The problem was that the safe was located in the same physical location as the production data. Had the tapes been stored even one mile away, the data wouldn't have been lost.

Wherever you live and whatever natural disaster you may face, such disasters aren't a common occurrence. Even if a tornado forms, it's still unlikely that it will hit any specific building. This company took the low risk of an extreme sort of environmental disaster for granted. It didn't accurately identify the impact of the risk (as defined earlier) of a tornado strike. Thus, it was very nearly put out of business completely. Had the company identified that impact and decided that the risk was so unlikely that further protection (other than the safe) was too expensive and unnecessary, then having no other environmental disaster protection would have been fine. The ultimate problem was that the company didn't even consider it as a possibility.

How SQL Server 2005 Would Have Helped

The ideal way to mitigate an environmental disaster is to have a copy of the data in a different physical location, at the very least. Database mirroring or log shipping would have protected not only against a fire or the destruction of the facility, but also against something as catastrophic as a direct hit from a tornado.

"Where is WHERE?" (Process Disaster)

Whenever I hear this DBA urban myth, it begins with, "I know a guy who has a cousin who knows a guy"—a good indicator of a myth. As the story goes, two consultants are working late on an online-ordering web site. It's late at night, and both consultants are starting to get a little punchy. They commence updating pricing for one category of products (there are more than 10 million products in the table). Consultant #1 issues the command UPDATE PRODUCT SET PRICE=1*1.1 and executes the query. He immediately panics, because he realizes he forgot to put a WHERE statement on the query. He proceeds to flip out. Consultant #2 calmly walks over to the server and disconnects the power. When the server comes back up, the database system rolls back the interrupted UPDATE statement. All is well with the world.

This is an excellent example of a process disaster, and one we've all experienced at one time or another.

The Scenario

This one is personal—very personal. In fact, I'm the subject of the story.

I was working on a massive data migration from one system to another, which meant changes in data layout, data types, and so on. Every test took an extremely long time to prep on the source side, to prep on the intermediary system, and to export from my system to a format that I could load into the target system.

It was late at night, and I had just finished loading all of the incoming data into my intermediary system. Of course, I had used scripts to organize the various modifications needed to convert the data to fit the new system. I had been doing this for about 27 hours straight, so all of the stored procedures I used were in the same query window. I'd just highlight what I wanted to run. (You should know that I'm prone to typos when I write.) For some strange reason, I highlighted the "cleanup" procedure and executed it. That stored procedure simply truncated every table in my intermediary system, including the lookup tables I used during conversion. As I hit F5 to run the query, I realized what I had done. Time crawled to a stop as I pushed the button. I could hear in classic slow-motion the sound of my brain saying, "NOOOOOOOOO!"

The Result

Because the stored procedure was simply executing TRUNCATE TABLE statements, everything happened quickly. The stored procedure finished in about two seconds. That's it; it was done. I had to start over from scratch. Of course, I had to reload all of the data, including the lookup tables. All of that took time, and I had a deadline to meet within three hours. I ended up missing the deadline (I did give my client a heads-up that the data would be late that day), and ultimately this ended up being the last project I did with that client. They weren't happy, and I completely understand why.

What Went Wrong

It was late at night, I was facing a deadline, and I just got sloppy. There's no other explanation. I didn't take the time to perform a backup after I loaded the data (again, I was concerned with the deadline), and my scripts didn't incorporate any sort of confirmation step. This is a classic process disaster—essentially, a user error for a planned activity.

Had I taken more care in double-checking my work, or had I taken the time to back up the database after the load, I wouldn't have been in that position. It was a painful lesson to learn, but things like this happen.

How SQL Server 2005 Would Have Helped

Ah, if I only had SQL Server 2005. Database snapshots are the ultimate tool when it comes to protecting against process disasters. Yes, I should have taken greater care in what I was doing, but as a fail-safe, I could have used a database snapshot as a response technique to my own carelessness.

What I would have done (and now do religiously) if I had SQL Server 2005 is create a database snapshot just before doing any work on the intermediary database, then perform my task, then remove the snapshot if the process was successful. In that particular situation, after the truncate operation completed, I could have simply snapped back to the database snapshot I created prior to making the mistake.

"No Electromagnets in the Data Center, Please" (Media Disaster)

A true media disaster, such as having hard disks or tapes physically damaged, is becoming a rare occurrence these days. In general, true hardware failures such as a server failing completely, are becoming more and more rare as technology improves. However, since a hard drive or a tape drive is magnetic storage, it's susceptible to damage from anything that generates an electromagnetic field (something even the human body does, to a very minor degree).

The Scenario

I didn't witness this one firsthand, but the person who did shared it with me. I confirmed later that this disaster really did happen.

The victim in this scenario was yet another manufacturing company. It had a great IT department, a well-organized on-site data center, and excellent IT and business integration. There was excellent communication among the people, whether they worked on the manufacturing floor, in finance, or in engineering or IT. For the most part, everyone got along well.

In the server room, rack-mounted devices were on the left, mid-range servers were on the right, and a storage cabinet containing a month's worth of tape backup history was at the end of the room. A few people were in the server room working on installing new equipment into the racks. Certain individuals from the engineering department had access to the server room. Those individuals doubled as backup help for cabling issues and miscellaneous IT tasks.

One of the non-IT people came into the server room and announced, "Hey, check out this cleanup device we got for the shop floor." It was a fairly powerful handheld electromagnet designed to pick up metal shavings and the like. This individual from engineering tossed a few dozen nails on the ground, pointed the magnet at them, and turned it on.

The device worked well; the nails flew to the magnet. Unfortunately, the individual pointed the magnet indirectly at the cabinet holding the backup tapes.

The Result

Fortunately, there was no destruction to either the Windows servers or the mid-range systems. The only items damaged by the magnet were the tapes in the storage cabinet. Essentially, all of the tapes were wiped clean by the magnet.

This IT department was extremely lucky. For one month, everyone held their breath as the tape library was reconstructed with current data. If, at any point, someone had requested a file from an older tape (which was actually quite common in this organization), they would have had to say, "Sorry, it's gone." Given that most of the requests were from executives, the "sorry" response would not have gone over well.

I'm happy to say that no harm ever came from this, and a number of people learned about the frailty of magnetic media.

What Went Wrong

While this situation does involve hardware and a user doing something, well, ill-advised, this is really a media disaster. By pointing the electromagnet at the cabinet holding the tape library, the individual created a field strong enough to scramble nearly every bit on every tape. This is an extreme case, but having something as simple as a TV or a radio resting on a server or next to a backup tape could have an effect.

How SQL Server 2005 Would Have Helped

The key to dealing with media disaster is redundancy of some kind. Using database mirroring or log shipping to keep a copy of data off-site would help. The BACKUP command now includes a MIRROR TO statement; when it comes to databases, transaction logs are critical. Using the MIRROR TO statement to create multiple copies on different magnetic devices minimizes the risk of losing a log file.

Recommendations and Caveats

The biggest problem with creating a disaster recovery plan is the risk of not being able to create one at all. What do I mean by that? Projects tend to fail, get forgotten, or get dropped for other "more pressing" issues. Most IT departments are doing all they can just to keep their heads above water, so any new undertaking is often frowned upon. You need to plan for disaster recovery, even if you can only take a small step, and you need to keep refining what you do. Disaster recovery is part of your job as a DBA. Don't forget these tips:

- *Rinse and repeat*: Disaster recovery planning needs to be an iterative process. It's a job responsibility, not a project to complete.

- *Understand that every disaster is a learning opportunity in disguise*: Every time you face a disaster, take something from it. No one can think of every situation in advance. It's when things truly go wrong that you really learn something.

- *Differentiate between mitigation and response*: Sometimes it's unclear whether you're dealing with mitigation or response. Clarify what you're working on. Mitigation is prevention; response is reaction.

- *Remember that response plans are not optional*: Some experts advocate spending a great deal of time working with mitigation planning. They say that if you can effectively prevent the problem from occurring, there's no need to come up with a response plan. I disagree. Everything fails sooner or later, including mitigation techniques. Always start with a response plan, then move to a mitigation plan if applicable.

Summary

In this chapter, I explored the aspects of a full SQL Server disaster recovery plan, from risk mitigation to response techniques. I then applied that discussion to actual disaster scenarios and deconstructed the issues. I explained how using SQL Server 2005 could have reduced the risk or improved the response capabilities. In the next chapter, I'll look at nontechnical, practical issues to starting disaster recovery planning within your own organization.

CHAPTER 12

■■■

Realistic Disaster Recovery Planning

It's easy for me to sit back and preach about disaster recovery; after all, this is only a book. The problem for all of us is that disaster recovery, like any other IT undertaking, never works according to formula once you step into the real world. All IT projects have a tendency to be problematic, but disaster recovery seems to be particularly problematic in the real world.

Many of my colleagues avoid the word "disaster" whenever possible. It's a negative word that naturally creates a negative atmosphere when used around others. They say that this negative atmosphere can essentially doom whatever you're doing, whether you're working on a project, training, or even selling consulting services. Instead of using the term "disaster recovery," my colleagues advocate using phrases such as "high availability" or "business continuity," both of which have a neutral, if not positive, connotation. I agree with my colleagues that words have all sorts of "baggage" attached to them, and the use of the word "disaster" does create a negative atmosphere. Where we differ is that I think that a negative atmosphere is actually a good thing to create.

If you've been reading this book at all, you know by now that I have no qualms about speaking my mind or calling things how I see them. I have no fear of negative words or wording something in a negative fashion. If I think someone says or does something wrong, I will tell that person—even an executive. However, I will always do so in a civil, polite manner, and I'll back up whatever I say with the *reasons* why I believe someone is wrong about a subject.

There are a variety of reasons why disaster recovery is at best a sensitive topic for any company. A DBA faces internal politics, personality conflicts, interdepartmental difficulties, and, worst of all, the need to justify the process to upper management. This chapter will explore the various difficulties involved in actually dealing with disaster recovery planning in your own environment.

Any business organization, whether in the private or public sector, is a country unto itself. It has a government of sorts, laws, political factions, biases, and personal conflicts. When you step into your company's facility, you almost need a passport.

Like most countries, companies find themselves divided within; differing groups have differing values. Some value the quality of the work they do. Some value the size of the paycheck they acquire. Some value their time away from work. Some value a specific management style. Some value nothing.

While undertaking disaster recovery planning, imagine yourself as an ambassador from a different country or someone vying for political office. To be successful, you need to understand the inner workings of this country, the various political factions, the bureaucracy, and so on. Once you stop looking at a company as a place to work and start imagining it as a place to live, understanding the complications and working around the roadblocks will cease being a mystery and will start becoming second nature.

Understanding Personality Archetypes

In addition to dealing with problematic situations that hamper the chance of success with disaster recovery planning, you'll also likely need to contend with personality conflicts (as if the planning process alone isn't difficult enough). Usually personality conflicts arise out of misunderstanding rather than true dislike. Everyone has his or her own personal triggers that can result in barriers. Once you understand what someone's trigger might be, you can avoid or repair damaged working relationships. The key is to first understand what motivates an individual to act in certain way.

The following subsections describe a few of the personality types I've encountered in my travels. Yes, this is armchair psychology. Yes, no one person fits neatly into one of these categories. Yes, this is simplistic.

The point is to give you a place to start, so you can take personality traits into account when attempting disaster recovery planning (or when living as a social being). You may disagree with my categories; you may have your own observations. If so, excellent! That means you're considering the subject in general. I'm not expecting everyone to agree with me, nor do I want anyone to take this as gospel. Everyone's situation is different, so all I ask is that you take something from this discussion and make it your own.

Note The personality types described in the following sections could apply to a person, a group, a department, or perhaps even the entire company. Also, everyone displays traits from more than one type. While reading, it may occur to you that I exhibit traits from at least three or four of these personality categories.

The Perfectionist

The perfectionist is perhaps the most difficult personality type to identify. Many people can be driven to perfection without outwardly saying so. While the typical perfectionist announces to the world that what exists is insufficient, other perfectionists might simply hide their work, destroy it, or have their dogs eat it. They'll do anything but let someone see work that they consider inferior.

What Is Valued?

Of course, perfectionists value perfection above all else, but that is an abstract concept. Nothing can be perfect, complete, or the best of all possible scenarios. The key to really understanding perfectionists is not in what they value, but in what they dislike—that is, anything that's imperfect, incomplete, or a compromise. This might seem like a positive quality trait, but perfectionists end up seeing only the negative in things.

What Problems Does This Create?

Any activity that is iterative is painful to perform for perfectionists. They keep seeing what isn't included in any given iteration. Any plan that admits to some deficiencies or compromises is essentially admitting that perfection can never be reached. That's like punching a perfectionist in the stomach.

   Unless activities are focused and straightforward, perfectionists have a tendency to never complete them. Large projects, complicated procedures, iterations, and anything involving trade-offs are things that perfectionists either attempt to prolong (in an attempt to get others to strive for perfection) or mentally check out of and feign participation. Such behavior does not lead to productivity. Unfortunately, disaster recovery planning encompasses almost everything that perfectionists dislike.

How Do You Deal with These Problems?

Perfectionists can complicate disaster recovery planning in one of two ways. First, they may try to make the process much more than what it is by increasing the scope, bringing up objections, and so on. Second, they may decide that their participation isn't really required, since no one listens to them when they voice their opinions on what *isn't* being addressed.

   There are two critical ways to assuage perfectionists. First and foremost, you must be able to assure them that their observations on what hasn't been accounted for *are* of use. Respond to objections with something like, "Excellent. No one thought of that. We need to add that to our list." This can go a long way toward keeping perfectionists involved.

However, if you're continually adding to the list, obviously nothing will get done. The second key to working with perfectionists is to present the current iteration as a single item to accomplish. If they point out a deficiency with the current activity that actually relates to the next step, you must try to get them to understand that their objection is to a separate activity. You must never dismiss what they say, because chances are, they are right. Perfectionists don't introduce complications just to be difficult; they really *see* the complication.

Both acknowledging their contribution and helping them maintain focus on an achievable goal can help put perfectionists at ease.

The Doomsayer

Ah, the warm embrace of despair. I know it well. Doomsayers are actually quite similar to perfectionists in terms of their resultant behavior. For doomsayers, however, not only is perfection unattainable, but no activity will succeed. This goes beyond simple pessimism. Doomsayers see everything as an impending world-ending comet strike.

What Is Valued?

It may seem as if doomsayers value nothing, but actually, they value everything. They don't want to see anything wasted or unsuccessful, so they're more inclined to pronounce an activity doomed to fail rather than have people invest time, energy, and resources in making it work. This applies in particular to new endeavors. Anything that veers from the status quo could potentially be a waste of everyone's time.

Doomsayers value cost—time, people, and money—above all else. They look for problems that will result in wasted cost and declare the activity doomed, hopefully before it even starts.

Wanting to "doom" something doesn't come from spite, a power trip, or anything malicious. Doomsayers sincerely want things to be successful. Current activities are known to be successful; new activities may be a complete waste of time and resources if they aren't successful. The mark of doom comes from a desire to maintain current productivity rather than wasting it on a flawed allocation of cost.

What Problems Does This Create?

If the activity isn't cancelled once doomsayers have declared the mark of doom, they'll cease to provide any constructive input (similar to the end result for perfectionists). Since disaster recovery planning is built almost entirely on possible scenarios and risks, doomsayers are uncomfortable participating in or endorsing such activities.

To further complicate the issue, doomsayers often have a great deal of influence over the decision makers within an organization. Since their declaration of doom is based on a rational objection to the activity, and their goal is to minimize wasted resources, decision makers tend to act on their recommendations. I've personally been involved in more than one project that was aborted due to the objections raised by a doomsayer.

How Do You Deal with These Problems?

The key to working with doomsayers is keeping cost off the radar. Usually activities that doomsayers declare to be doomed are large projects that involve a significant percentage of people and have quantifiable monetary costs. Essentially, projects are the target for doom, not day-to-day activities.

If you keep the focus of disaster recovery planning to a day-to-day activity (I believe it should be an ongoing job role of a DBA), the likelihood that it will have the gravity to attract the attention of a doomsayer is low. Keep the process iterative, and reduce any specific requests for resources (whether personnel or financial) to a minimum. Doomsayers probably won't see a risk to productivity (or at least other risks will take precedence).

Should a doomsayer be directly involved in disaster recovery planning and declare a mark of doom, you must react in two ways. First, don't argue or downplay the objection raised (unless it's without merit, in which case this isn't a doomsayer that you're dealing with, but a simple miscreant). Acknowledge that the objection is valid. Second, start a dialog about how the objection should be handled. Shutting things down completely is only one approach. When beginning that dialog, say to the doomsayer, "That's an excellent point. What would you suggest we do instead?" Doomsayers are rational, albeit a bit defeatist in their viewpoints. While they may not have the creativity to consider different approaches, they will listen to alternate courses of action.

The Isolationist

One key to successful disaster recovery planning is the involvement of multiple groups from all parts of the company. You don't want just the IT department involved. You also want finance, sales, purchasing, and other critical stakeholders involved. Isolationists want nothing to do with other groups. Isolationists are usually born out of a failed joint project, difficulties in working with others, or experience with others meddling in their particular area of expertise.

What Is Valued?

In a sense, all isolationists want are respect and privacy. They don't want to have anyone glibly summarize what they do or speak about them in the third person. (FYI, never talk about someone in the third person when they're either part of the conversation or a recipient of a written conversation. This is perhaps the most demeaning thing you could do to someone.) Isolationists value being recognized as an individual. They want specific areas of responsibility, and they want the boundaries of those areas of responsibility to be respected by others.

What Problems Does This Create?

As you may expect, isolationists can be difficult to bring into a group activity. They've probably become isolationists through negative experiences, so promises that "this will be different" rarely work.

If you need to work with isolationists (whether in a technical role or a business role), you must somehow gain access to their area of expertise. They're unlikely to provide that access willingly, and forcibly doing so (by going above their heads and making the request from their management) will result in only more alienation and a greater desire for boundaries. Appealing to a higher authority may get you results, but you'll make things worse for the next time you need to work with the isolationist.

How Do You Deal with These Problems?

Keep in mind that isolationists value respect and privacy. Once you bring them into the fold of your disaster recovery planning, always say something like this: "So James, this is your area of expertise. What do you think?" Never try to speak for them, never try to summarize what they do without validating the summary with them, and *never* begin with assumptions regarding their area of expertise. For example, you may question someone who specializes in .NET Web development by starting off with, "So, John, you're a specialist in .NET Web development. How would you approach creating an effective user interface?" That simple acknowledgment makes all the difference.

Involve isolationists as soon as possible. If your activity will ultimately affect them, waiting to ask for their input deep into the process will come across as a lack of respect. Never make demands on them, and never try to force them out of isolationist mode. Be satisfied getting the information or involvement you need.

The Information Hoarder

Similar to isolationists, information hoarders want the boundaries between their responsibilities and the responsibilities of others to be clearly defined, respected, and, most importantly, enforced by management. If there is no external enforcement of boundaries, they will take matters into their own hands consciously or subconsciously, implicitly or explicitly, to prevent others from crossing those boundaries.

What Is Valued?

On the surface, the issue at hand appears to be one of ownership. Like isolationists, information hoarders seek to prevent others from gaining access to what they consider their own responsibility, from detailed involvement to the smallest piece of information. However, ownership is not the driving force.

Information hoarders hold onto their area of expertise with an ironclad grip because they value their jobs—not just their particular job role, but employment altogether. Information hoarders are typically in charge of older, legacy systems or traditional business practices, so activities that require their involvement can often be interpreted as the harbinger for their ultimate unemployment. For example, someone who supports an older database technology (not just older in years, but in the version level) may refuse to share information out of fear that the technology will be subsumed by a newer one. The result for them would be an unmarketable skill set, so their future employment both with the current company and potential new companies would be at risk.

What Problems Does This Create?

Information hoarders are the one personality type whose actions taken to block access to critical information can be malicious in intent. Because they believe their very livelihood is at risk, some information hoarders will go to great lengths to hamper anyone else's attempt at gathering pertinent information or stepping into their area of expertise. I've even seen an information hoarder goes so far as to frame another employee in an attempt to get that employee fired. This was an extreme, unfortunate case in the mid 1990s, and I haven't seen something that severe since.

Information hoarders who hold data critical to the success of your disaster recovery planning may fight access implicitly, or they may respond aggressively. They even may make a preemptive strike. Under no conditions will they give up their information willingly.

How Do You Deal with These Problems?

There is both good news and bad news when dealing with information hoarders. The bad news is that the steps you take to put information hoarders at ease may not matter at all. The good news is that there are some simple techniques you can use (if the information hoarder is capable of listening) to break down the walls created to keep you and your information-greedy mitts off.

The key is to somehow establish quickly that the information hoarders' jobs are not in jeopardy. It's useless to simply get someone from management to say, "Your job is not in jeopardy." In an age where the average worker will go through 15-20 jobs in his or her lifetime, corporate loyalty to employees is a rare commodity.

Get on the good side of information hoarders by involving them in whatever project you're undertaking by giving them something new that they can hoard. It's unlikely that you'll ever change the behavior of a true information hoarder, so instead, use it to your advantage. Give these employees new, specific, and possibly even esoteric areas of knowledge.

The Territorialist

I am the proud owner of two huge, well-trained German Shepherds. Most animals have some sense of their territory. German Shepherds are the textbook definition of a territorial animal. Like many breeds, an untrained German Shepherd can result in a very unpredictable and potentially dangerous dog. My dogs understand what constitutes their yard, their house, their cars, and their neighbors. Enemies who enter this territory, such as delivery trucks or the evil postal service, must be properly warned with eardrum-shattering barking. As long as these enemies don't enter the territory, they only receive a warning "woof."

I'm certainly not equating territorialists to animals, but the drive and behavior is simple, albeit with less barking. Territorialists are somewhat similar to isolationists and information hoarders, but what they value most is different.

What Is Valued?

The main value of territorialists can be summed up in a simple sentence: "I know more than you." Whether it's true or not, territorialists believe that they're the experts in any given area (technology or business). To question them is an insult; they believe that everyone should acknowledge their status as an expert. More often than not, territorialists are experts in their field or business area. Like most personality types, any complications that territorialists introduce into an activity are done so with the best of intentions. Territorialists want nothing more than to make sure everyone understands how things *really* work.

What Problems Does This Create?

Territorialists are one of the few personality types that tend to rub people the wrong way. No one wants to be told they're wrong, especially in public and by someone who places himself above question. Mostly due to the directness of their nature, territorialists tend to be viewed as arrogant and abrasive, which is unfortunate.

Although rare, territorialists may think they know more about a particular subject than they actually do. This can be especially damaging if it happens on a large project with multiple representatives from the same technical or business area involved. Territorialists can also unintentionally cause discontent with the people involved in the process.

Their confidence implies a certain level of inflexibility. Their attitude implies that their word is scripture.

How Do You Deal with These Problems?

The first step to minimizing the potential distractions generated by territorialists is to restrict their participation in disaster recovery planning. Include only one territorialist per technical or functional area. This prevents potential clashes between fellow "experts."

If you're working with territorialists who you know to be incorrect about a particular fact, always try to convey the correct information in private and in a way that makes them feel that they came up with the idea in the first place. Perhaps give them a gentle nudge in the right direction, or ask them to validate a claim just to be 100% certain of it. Calling them out in public or directly debating an issue will almost certainly damage any working relationship with a territorialist.

Note While a true territorialist does have a high level of expertise in a subject, no one knows everything. If you ever encounter a colleague, instructor, or presenter who claims to know everything there is to know about a certain subject, get up and walk out of the room. No one knows everything about any specific subject unless it is very limited in scope.

The Holist

Holists are one of the most well intentioned yet distracting personality types when it comes to disaster recovery planning. They have a tendency to take any simple activity and turn it into a grand endeavor. In an effort to make sure that everything and everyone is involved in the process, they can take a task that requires the input of two or three individuals and turn it into a massive project involving dozens of members with applicable yet marginally useful input. They take something that should last no longer than 15 minutes and turn it into a multiweek project.

What Is Valued?

Holists mean no harm; in fact, they want nothing more than to see things succeed. The fact that they ultimately end up lengthening the disaster recovery process is just an unfortunate side effect of eager participation.

Holists don't intend to complicate things or make activities overly complex. They sincerely want everyone to be successful. However, they believe that the key to success is ensuring that everyone who might have valid input about any given activity is given the opportunity to provide that input. This means not only taking the time to collect that input, but also taking the time to identify who may have that input (as well as convincing those people to share it).

Completeness of information is the sole objective of holists. They're motivated by knowing that the correct decision or action has been taken. Without that complete picture and all relevant input, any decision or action is automatically suspect.

What Problems Does This Create?

Holists prolong any activity far past what is necessary. For holists, there is no such thing as a "good enough for now" approach if individuals with input have not been consulted. Holists are different than perfectionists, because if all applicable parties have been included, they'll accept the "good enough" answer.

The participation of holists can potentially negatively affect the other participants. Holists all but demand the input of others, often against their will. Would you want to be dragged into a meeting, only to sit for two hours while everyone answers a single question? I sure wouldn't.

How Do You Deal with These Problems?

The key to working with holists is compromise. As with the other personality types, don't simply dismiss their requests for a wider range of input, because their requests are probably valid. You have to learn to minimize the impact of the requests.

Keep the subject of any given activity very focused. When working on disaster recovery, you might create very specific steps, such as backup/recovery planning and specific mitigation techniques. An iterative approach is useful. Try to keep holists focused on the individual steps of planning, and hide the larger picture from them. However, this won't always work, because holists tend to seek out the big picture.

You can also allow input from individuals with peripheral information related to a specific activity, but in a way that requires as little of their time as possible. Send the request for information via e-mail, or simply ask a question in passing. Of course, this is difficult to do if the holist is playing the role of project manager. That's where lengthy meetings come in.

The Pacifist

Having a rational argument can be one of the most productive activities in a group atmosphere. You learn a lot when two people who don't agree start debating an idea. Pacifists, however, view confrontation of any kind as counterproductive. Like holists, they can be particularly distracting when it comes to disaster recovery planning.

It usually doesn't matter if the confrontation is amicable or hostile. Either way, pacifists always attempt to stop the confrontation outright, or at the very least act as a mediator. Pacifists who find themselves involved in a confrontation quickly back down from their point, potentially discarding extremely useful information.

What Is Valued?

Pacifists don't necessarily fear confrontation, but even if they do, that isn't the motivation. They believe that the most productive environment is a harmonious one. They think that nothing positive comes from confrontation, which ultimately does nothing more than waste everyone's time.

■**Note** I, of course, disagree with the concept that only harmony leads to positive results, while discord does nothing but distract and destroy. Not all of you will agree with me on this; you might have the personality type of an arguer. It's true that some people argue for the sake of arguing, but I believe that behavior is driven by something else (such as the fear of losing a job, as the information hoarder fears). As I've said, I'm not expecting everyone to agree with me. What I want is for everyone to consider these topics within the context of their own job.

What Problems Does This Create?

When pacifists participate in a conflict, they back down. Let's say a pacifist happens to be the resident expert on SQL Server and is recommending the best method for backup/recovery, only to be countered by the resident Oracle expert. Chances are that the SQL Server expert knows his platform better than the Oracle expert would. When the pacifist backs down, the result may be a backup/recovery plan that's not only far from optimal, but completely invalid.

Pacifists who are in a team leader role attempt to put a halt to arguments, whether rational or emotional. My academic background is in philosophy, which essentially reveres the art of arguing. (A question is considered philosophical if no book holds the answer.) Arguments, even emotional ones, often uncover valuable information, usually once the point of contention is uncovered.

How Do You Deal with These Problems?

Pacifists are the most difficult personality type to overcome, primarily because they can be difficult to detect. If they're involved in a confrontation, you'll probably have to argue for them as a sort of proxy. However, arguing on behalf of such people can be difficult, because they won't be willing to tell you what their concerns are until you extricate them from the confrontational situation. But it is paramount that you try to argue on their behalf. Restate what you think their point is, and ask if you're correct. Keep poking and prodding until the crux of the confrontation is made apparent. (Speaking to them alone, away from the source of confrontation, can help too.)

If a pacifist is in the role of a project manager, attempt to take the argument out of the hands of the participants. Make both sides present their case to you, then evaluate both positions in an all-inclusive discussion. If you can do this effectively, the pacifist project manager will no longer see a confrontation, but instead will see a harmonious discussion of the issues.

Tip If you want to further explore the topic of human behavior, don't read Freud, Jung, or any other psychologist or philosopher. Read Shakespeare. There's a reason that The Bard is still one of the most respected writers in history; he has a fantastic insight into human nature, which he can demonstrate in a word or two. Shakespeare can be difficult to read, since every play is really a poem. If you prefer a more visual experience, see the plays performed live. Even if you don't fully understand the dialog, you'll quickly understand what is happening. Just don't walk around the office uttering things like, "What fools these DBAs be!" or "All the world's a database, and all the people merely bits upon the disk." I can say from experience that few appreciate it.

Overcoming Roadblocks

Whether working for a company directly, as a contractor, or as a consultant, most people face the same problems. In addition to the different personality types that may pose a problem, there are also institutional and logistical barriers to overcome. I'll describe some of these barriers in the following subsections.

A word of warning: you won't always be successful in dealing with barriers, and at times, you may face a situation without an apparent solution. In such instances, disaster recovery planning is essentially dead. However, don't take the defeat personally or let it demoralize you. Project failure happens, unfortunately more often than I'd like to see. Above all, don't take a failed project as a sign to give up. Do what you can, wait, and then try again. Persistence without becoming a pest will pay off, eventually.

IT VS. IS VS. EVERYONE ELSE

The department that handles computer-related activities is usually referred to as Information Technology (IT), Information Systems (IS), or some slight variation thereof. While the role of this department within any given business is becoming clearer each year, IT/IS still tends to be a catchall department for anything having to do with technology. And in many organizations, there is a schism of sorts between the rest of the business and the technology side of the company. No one really knows what those who work in IT/IS do, nor do they want to know. Similarly, those in IT/IS are often focused more on technology per se than on the business of the company of which IT/IS is a part. My guess is that most of you reading this feel some sort of segregation from the rest of the business, whether in a good way or a bad way.

I think of IT and IS as two separate departments within an organization, although this is rarely the case. IT is responsible for infrastructure—that is, networks, servers, storage, and so on. Essentially, IT handles hardware and standard software installations, such as Windows and Office. IS deals with custom or third-party applications that are used to facilitate business processes. Developers, business analysts, and the like comprise this group. And then we have the poor DBA, who has one foot in each department (a rant for another time).

IS should interact with business units on a regular basis. The sole responsibility of IS staff is to create or maintain applications for use by the business units. There was a day when IS would drive what the business units would use; thankfully, that trend is beginning to stop. The problem with simply creating an application (or purchasing a third-party one) in a semi-vacuum and delivering it to a business unit is that the business process must conform to the application. It really should be the other way around. Technology does not solve business problems– (another rant for another day).

Currently, most business units see the support of their applications as being totally within the hands of the mystical IT/IS staff. This means that most business units believe IT/IS is solely responsible for supporting these applications. This viewpoint must change. As much as IT and IS need to pay more attention to the business processes they support, business units must be aware of the technology requirements behind their processes. They also must take responsibility for certain decisions, such as acceptable data loss, acceptable downtime, and so on. Right now, most organizations have an "us vs. them" mentality regarding business and technology. Both sides need to take responsibility and have at least a basic understanding of what the other does.

Roadblock: Lack of Awareness

All too often, companies either are oblivious to disaster risks or downplay the likelihood or the impact of their occurrence. Whether it's a case of pure ignorance or wishful thinking, lack of awareness is a very real problem you're likely to encounter when it comes to disaster recovery.

Description of the Roadblock

When it comes to raising awareness, strangely enough, the first person to start with is you. You might be thinking, "Aren't I already aware of the need for disaster recovery planning? I'm reading this book, after all." However, you'll face a lot of roadblocks on the way to a disaster recovery plan. Think about what your job is like right now. How much time do you have devoted to disaster recovery planning? My guess is little or none, unless your company is in the middle of a disaster recovery (DR) project. If your job is anything like the majority of DBA positions, you're probably doing all you can just to keep your head above water. It is surprisingly easy to let disaster recovery slip off your radar while you scramble in your day-to-day duties. I experience the just-keeping-my-head-above-water syndrome myself.

The real problem is trying to raise the awareness of your team, your peers, your management, executive management, and business units. It's actually easier if your peers and management have no understanding of disaster recovery planning. It's more difficult when every level has its own distinct concept of what disaster recovery planning means. As I mentioned in Chapter 1, I'm presenting my understanding of disaster recovery planning, but it isn't the only available approach. You may disagree with me, but at this point, (I hope) you will have identified what approach will work for your company. If everyone in your company has a different viewpoint, you first have to gain consensus before you can undertake some of the larger, cross-department planning.

This particular roadblock can appear within your team (fellow DBAs), individual peers, management, and so on. I'll examine each group in detail, first starting with how the roadblock can occur.

Your Team

Sometimes convincing your fellow DBAs that disaster recovery planning is needed can be extremely difficult. The problem is that they are in the same position as you—that is, doing all they can just to keep their heads above water. The usual protests from other DBAs include:

- "We've already got a backup plan. What are you talking about?"

- "I've got enough to do as it is."

- "Duh, we already have a disaster recovery plan—that's why we carry pagers."

- "Management will never let us do this; just give up on it."

- "Where do you guys want to go for lunch?"

The general issues you'll see involve either a lack of understanding of what disaster recovery planning is, a preconceived notion of what disaster recovery is, or just plain apathy or despair.

Your Peers

By *peers*, I mean your colleagues in IT/IS—individuals who should understand the technical risks involved as well as the need for some type of disaster recovery planning. I do recommend that you stick with database-level disaster recovery planning to start with, but eventually you'll need to work with the server management team, the network team, and so on. They will have comments similar to your team:

- "My boss will never let me have time to work on that."

- "We already have what we need in place. Worry about your own stuff."

- "That's not my problem."

Not only will you face the usual ignorance or apathy, but you may face a layer of hostility as well.

Your Management

Hopefully, you only have one immediate manager. (Some employees have many direct managers, but let's not go there for sanity's sake.) These are some direct quotes from discussions I've had in the past at people at the managerial level:

- "Great idea! Good job! I just need to run it past my boss."

- "Great idea! Write up an official proposal and e-mail me."

- "Great idea! Oh, by the way, everyone else has vacation next week, so you have to carry the pager."

- "Are you saying we don't do backups right now?"

- "We already have an outside vendor who does that."

- "I don't get it. What?"

Not only will you get the usual ignorance or apathy, but you may just get the brush-off as well. Be very, very wary of extremely enthusiastic responses followed by requests for more information or a quick subject change. When that happens, it's a pretty good indicator that there is no intention of following through with your recommendations.

Executive Management

Hopefully you personally won't be in a position where you'll need to approach executive management to discuss the need for disaster recovery planning. If you are, you'll need to be careful. This is usually where things get blown well out of proportion, as the following quotes demonstrate:

- "We'll be budgeting for a business continuity (BC) project next year."

- "We just don't have the budget for that right now. Talk to me again in October next year when we work on the yearly budget."

- "How did you get in here? Get out of my office before I call security."

Executive management likes to use faddish buzzronyms such as DR, high availability (HA), and BC. These can be dangerous! Mentioning one of these abbreviations to the wrong executive might turn the small, disaster recovery project that you have in mind into a multimillion-dollar, multiyear project (which, as you might expect, will probably fail).

Another issue with approaching executive management—and I hope no one ever encounters this problem—is that they might even react in a hostile manner over your having the audacity to schedule time with them. Tread carefully if you begin to receive hostile vibes.

Business Units

This is by far the most important group when it comes to simply raising awareness. Most organizations treat IT/IS as an island. The other business units believe they shouldn't need to worry about "techie" things:

- "And you're talking to me because . . .?"

- "I thought you guys took care of all that stuff already."

- "Disaster? What, is someone getting fired?"

- "Uh huh. Uh huh. Uh huh. OK. Uh huh . . ." (followed by lots of nodding with a slightly glazed look in the eyes).

Generally, at this level, you'll find complete ignorance about what you're discussing. You may have your hands full just trying to keep everyone's attention.

Techniques to Remove This Roadblock

Try to do anything you can to remain focused on disaster recovery planning. If your company is heavy on time scheduling and meeting notifications, schedule a 15- to 30-minute meeting with yourself on this topic every day. If your organization is a bit more informal when it comes to planning activities, a simple sticky note on your desktop reminding you to take some time to plan is a simple but effective start (unless your monitor is already covered with 200 sticky notes). Also, try to force yourself to come up with a new risk on a weekly basis. Set some sort of short, achievable goals toward identifying new items to include in your plan.

Again, I'll look at each group when evaluating techniques for removing the roadblock, starting with your team of DBAs.

Your Team

The key to raising awareness within your own team is to start with informal discussions (sometimes on a one-on-one basis). The idea is to plant seeds so that when the topic comes up formally, everyone already has been introduced to the idea of disaster recovery planning.

Never make the mistake of trying to present this as "your" idea, even if that's the case. It may then appear that you're looking to just boost your own value in the company or climb the corporate ladder. Even if you head the charge, try to give the impression that this is a group effort (ultimately, it should be).

Your Peers

This is a tricky situation, because no one likes someone poking around or questioning what he does. Again, informal discussion prior to any formal introduction to disaster recovery planning is extremely helpful. It can also be helpful to have strategic allies within any given department. A friend on the networking team can go a long way toward creating an open environment to discuss the need for disaster recovery. Always use this approach in earnest; don't make a friend just for this purpose.

It also may help to go to your peers for advice on the matter. Asking someone out of the blue how she would approach disaster recovery is invasive. Asking her how she would approach disaster recovery in the context of seeking advice is a passive inquiry. You'll have a lot more luck with the latter than the former.

Your Management

I strongly recommend that you don't attempt to drive a disaster recovery planning process until you spend at least a year at a company. Not only will that help you in establishing credibility, it will give you time to learn the personalities of your coworkers. This is especially important with your manager. Often you won't get any direct objection to what you're proposing, so you'll need to be able to read the sign that the discussion is falling on deaf or dismissive ears.

If you're being dismissed outright, back off and try again another time. You never know what may be driving your manager's rejection. It could be because he believes you're wrong, won't succeed, or are incapable. It could also be because he just got yelled at by his manager, because he's having troubles at home, and so on.

It also may be useful to simply start working on your disaster recovery plan within the context of the databases you support and come to your manager with examples in hand. It's much easier to see the value in something when you have something concrete to look at. This approach also gives your manager something concrete to show his manager, making it easier for him to approve whatever time you need to spend on disaster recovery planning.

Executive Management

You should only need to approach executive management in an extreme situation. Even if the meeting is successful, approaching executive management has consequences. You'll probably alienate most of your coworkers by going above their heads.

Above all, make sure you know your organization well enough to know if you will even be taken seriously. Many managers or executives state, "My door is always open," But that doesn't mean it is. That statement might just be a team-building tool. Here's a good indicator of whether or not executive management is approachable: when you say "hello" or "good morning" on an elevator, do they respond in kind? Do they actually know your name? If they don't, don't even consider approaching executive management to discuss disaster recovery planning.

Unlike when meeting with your management, having piles of documentation in hand when meeting with executive management will actually detract from the discussion. Executive management usually has very little time to start with, so anything other than a one-sheet example will be politely discarded ("I'll take a look at this later today"). At this level, you really need to work on your pitch. You're going to get five minutes to establish interest in the subject, and that's it. Be pithy.

Business Units

The quickest way to lose a business-unit audience is to jump into any sort of technical jargon. Even if you use only one term early on, your audience may check out and not listen to the rest of what you have to say. Keep things simple, and keep things focused.

This is another situation in which approaching the discussion passively (i.e., asking for their advice or input) can have a dramatic effect on whether or not you're even heard. Always talk in terms of implications, both from a risk and a cost perspective.

Another quick road to failure with a business group is to walk into the room or office and ask, "So, what do you do?" Take the time to learn something about any perspective business unit before talking with the people involved, and try to summarize to them what you think their needs may be and why disaster recovery planning is important to them. It's fine if you get something wrong. In fact, that can actually be constructive to the dialog. Because you've shown some level of understanding what they do, they'll be more inclined to provide you with information. It's sort of like being in France and taking the time to learn a little French. Even though they'll correct you or ask you to speak in English, you'll be treated with *much* more respect than the average tourist.

Roadblock: Lack of Management/Executive Buy-In

Assuming that you've raised awareness of the need for disaster recovery planning, you still need to get the buy-in from management—that is, the time or the financial resources to achieve what you'll be doing. The general solution is to present disaster recovery as an ongoing cost of doing business—a necessity much like pens and sticky notes.

Description of the Roadblock

Overcoming the first hurdle of awareness can often lead to running into a wall of "we just can't afford this." I've run into that wall more than once, and it knocks the wind out of you. Working as an internal employee, nothing is more demoralizing than hearing that you have a good idea but that it's not good enough to invest in.

Usually the issue is one of cost, either from an actual financial perspective, a time perspective, or a logistical perspective of getting people to work together. An indirect reason that cost can be an issue is that the higher you go in management, the larger the "picture" of the organization you see. While your immediate manager may see the value in something that you want to do, his manager may not know enough about your job to see that same value.

Using a cost-justification technique to approach the financial aspect of executive buy-in is nearly guaranteed to fail. The reason is that in the best case, spending on disaster recovery is like spending on insurance—hopefully nothing will happen, and the money will be "wasted." (Not truly wasted, but think about how much better you feel about your auto insurance when you can actually file a claim.) It's often difficult to convince an executive to spend money on something that is highly unlikely to be needed or that won't be used on a routine basis. At least, it's difficult to use the argument that the investment will pay for itself in the same way as new energy-efficient windows on a house.

BUSINESS COST VS. ROI

The topics of cost justification and disaster recovery just don't mix. I've seen Chief Financial Officers (CFOs) panic when told that a disaster recovery plan is now required by some regulation or law. The expectation is that putting the plan into action will cost a lot of money and that they'll have nothing to show for it.

The difficulty when discussing funding for anything related to disaster recovery is explaining the subtle difference between a purchase that's a cost of doing business vs. a purchase that has an expected return on investment. I've encountered numerous layers of management—even CFOs— who don't understand within IT/IS the difference between a business cost and an investment with an expected return.

Company spending falls into two categories: the cost of doing business and an investment. The terminology changes from organization to organization, but the basic idea remains the same: spend money to make money. Spend money either to support or expand existing infrastructure, to create new business activities, or to improve existing ones. Examples of cost-of-business spending include

- New-employee needs (such as desk, chair, phone, computer, software, and so on)

- Facilities management

- Legal services and insurance

  Examples of investment spending include

- Custom software development

- New product development

- Research and development

- Company expansion

During the dot-com boom, the industry's fast adoption of new technology and incredible success stories led most companies to give IT/IS a blank check. There was no need to justify any specific expenditure. Companies spent massive amounts of money on questionable purchases, which led to the expectation of huge returns on investments. Since the dot-com fallout, IT/IS spending is usually scrutinized to the point of paranoia. Unless it has sponsorship from executive management, something that isn't presented as a cost-of-business expenditure has a low likelihood of being approved.

Techniques to Remove This Roadblock

When seeking management buy-in, *never* respond to objections by trying to justify the cost involved. To remove the cost factor, you need to somehow work disaster recovery planning in as a cost of doing business. Present it as a necessity no different than supplying a desk or a phone to a new employee. By approaching disaster recovery in small bites, you can change management's perception of it from a wasted investment to a necessary cost.

Always present disaster recovery planning as an ongoing, iterative process (which it should be). The cost should be stretched over an extremely long period of time, often to the point of not even being seen. Management has a tendency to see DR as a project, not a job responsibility. Therein lies the key to gaining support. In fact, if done correctly, management may not even consider cost.

Also, never try to use cost-justification. It just won't work, because disaster recovery cannot be cost-justified. Period. It's like trying to cost-justify the purchase of insurance. In the best case scenario (the ultimate payoff of the investment), the money is thrown away.

Roadblock: Lack of Staff Buy-In

Just as you must get management buy-in, you must get staff buy-in as well. Believe it or not, workers don't always just fall in line with what management wants. You have to sell your ideas downward, laterally, and upward. From a staff point of view, disaster recovery (as I've said in other sections of the book) *must* be seen as an ongoing job function, no different than filling out a weekly status report. In fact, it should appear on that report!

Description of the Roadblock

Building support amongst staff may seem like an unnecessary step. Wouldn't the full support from management ensure staff participation? In the best of all worlds, yes, that would be the case. However, we don't live in the best of all worlds. If the need to create a disaster recovery plan comes as a top-down directive, you may even encounter a sort of insurgency that opposes the planning and does whatever possible to derail it.

You also may alienate your coworkers indirectly while getting executive buy-in. They may believe that you're adding to their workload, and like everyone else, they're probably doing all they can just to keep their heads above water.

■**Note** Ultimately, disaster recovery planning, being a proactive activity, should help reduce one's workload. One client I worked with went from having DBAs spend an average of 18 hours a month in some sort of disaster response situation to only one hour per month after putting a disaster recovery plan in place. (Many of the previous disasters had been user- and process-based.)

Techniques to Remove This Roadblock

Again, the key here is to focus on disaster recovery planning as an ongoing job role, not a project. Emphasize that it won't require a great deal of anyone's time, because it will be approached slowly on an ongoing basis. Unfortunately, after establishing executive buy-in, the concept of disaster recovery planning as an ongoing process may turn into a company-wide project, despite your best efforts to prevent that from happening.

When it comes to alienating your coworkers, some of that is out of your hands. If, after you get management buy-in, the project is presented as *your* idea, there's no way to prevent some people from being miffed. If you can, try to remove yourself from the equation as much as possible. Better yet, present your approach with a team of people when establishing management buy-in. Keep the focus as impersonal as possible.

Roadblock: Issues with Job Role vs. Project

As hinted at in the previous section, disaster recovery planning has a tendency to evolve into a huge project. Guard against this problem by always emphasizing the job-role connection. Another useful technique is to avoid the use of the word "project" at all when talking about disaster recovery (or even the phrase "disaster recovery").

Description of the Roadblock

The misguided evolution of disaster recovery into a huge project is usually due to executive management participation and the ubiquitous buzzronyms they encounter, such as DR, HA, and BC. Other times, it can just grow naturally as more and more individuals get involved. Someone decides a project manager is needed, and from that point on, it's labeled a "project."

As I've advocated throughout this book, disaster recovery planning needs to be an ongoing, iterative *job role* in order to be effective. My experience with projects in general is that the larger they are and the longer they take, the less likely they are to be successful. Many of those involved in large projects tend to feel the same way and give up early on, often killing a project before it gets off the ground.

It is critical that you retain that job-role approach to planning. Putting all the separate pieces together can be difficult to do without someone who has the responsibility of handling those logistics, but it doesn't need to be a project manager.

Techniques to Remove This Roadblock

First, you must ensure that the concept of disaster recovery as a job role is not only understood by all, but embraced. Whenever discussing disaster recovery, say "job role" as often as possible. If someone uses the word "project," gently correct them by saying something like, "Well, this is really more like integrating job roles between departments." Avoid uttering the word "project," and use the term "job role" until you're blue in the face.

Never use buzzronyms, whether spoken in meetings or written within documentation. It can be easy to fall into the temptation of abbreviating disaster recovery planning. Notice how I make a concerted effort to always use the full spelling rather than the acronym? (My mother, who was a high school English and grammar teacher—yes, I had my mom as a teacher one year in high school—would chastise me for being so repetitive in my writing.)

Another key to establishing the job-role concept is to embrace it personally. Assume that it is one of your job rolcs, and encourage others to personally embrace it as well.

Roadblock: Ineffective Discovery Process

From my consulting experience, I've found that simply asking people what they need or what they have is rarely a sufficient means of discovering information. Discovery is no different when working internally.

Description of the Roadblock

Have you implemented some sort of technology or process only to have someone come to you afterward and say, "But what do we do when we want this?" Personally, I find nothing more frustrating than surprise requirements that crop up after a technology or application has been completed. Disaster recovery planning is not immune to such surprise requirements.

Because I work as a consultant, I have the luxury of demanding a discovery process— that is, time to do nothing but look for requirements. If surprises occur later, I didn't do my job very well. However, surprise does happen, and it continues to happen, regardless of the activity I'm doing. No one can think of everything on his or her own.

Techniques to Remove This Roadblock

When performing discovery, I try to include as many people in the discovery process as possible, or at least attempt to identify who may have additional input. Avoiding surprises in disaster recovery planning works the same way.

Usually with disaster recovery, the surprises come from a business unit's "true" requirements. Be sure when performing discovery to take the time to truly understand what a business unit's requirements might be. Keep in mind that what the people in that business unit tell you is a requirement might not be the real requirement that they need met. Reword and repeat back to whomever you're talking to. You may be shocked at how often the response will be, "No, that isn't quite it."

Roadblock: Ineffective Communication of Risk

The word "risk" has its own baggage—some good, but mostly very heavy, ugly baggage, like those huge oversized pieces of luggage covered in some '70s upholstery style. As a natural course of human nature, people often avoid the word "risk" and any thought of possible repercussions until the last minute. (Sadly, I admit that I'm a bit of a procrastinator. It's a problem for me, but I'll deal with it tomorrow.) Somehow, someway, you need to make each functional group (IT, business groups, management, and so on) aware of the risks it faces.

Description of the Roadblock

When working in a disaster recovery situation, it's common to have to resort to the worst-case scenario to return to an operational status. Perhaps that means a loss of a single day's data. When that happens, the business owners of the system will often say that isn't acceptable, even if they signed off on the disaster recovery plan themselves. Whether they didn't understand the implication of the risks or implicitly or explicitly refused to take responsibility, this makes any disaster recovery process very difficult.

Techies usually understand the various risks and their implications, and we often take it for granted that others will as well. Something such as the impact of downtime might seem so obvious to us that we don't press it enough when talking with business units. Just because a business owner signs off on a particular approach doesn't obligate her to taking responsibility unless she truly understands what she's signing (the legal concept of signing something "under duress").

Techniques to Remove This Roadblock

While most of the work I do is consulting, I do teach on a regular basis as well. One thing I know from experience is that you can't teach something unless you truly understand it yourself. Given that idea, have the business owners explain back to you what the implications are of the plan they're approving. If there is any hesitation, they don't fully understand.

Using the same approach, have the business owners write the section of the sign-off document that explains what the implications are. Again, you'll quickly see if they understand or not.

Note I believe that we techies have a responsibility to ensure that the nontechnical people in a business understand the implications of anything that we do. Who else is going to ensure that kind of understanding? Taking it for granted that a nontechnical person will understand the implications of technical activities is not only unwise, but I believe it is also unethical.

Roadblock: Silos

If your technology people are organized into well-defined and isolated groups, you'll have a problem getting those people to work against that group structure when planning for disaster recovery. You need someone capable of bridging the gap between the various *silos*.

Description of the Roadblock

There is a school of thought in management that says the most efficient way to organize IT resources is to group them into their specific areas of expertise. All of the DBAs are in the same group, regardless of what systems they support. The same goes for developers, server administrators, and network administrators. Even project management is often a separate group. The idea is that the groups will act as a collective brain trust and learn from each other.

I have seen organizations in which this type of organization structure works, but more often than not, it leads to silos—that is, individual groups with no knowledge or interest in what any other group is doing. When a business unit encounters a technical problem, the problem is often bounced from silo to silo. The networking group says, "It isn't a problem with the network. Go to the database group." The database group says, "It isn't a problem with the database. Go to the networking group." Not only is this extremely frustrating for the business unit, but it also creates distrust in anything IT/IS does.

Even if this organizational structure isn't intended, silos can evolve naturally when communication is a problem. Even if your organization isn't structured by silos, be on the lookout for groups or subgroups that have created their own private silos.

Techniques to Remove This Roadblock

Whether silos are deliberate or not, communication is the only way to overcome the almost literal walls that silos create. Establishing strategic allies within silos can be very useful, but often more dramatic measures must be taken. (As I've said before, don't be crass enough to make a friend just for the purpose of establishing a line of communication; it will come back to bite you.)

If the concept of a *business liaison* doesn't exist in your silo infrastructure, someone will need to step up to the plate and take on that role (often in addition to whatever role he normally plays). Someone will need to bridge the massive gap between technology and business, as well as the individual gaps between IT/IS silos.

I won't pull punches here: this is extremely difficult and painful to accomplish. You'll have to force people to talk to one another, or you'll have to have them all talk to you, and you'll need to play the role of translator. It can be time-consuming, frustrating (no one wants to leave their silo), and thankless, but it must be done.

Roadblock: Banging the Gong

There is one more barrier to discuss: trying too hard to work around the previous barriers. I refer to this tendency as "banging the gong."

Description of the Roadblock

I've learned this the hard way: if you walk around essentially banging the gong—that is, doom-saying and ignoring any internal delicacies—you will alienate everyone with whom you need to work, ensuring your failure. When encountering extremely difficult infrastructures, I have used this noise-making approach. While it got things moving, it did not endear me to anyone. Still, I was happy in that I accomplished something positive, even if it meant losing future work with an existing client.

Techniques to Remove This Roadblock

As a consultant, I could walk away with some level of satisfaction, but if you bang the gong in your organization, you'll have to live with the consequences. (Get used to eating by yourself in the cafeteria.)

A better approach to a problematic environment (one that wasn't open to me in my example) is to back off and try again. You can be persistent without being outright annoying. Bring up the topic of disaster recovery planning often, but when met with fierce resistance or mollifying apathy, stop. Wait a few months, then try again. Organizations change over time, both in personnel and in attitude. Eventually, someone will listen. Plus, nothing prevents you from embracing disaster recovery planning in the work you do.

Caveats and Recommendations

This chapter has basically been a huge list of recommendations on how to deal with disaster recovery in your own organization. Some of these caveats and recommendations are critical.

- *Avoid buzzronyms*: Avoid using acronyms such as DR, HA, and BC. Acronyms in general are a bit clichéd, in my opinion, but the use of these particular terms often evokes fear.

- *Beware of the landslide effect*: If you're starting disaster recovery planning from scratch with SQL Server, other groups can have a tendency to tack their own planning on to yours. This is fine, as long as it happens in a controlled manner. Make sure your work isn't swallowed up by other groups. This can often result in the declaration of a "DR project."

- *Don't undermine existing activities*: If you alienate anyone, from coworkers to management, by either deliberately or accidentally undermining or detracting from the work they do, you will be eating alone in the cafeteria. And your attempts at spreading disaster recovery planning will be met with hostility at every turn.

- *Avoid scare tactics*: Never resort to scare tactics—for example, "If we don't do this, we'll lose all of our data." In my experience, negative approaches to any sort of discussion make the problem even more difficult to deal with.

- *Don't stop*: Disaster recovery planning should be an iterative process—a job role, not a project. When working with others, you must reinforce this concept above all else. When faced with extreme resistance, it's fine to back off for a while, but always come back and try again. Defeatism is not allowed.

Summary

In this final chapter, I've explored some of the practical (or impractical, depending on how you look at it) aspects of attempting disaster recovery planning within your own organization. It would be nice if we could simply approach the topic of disaster recovery from a purely technical point of view, but the unfortunately complicated reality of the situation is that successful disaster recovery plans require the participation of the entire business, not just IT/IS.

Maintaining the concept of disaster recovery planning as part of your job description is the key to its success. Large DR/BC projects often fail or become outdated by the time they are implemented. The job-role approach implies small, iterative steps, hopefully ensuring that at least *some* action will be taken in a timely manner.

Finally, it is your responsibility to ensure not only the participation of the rest of the business, but a true understanding of what is being done. This may be an unfair requirement, but someone needs to begin building a bridge between technology and business. It might as well start with you.

■■■

SQL Server 2008 Considerations

At the time of this writing, SQL Server 2008 is well into the CTP process. The goal with the CTP process is to expose only features that are considered near completion—no beta features with significant issues. This means that we won't know everything about what the final product will include until the release to manufacturing (RTM), which is the official release.

This also means that by the time you read this appendix, chances are it will be slightly out of date. No worries. The fundamental changes in most features have been revealed by this point, and any that haven't been will be covered in an appendix available on the Apress web site (www.apress.com).

▮Note All information in this appendix is based on the November CTP.

Backup/Restore Improvements

The majority of the backup/restore features remain the same in SQL Server 2008. It still features full, differential, and log backups; file and filegroup backups; piecemeal and page-level restores; and so on. It still offers the same basic Full Recovery, Bulk-Logged Recovery, and Simple Recovery modes. For the most part, Chapters 2, 3, and 4 still apply, even syntactically.

However, there are some notable improvements to backup and recovery in SQL Server 2008. These improvements make your job easier and enable you to protect your database against loss and damage more efficiently. The subsections that follow describe these new features.

Tail-Log Backups

SQL Server 2005 was nice enough to warn you to back up the tail of the transaction log (those transactions in between log backups) if you tried to overwrite an active database. SQL Server 2008 brings even greater attention to the tail-log within the GUI. As Figure A-1 shows, you now have the option within the GUI of backing up the tail-log and leaving the database in a NO RECOVERY state.

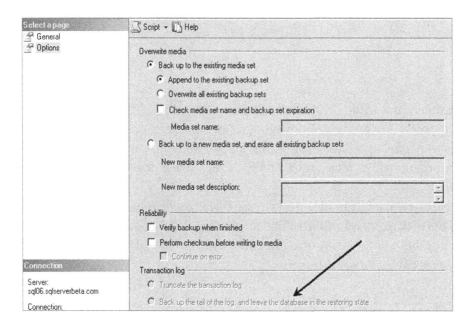

Figure A-1. *The option to back up the tail-log and leave the database in a* NO RECOVERY *state*

This new ability to leave the database in a NO RECOVERY state after backing up the tail-log may seem like a relatively insignificant change, but I've seen far too many tail-logs destroyed by accident (usually followed by the question, "So how do I get those changes back?"). Anything that raises awareness of the need to perform a tail-log backup is good, to my mind.

Native Backup Compression

SQL Server 2008 finally provides a native method for compressing backups. If you've ever looked closely at the size of an uncompressed backup, you've seen that it is generally the same size as the original database. Since everyone seems to agree with the mantra, "Disk is cheap," databases tend to grow at an alarming rate. That means the backups of those databases grow as well.

To compress backups with SQL Server 2005 and earlier, you had to either purchase a third-party SQL Server backup utility or include some sort of file-based compression action after the initial native SQL Server backup. With SQL Server 2008, compression is now supported with each and every backup (see Figure A-2).

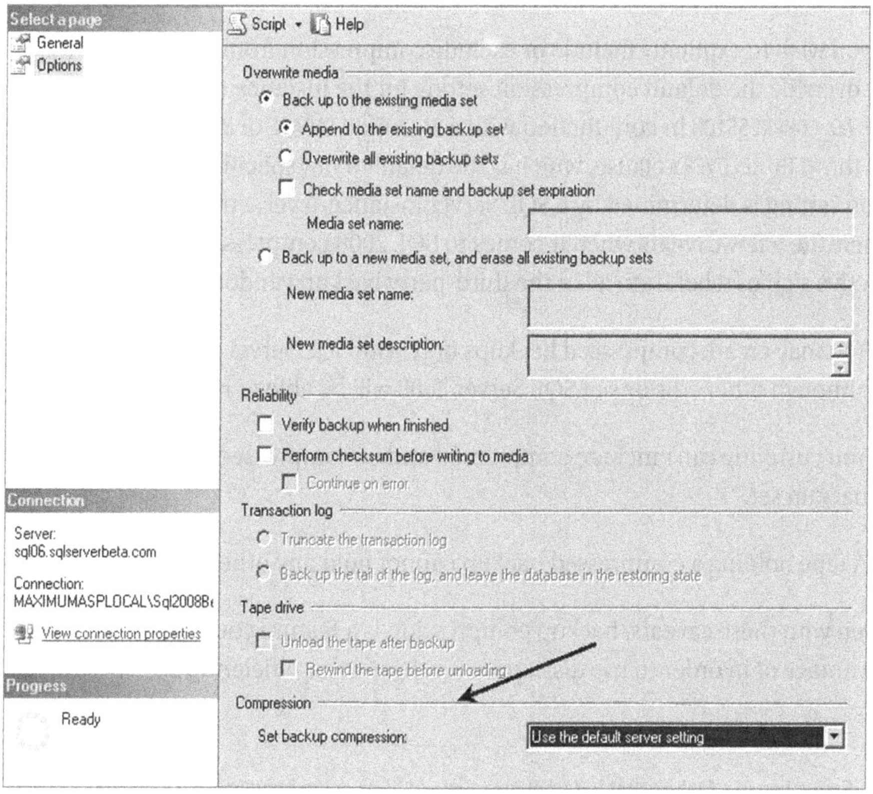

Figure A-2. *Every SQL instance has a default compression setting (on or off), which you can override during each individual backup command.*

Backup compression is either on or off; there are no varying levels of compression to set. To enable backup compression at the instance level, you would use the sp_configure command (I'm hoping that by the time of release, you'll also be able to use the ALTER SYSTEM command):

```
sp_configure 'backup compression default', '1'
```

Even with compression enabled, your backups will not necessarily shrink by the same ratio. For example, if the database contains lots of character data, it should have a high rate of compression (plain text compresses nicely). If the database contains binary data types such as TEXT, IMAGE, or VARCHAR(MAX), the ratio may be slightly less. To check the ratio of any current backup, a new field called Compressed_Backup_Size has been added to the MSDB..BACKUPSET table. The following simple query gives you a compression ratio for an individual backup:

```
SELECT backup_size/compressed_backup_size FROM msdb..backupset;
```

If you wish to explicitly include or exclude compression from a single backup, you simply override the default compression setting for the instance using WITH COMPRESSION or WITH NO_COMPRESSION in conjunction with a BACKUP DATABASE or BACKUP LOG command. Unlike the WITH RECOVERY clause, which is the default if not specified, the default compression setting is determined by a SQL Server instance-level setting.

There are a few caveats when it comes to SQL 2008 compression (I think I just heard a collective sigh of relief from all of the third-party backup vendors out there):

- You may create compressed backups only with SQL Server 2008 Enterprise Edition, although other editions of SQL Server 2008 will be able to restore them.

- You currently can't include compressed and uncompressed backups in the same backup set.

- A tape holding a compressed backup cannot hold any other NTBackup files.

Even with these caveats, backup compression is a feature you'll want to consider taking advantage of in order to use disk space (or tape) more efficiently.

Note Encryption is a feature that is sometimes thought of as going hand in hand with compression. SQL Server 2008 still doesn't provide encryption for a backup (just the same basic password protection), so I see a lot of room for improvement here. Let's hope we see that improvement soon.

FILESTREAM Data

One of the more significant improvements in SQL Server 2008 is the ability to store binary objects as files on the operating system, not within 8K data pages. Previous to SQL Server 2008, all binary objects, such as Word documents and image files, had to be stored as either TEXT, NTEXT, IMAGE, VARCHAR(MAX), or VARBINARY(MAX). Each of these data types organized information in terms of 8K pages, which led to a lot of wasted space. A 9K .jpg file, for example, resulted in 16K minimum in terms of storage space used. This not only meant a larger database and, hence, a larger backup, but also a slower application.

A traditional alternative to storing binary objects within the database would be to simply have a VARCHAR field record the literal or relative path to the binary file itself (e.g., a value such as C:\WordFiles\WordDoc01.doc). The path approach had drawbacks of its own:

- Files were not controlled by SQL Server.

- Files were not included with a SQL Server backup.

Because there was no direct relationship between the file and the database in the traditional scenario, disaster for one (a lost database or lost file) meant disaster for both.

With the inclusion of FILESTREAM storage in SQL Server 2008, you can combine the benefit of efficient file storage with the benefits of tightly coupled data stored within the database itself. When you make use of FILESTREAM storage, you need to also make use of a filegroup—for example:

```
FILEGROUP FileStreamGroup1 CONTAINS FILESTREAM
( NAME = FileStreamDBResumes,
FILENAME = N'D:\test\Resumes')
```

The FILENAME property for the filegroup points to a directory structure. The final directory listed (Resumes, in the example) is created automatically; the rest of the directories must already exist. Within the base directory, SQL Server 2008 places a filestream.hdr file and a subfolder called $FSLOG. SQL Server 2008 uses these to control the FILESTREAM data and ensure transactional consistency when working with FILESTREAM data. When SQL Server is running, all FILESTREAM directories are locked and controlled only by SQL Server.

How does the ability to store large objects as files in the operating system affect the disaster recovery landscape? For starters, you need to take care not to allow users to manipulate those files outside of the context of SQL Server. Also, when the database is backed up and later restored, all of the FILESTREAM data moves along with it. Finally, since a FILESTREAM is represented within SQL Server as a filegroup, it is possible to include or exclude that FILESTREAM from a complex filegroup backup/recovery plan, to use piecemeal restore, and so on. This ability to include or exclude data from backups is a significant improvement when it comes to working with binary data.

A WISH LIST

Unfortunately, SQL Server 2008 still retains a number of misleading features. I would like to think that by the time SQL Server 2008 is finally released, some of these annoying features will be changed:

- *Default recovery after a restore*: It is still far too easy to recover the database in the midst of a restore process. If left unspecified, the default action for a RESTORE DATABASE or RESTORE LOG command is WITH RECOVERY.

- *Misleading Backup and Restore screens in the GUI*: SQL Server 2008 uses the same GUI tool design for the Backup and Restore screens. The Backup screen still has that same Backup Location list box, which can give the impression that selecting a file in that list box means that the backup will be stored in that file. In reality, having multiple files in the Backup Location list box means that the backup will be striped across all files.

Both of these examples seem simple enough to change, but perhaps I shouldn't complain. At least what I've said in Chapters 2 and 3 still applies to SQL 2008.

Database Mirroring Improvements

As you might expect, SQL Server 2008 also makes improvements to database mirroring. There aren't any fundamental changes: mirroring still works basically the same, and the different modes of mirroring available remain the same. Rather, the changes lean more toward fine-tuning than redesign.

Automatic Page Repair

The one exception to what I just said about fine-tuning is the new feature of automatic page repair. If the principal and mirror are in a synchronized state, page-level errors occurring at *either node* are repaired automatically. If a mirror detects a corrupt page, it will request a replacement from the principal. If the principal detects a corrupted page, it will request a replacement from the mirror. It's like having an off-site mechanic continually fixing your car.

Database Mirroring Tuning

SQL Server 2008 also includes some much-needed improvements to the speed of database mirroring operations. These improvements include

- *Log compression*: Data changes sent over the network from the principal to the mirror are now compressed. Given that those data changes represent fully logged actions that are sent over the network (including an image of the *before data*, the text of the statement making the change, and the *after data)*, this compression can result in a significant speed improvement.

- *Mirror server write-ahead*: The mirror server now moves ahead asynchronously, writing log information out to its transaction log, regardless of whether it's waiting for further log buffers from the principal.

- *Log cache tuning*: Improvements to in-memory log caches maximize the amount of log data that can be sent from a principal to a mirror at any given time.

What do all of these changes mean? For one, synchronous, two-phase commit operations will have less of an impact on the user experience, meaning fewer lags between data entry operations. Also, asynchronous configurations are more likely to stay in a synchronized state. The bottom line is that these changes are good news for everyone using database mirroring.

Change Tracking

With the growing emphasis on legal requirements, as noted by the Sarbanes-Oxley Act of 2002 and the Health Insurance Portability and Accountability Act (HIPAA), being able to have true change history is critical. SQL Server 2000 and SQL Server 2005 offered C2 auditing, a government specification (see the Divisions and Classes section at `http://en.wikipedia.org/wiki/Trusted_Computer_System_Evaluation_Criteria`). SQL Server 2005 included even more attempts at tracking changes, such as Data Definition Language (DDL) triggers and event notifications. SQL Server 2008 includes a new feature called Change Tracking, which comes much closer to meeting many legal requirements for auditing than any of the earlier features.

You can enable Change Tracking at the entire database level, as shown in Figure A-3, or at the individual table level. Once enabled, tracking is maintained for a set amount of time and is performed synchronously when Data Manipulation Language (DML) events occur.

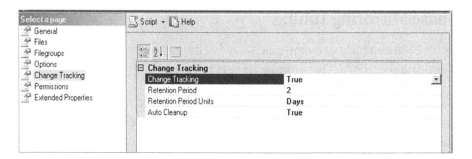

Figure A-3. *The new Change Tracking feature provides automated cleanup.*

AUDITING TO MITIGATE USER DISASTERS?

Many of the existing features in SQL Server 2005, such as DDL triggers, event notification, and the OUTPUT clauses, are geared more toward auditing data rather than mitigating or responding to user disasters. At the moment (and I reserve the right to change my mind in the future), I include SQL Server 2008's Change Tracking feature in the same category of data auditing rather than one that relates to disaster recovery. The problem with user disasters is that the actual problem is rarely known. Yes, you could use Change Tracking to attempt to recover specific changes, but you would need to know exactly what the issues are to determine exactly what changes need to be recovered.

I may change my mind on the utility of Change Tracking as a disaster recovery tool the more I work with it as SQL Server 2008 becomes prevalent in the workforce. It's good to keep an open mind on new features like this.

Change Tracking can potentially place a heavy load on your storage system and on your server in general. Unlike Change Data Capture, a SQL Server 2008 feature that provides similar functionality, Change Tracking is performed using a sort of two-phase commit. Change Data Capture, on the other hand, works by reading from the transaction log. These features definitely add to the ability to handle user disasters, but upon initial review, I wouldn't consider them a panacea to the problem.

Index

You Need the Companion eBook

Your purchase of this book entitles you to buy the companion PDF-version eBook for only $10. Take the weightless companion with you anywhere.

We believe this Apress title will prove so indispensable that you'll want to carry it with you everywhere, which is why we are offering the companion eBook (in PDF format) for $10 to customers who purchase this book now. Convenient and fully searchable, the PDF version of any content-rich, page-heavy Apress book makes a valuable addition to your programming library. You can easily find and copy code—or perform examples by quickly toggling between instructions and the application. Even simultaneously tackling a donut, diet soda, and complex code becomes simplified with hands-free eBooks!

Once you purchase your book, getting the $10 companion eBook is simple:

❶ Visit **www.apress.com/promo/tendollars/**.

❷ Complete a basic registration form to receive a randomly generated question about this title.

❸ Answer the question correctly in 60 seconds, and you will receive a promotional code to redeem for the $10.00 eBook.

THE EXPERT'S VOICE™

2855 TELEGRAPH AVENUE | SUITE 600 | BERKELEY, CA 94705

All Apress eBooks subject to copyright protection. No part may be reproduced or transmitted in any form or by any means, electronic or mechanical, including photocopying, recording, or by any information storage or retrieval system, without the prior written permission of the copyright owner and the publisher. The purchaser may print the work in full or in part for their own noncommercial use. The purchaser may place the eBook title on any of their personal computers for their own personal reading and reference.

Offer valid through 9/08.